The Parallels of Dita

Surviving Nazism and Communism
in Lithu~~ania~~

GW00630522

a memoir

Silvija Lomsargytė-Pukienė

translated

by

Al Zolynas

Lymer & Hart
Rainbow, California

Lymer & Hart
  an imprint of Garden Oak Press
1953 Huffstatler St., Suite A
Rainbow, CA 92028
760 728-2088
lymerhart@gmail.com
gardenoakpress.com
gardenoakpress@gmail.com

© *Silvija Lomsargytė-Pukienė   All rights reserved*

Translation © Al Zolynas   All rights reserved

No part of this book may be reproduced, stored in a retrieval system or transmitted by any means without the express written consent of the Publisher.

First published by Lymer & Hart/Garden Oak Press on November 1, 2021.

ISBN-13: 978-1-7350556-0-2

Library of Congress Control Number: 2021942032

Dita. Paralelės [Dita. Parallels]: originally published in Lithuanian by Jotema Press, Vilnius, Lithuania, in 2004.
    ISBN: 9955527773   LCCN: 2005356120

Printed in the United States of America

The views expressed in this memoir are solely those of the author and translator, and do not necessarily reflect the views of the Publisher, and the Publisher hereby disclaims any responsibility for them.

In memory of my father, Samuel

The Parallels of Dita

Surviving Nazism and Communism in Lithuania

a memoir

Silvija Lomsargytė-Pukienė

translated

by

Al Zolynas

1
Freedom Avenue

The gnome fountain

S earch for your fortune every day," the old calendar urges.

I'm searching, I'm searching—I say almost aloud, understanding less and less what that fortune may be the more I seek it.

Maybe someone can tell me what it is?

Many seek it, but no one seems to know what it is.

Can it be we search all our lives for what we don't know?

Over thirty years ago, returning late at night to my place in Vilnius (the first apartment I owned though I was already in my late thirties) even as I was locking the door, I could hear chirping inside. Aha, it's already past midnight. I knew my children were sleeping peacefully.

"Perhaps I'm fortunate now," flashed through my mind.

A cricket lived behind our gas stove all winter long. He'd begin his chirping only after midnight so as not to bother anyone. In the spring he disappeared. In the summer, staying with relatives by the seaside, I ask:

—Could you please give me a cricket?

At first they didn't understand what I wanted, as if they didn't hear me correctly.

Oh, those town folks, they'd say, and shrug their shoulders like the rational western Lithuanians—*lietuvininkai*—they knew themselves to be. They explained that in the modern-day village there are no more crickets, and if they were ever to come across one they'd kill it with boiling water. Just so its chirpings wouldn't interfere with anyone's sleep.

Instead of a cricket, they gifted me with an old horseshoe. A fairly beaten up and rusted one. Seems it had spent more than a winter or two mired in puddles and kicked along the paths of seaside villages. If you really need all of that good fortune, their looks seemed to say... but generally those kinds of superstitions are not good....

We nailed the horseshoe to the door on the stairway side, so the approaching good fortune would have no doubt on where to enter.

3

Well, come then.

And while it's coming, I'll return, for now, from where I came.

I return to Kaunas and to that time known as between-the-wars.

•

...Kaunas begins for me at the railroad station square where the black carriages stand. The carriage drivers sit up high on their seats and together with their carriages are known as *izvoščikai*. When it rains they pull a rounded cover over the passengers, much like the roof over a child's stroller, only larger. Passengers can cover their knees and laps with a black tarp that fastens along the sides. The carriage fits four or five passengers, much like a taxi today—except that half of them sit on a soft leather seat and the other half opposite on a hard fold-out bench. The horse clops apathetically along Kaunas' streets, many of which are still unpaved. Soon those *izvoščikai* will no longer be needed, nor their sluggish horses with their randomly dropped "road apples."

On Vytautas Prospect (Avenue), not far from the station, stands a policeman. And needless to say, he is tall. In those days all policemen were tall. His uniformed cap, adorned with a cockade, stretches him to even a greater height. He looks dignified, though undoubtedly he's just an ordinary village boy, "not long off the plough."

•

It's hard to imagine Kaunas without Freedom Avenue. Starting from Vytautas Park's wooden gate it's a rather modest street, but from the *Soboras* (a real Kaunas old-timer would not refer to it as Garrison Church or the Church of St. Michael the Archangel) to Vilnius Street it's an avenue planted with many linden trees and sparkling with shop windows everywhere. From the "Agfa" firm Mama buys a modern camera with bellows and some film. "Telefunken" offers the latest radio sets. During Easter season the firm's window displays chirp with little live yellow chicks. Arkus, the cloth merchant, has hired a little person for his shop window. He's a dressed up little man of indeterminate age, with a face as wrinkled as a balled-up wad of paper, decked out in coat and tails and patent leather shoes. All day long he'd clamber up and down and over the piles of cloth bolts.... I look at him, my nose pressed against the glass, and feel a little envious—how fine it must be for him there. From the Markus con-

4

fectionary shop come the aromas of almond cakes and cinnamon buns... I'm most drawn by the "Tilka" chocolates and the ice cream. That prewar ice cream, those variously colored balls, plopped on stemmed glass dishes. And of course you'd always get a glass of water! And almost on every corner were the white-robed sausage sellers. A serving would be laid out on a cardboard dish—a fried bun, a sausage, and a puddle of mustard. From a distance I see a whole cloud of balloons. The man holding them on a stick seems as small as an ant. I choose a red balloon with ears that remind me of Mickey Mouse.

The company *Pienocentras* ("Milk Central") builds huge quarters on the corner of Freedom Avenue and Daukantas Street. In that building there's an elevator and an elevator operator, still a rarity in those days, and fashionable apartments facing the busy street. On the other side, you have the movie theater "Triumph" (later the "Mercury" store).... How small those people are, and they all go to the movies whenever they want to, I think to myself, looking down onto Freedom Avenue from the fifth floor of Mama's friend Nina's apartment.

In the "Batia" shoe store a true miracle—there's a little room containing a special box with a little window on the top and a hole in the bottom. You place your foot with the shoe you're trying on in the box through the hole, press a button, look through the window and know if the shoe's not too tight on your foot and fits you properly. For me, the distance from the hole to the little window is too far, and Mama has to be the one to determine whether a shoe fits me. What a pity I don't get to see my foot through that window.

In the bookstore I see something terribly desirable—two little picture books. They're cut up so that one is in the form of a little girl, the other a bear cub. How I want them...

—Buy them for me,—I ask.

Mama replies with a sacred phrase I can't stand but one I'll hear many times and, later, one I'll repeat myself over and over, even to this very day:

—I don't have the money.

Work a little, work a little more, and then you'll have some, my kids used to say.

—How can you have any, when the light is always on in your hallway?—says my little grand-daughter when I refuse to buy her a stick-limbed Barbie doll.

...Christmas approaches. Lights twinkle along Freedom Avenue.

Lithuanian lass, daughter of open fields,
With your eyes the color of sky,
Lithuanian lass, I am your slave,
My heart belongs to you...

—sings Danielius Dolskis, a star of Kaunas from that time, a Jewish immigrant from Russia who learnt Lithuanian surprisingly quickly. I'm not there yet, and my future papa, as if winged, flies down Freedom Avenue toward my mother-to-be with a bouquet in his hand and a heart belonging to a *lietuvaite* (Lithuanian lass) in his breast.

And later, there is me.

It's the last Sunday,
Today we'll separate...

—sings another star, a local one, Antanas Šabaniauskas.

The shop windows compete with each other. Colored light runs through letters made out of wreathed and twisted glass tubes. It fills the tubes, then dies, then starts up again. A brand new innovation. But how I want those books... I head home disappointed and sad. Fortunately, Christmas arrives soon and Santa Claus makes me happy.

Money—the litas, the mark, the ruble, and again the litas—in our family at all times there was never enough.

•

In The Swans pharmacy on Daukantas Street, two white swans, one in each window, necks curved, look to right and left. Both the pharmacy and the two swans disappear during the second Soviet occupation. Many years later I come across one in the Pharmacy Museum on Town Hall Square. It fills me with joy, like meeting up with a long-lost friend. Throughout my childhood, my pediatrician Andrius Matulevičius, always recommended The Swans pharmacy. From there came a frighteningly large syringe and needle that he used to inoculate me in my rear end when I was sick with diptheria.

Doctor Andrius Matulevičius was not a big believer in medicines. For minor illnesses he'd recommend mashed bananas with orange juice. During the German occupation when I'm seriously sick again, Mama, unable to find our good doctor, approached another well-known pediatrician, Vincas Tercijonas. But he won't make a house-call unless

6

you send a car for him. During those times, people were already starting to change.

•

I become feverish and delirious; Mama runs to a nearby physician, Vytautas Juškis, who specializes in skin and venereal diseases. He doesn't turn us away. He heals what comes before him, as he understands it. Juškis' house used to be one of the most modest ones on Vaižgantas Street.

...From The Swans pharmacy you can almost reach your hand over to the garden of the War Museum.

—Greetings, Sir,—I politely address the "little person" statue, as I always do each time I come to the garden with its little fountain. The fountain's iron gnome says nothing back. I know he only pretends to be grumpy. For so many years he's been tearing with his bare hands at the rock face from which spurts a fountain of water. Thousands of little girls have stood in front of that fountain. The worried little man tries to find me among those thousands. It's hard for him to remember—but he does—the former days when the fountain was beautiful with its golden fish, rather than filled with trash and dull coins. The little girl Dita marveled then at the little man's diligence.

Today, the old woman Dita looks at him with the same fearful respect. The garden and memorial have been re-created to look almost exactly the same as before. The Soviets had swept the grounds clean of all crosses, the piled-stone monuments, the altar, the Statue of Freedom. But they didn't touch the gnome. Perhaps he didn't look threatening enough. He didn't stand for any ideas.

I still hadn't learnt to read, but I knew where the busts of Maironis and Basanavičius were. And not only where they were, but also what they were. More or less—not yet having had my first lessons in patriotism. Those lessons were also on the modest covers of my school notebooks—as portraits of Vincas Kudirka, Žemaitė, the ruins of Trakai castle... The covers were simple, single colored. Poor cousins to today's notebooks. Back then no one made fun of the idea of patriotism, love of one's country, freedom, the tri-colored national flag.

So.

They swept it all away and not only from the surface. They dug out the remains of the Unknown Soldier and no one knows where they put them. Later, not far from that spot, they buried the poet, Salomėja Nėris. Only after many years was she finally transferred to the Petrašiūnai Cemetery.

Those times you could call the excavation years. Historians and museum archivists, in restoring the statues and memorials of the War Museum's grounds, searched everywhere for the Unknown Soldier's remains, but did not find them. Earlier, the Soviets were unable to find the bodies of Darius and Girėnas[1], which had been secretly removed from their mausoleum and hidden away. Much later, after the nation's regained independence, the responsible officials somehow allowed the nationally known priest and poet Ričardas Mikutavičius—killed by criminals—to be buried as an unknown person, with no honors. Eventually his body was disinterred and reburied in the Petrašiūnai Cemetery next to Salomėja Nėris'grave. Now the two are side by side. Probably two of the most controversial yet highly-respected people in Lithuania.

•

...The transfer of Salomėja Nėris' remains from the War Museum's grounds doesn't happen right away. The planned ceremonies hit a snag and are postponed. It seems that the remains are not buried directly under the gravestone and monument. A fair amount of searching needs to take place and finally a lot of jack-hammering at the concrete panel under which they're finally located. The remains are solemnly carried to Vytautas church where, at that time another poet, Ričardas Mikutavičius, is the parrish priest.

The next day the coffin is transported to the cemetery. But what happened the night before?

Father Ričardas comes from his nearby apartment, unlocks the church doors, and approaches the coffin. He lifts the coffin's lid and unseen by anyone he lays a rosary on the white bones of the poet. A rosary gotten from the very hands of the Pope.

•

—May all be forgiven you—prays the priest, and all the dark vaulted space seems to look on approvingly.

---

[1] Steponas Darius and Stasys Girėnas, Lithuanian-American pilots, flew across the Atlantic in 1933, crashing and dying in Germany just short of their goal, Kaunas. The flight was a significant accomplishment in the history of aviation and also stands as the first transatlantic airmail consignment.

—God has forgiven her all—says the priest to me in the ancient Vytautas church, restored and decorated as a result of his attention and concern, when I arrive the next day with a microphone to interview him for the radio.

By the gnome fountain, then. . .

. . .and now.

note: the gnome fountain stands in the garden of the Kaunas war museum.

9

The bell clangs... My heart is pierced
By moaning, weeping...
Surely that's not my coffin they're carrying...
My days run forward happily!...

•

Nėris wrote this verse in 1921 when she was 17. And this, in 1944, a year before her death:

Unrested, without food or drink,—
The she-wolf stumbled through the fields.
Gripped by fear, the sick beast
Was called by the forest's green depths.

By dusk of velvet moss
She's lulled into eternal sleep...

If only my homeland would meet me like that!
How hard it is, how I pity myself.

•

These verses were not typical for the Salomėja, whom some honored, others reviled. Nor for the Salomėja, whose verses rang from the youthful lips of my generation, cultivated our literary taste, helped name those newly born feelings of love. Nor for the Salomėja, who still echoes in my heart in the voice of my girlhood friend Rena.

•

...At the end of Freedom Avenue a narrow archway lets you into a yard, where stands the small church of St. Gertrude. Most people call the place Šaritės (Charity) Church, or just Šaritės. The church was first made note of in the beginning of the sixteenth century. At one point, alongside the church lived a group of nuns, the Sisters of Charity. The nunnery grounds stretched alongside the banks of the *Nemunas* to the Carmelite church. The sisters used to grow vegetables and look after the poor. The prospering city's development swallowed the sisters' gardens and finally even the order itself. The church, undergoing renovation and "im-provement," lost its gothic appearance, its frescoes, its tapering windows.

Many had the habit, walking down Freedom Avenue, of turning into Šaritės, kneeling, and asking for some small favor. That short stay, you could say was like getting a little pet from the Almighty. A short stay—a small request, and a short thanks.

10

—Please, Lordy (*Dievuli*), let me meet up with Juozas.
—Thanks, Lordy, for helping me pass my exam.

•

...The Šaritės churchyard is thick with green bushes and trees. Behind them hide two teenage girls who amidst coughs try to inhale the smoke of cheap "*Moka*" cigarettes. Those teenagers are the high schoolers Dita and Protelė. The daughter of the composer Mikas Petrauskas lives on Kipras Petrauskas Street (named after his brother, a famous opera tenor), in the Petrauskas house, first floor. Neither for her nor for me is it necessary to walk to school via Freedom Avenue, but somehow we two always end up there. And we don't forget to stop by Šaritės.

The Soviets convert the little church into a pharmaceutical warehouse. Garages sprout on the approaches to the church. Finally, they decide to expand the existing communist bureau for their local leaders, and within a few steps of the church they begin to erect an especially solid-looking building. Meant to stand for a thousand years. Like that Reich of Hitler's. The unwanted soil is carted out of town along with the bones and skulls of nuns who'd been buried there long ago.

Just before Lithuania's Independence[2], when I arrived at Kaunas on a work assignment, I see such a sad scene at Šaritės. I complain to the then Culture Fund's chairman, professor Česlovas Kudaba. But the professor is not omnipotent, and his eyes fill with sadness.

—I know,—he says,—I've seen it. And I also spoke to the head of that office. The director first enquired "who I thought I was," and then said, "For the sake of some old antique, no one is going to halt the building of a project already in progress."

•

The enlightened Česlovas Kudaba's memory will last a long time, but who will remember those functionaries? Even their surnames? During the Independence movement—the very Rebirth of the nation—the huge foundations were dismantled, the pits filled in and leveled. Šaritės regained its original form and purpose. They repaired and restored it; only the central altar up to now remains as it

---

[2] The second Lithuanian independence, March 11, 1990—the Day of Restoration of Lithuanian Independence.

11

was during the time of the church's use as a pharmaceuticals storehouse—beaten up, dirty, peeling. Strange. Between the newly cleaned walls, the altar still glows with the truest, purest light. Your eyes, having run through the small space of the church, stop on the altar and seem to see God's face there. At least for a short time, your heart is relieved and at peace. But the dish to take that feeling away in is so shallow, and the drop in it is so tiny... Surely I'll spill it, won't be able to carry it. Truth be told, where am I to take it anyway?

•

Today's Freedom Avenue empties around nightfall, even though the shop windows are twice as spacious as before and glow with sterile lights. In the years of my girlhood, the darkening Avenue filled up with people, and you could meet anyone you wanted to there. If you went up and down a few times between the Soboras and the Šaritės' gates it was called "šlifuoti," or polishing. Freedom Avenue was "polished" by pupils, students, all sorts of folks of differing ages from all the various districts of Kaunas—Žaliakalnis, Šančiai, Slabada, Senamiestis... Ah, if only we all could gather here now!

Afternoon. The start of summer. 1940. Freedom Avenue is full of people. They're not going anywhere. They stand on the sidewalks and look into the street. Down the Avenue flows the stream of a dimly colored foreign army. At that time I only sensed, but now well know, why my mother wept, why many people wept as they looked on at the puffed up men in their strange uniforms. They did not yet resemble the short-statured brutes with Asiatic features and small-peaked caps who were to come later, the ones who within a year will stuff cattle cars full of terrified Kaunas residents.

The smell of army boots and cheap soap overwhelms the aroma of cinnamon from Markus' confectionary.

I didn't know then what freedom smelled like. It was just there. As ordinary as air. You breathe it in—you breathe it out.

The Statue of Freedom still stood in the War Museum grounds.

Crying was not enough then. It was not enough to grasp that this was freedom's burial.

—What does it mean, CCCP?—I hear myself asking.

—In Lithuanian, that would be SSSR (USSR), the Union of Soviet Socialist Republics.

•

12

Not everyone wept.

"We met the Russians with flowers and song," remembered Cilė Žiburkienė, the granddaughter of Plungė's rabbi in 1944.[3]

"No, that was not an occupation," agrees Rachelė Margolis in that same book. Her parents were from Vilnius, and after the October Soviet revolution of 1917 they returned here from Russia. As she herself affirmed, "They ran from the Soviets."

Unanswered questions pour over me from Freedom Avenue's linden trees. Why were the flowers and songs necessary, Cilė? If not an occupation, then what, Rachelė? And why did your parents flee the Soviets? Why was the Lithuanian army in shining readiness at that time, if not for defense? What price did Juozas Urbšys, the foreign affairs minister, have to pay for accepting the Soviet ultimatum? Only eleven years in solitary in a Soviet cell for himself, and solitary for his wife, Marija Mašiotaitė, too?

At the beginning of 1990 Juozas Urbšys inscribed his memoirs for me with a trembling hand. And "good wishes" above his signature to my children, Paulina Eglė and Martynas Žilvinas. He was ninety-four then. In a year he was dead. When I visited him, the former minister lived far from the center, in block housing, "near the tank," as Kaunites used to say. As angry fate had it, that tank stood for many years, not only as a monument but also as a stern warning, with its barrel pointing at the window of the foreign affairs minister of the "liberated" state. But there came a time when the tank, named the "Josef Stalin," was hoisted up and carried away. A cross was erected in its place. One night some unknown vandals knocked the cross down. Now, there's an entire hill of crosses there. They won't knock them down in one night.

•

After the war, it was fashionable to call Kaunas a city of speculators, swindlers, and scammers—without any subtlety of spirit. Even though the light of Maironis, and Vaižgantas, and Krėvė, and Putinas, and other famous Lithuanian writers, still shone over it, those who didn't want to see it didn't.

---

[3] *Lithuania's Jews, 1918 -1940. Echoes from a Lost World* ("Lietuvos Žydai, 1918-1940. Prarasto pasaulio aidas"), ed. by Ives Plasseraud ir Henri Minczeles; trans. by Elena Belskytė and Liucija Baranauskaitė—VG: Baltos lankos, 2000.

A certain science professor, after having listened to my many biting pronouncements about the city of Kaunas, finally unable to stand it any longer, asked me:

—Why do you love Kaunas so painfully?

Then I really thought about it. Why, indeed?

Not only because it's my birthplace.

Here, the fountain's sullen gnome still tears persistently at the rock face.

Here, Daddy and I walk down Freedom Avenue to the photo gallery "Zinaida" near the post office and get ourselves photographed in an embrace.

Here echo and fade the steps of my first love.

> *When wisdom entereth into thine heart, and*
> *knowledge is pleasant unto thy soul.*
>
> Proverbs 2: 10

> *A time to rend, a time to sew;*
> *a time to keep silence, and a time to speak.*
>
> Ecclesiastes 3: 7

2
In the Purickis House

On the Purickis' balcony

The Purickis house on the bluff of Vytautas Hill shines from afar with its white walls and large windows. You can see it all the way from Aleksotas Hill.

The doctor of philosophy, diplomat, and publicist Juozas Purickis, who died in 1934, had left that five-storey building to his wife who was living on Vytautas Avenue at that time.

Below in the valley, Kaunas was expanding, a young and energetic city. The grand official buildings were erected by the state, while all kinds of officials, lawyers, teachers and other well-to-do citizens had private houses and cottages built. The wealthy particularly favored lots on Vytautas Hill and on *Žaliakalnis* (Green Hill). Especially desirable were the gentle slopes of the *Naujamiestis* (New City). New two-storey brick buildings climbed up and down the slopes... Thus the new streets of *Trakų, Sopranų, Tenorų, and Bosų* appeared, lined with fresh and bright new homes. The granite Būgos Steps linked Vytautas Hill with the valley below.

Today, on Vytautas Hill and *Žaliakalnis*, there are a lot of new buildings too. But today's landlords don't bother renovating the old houses; they just stick on new extensions. The extensions, frequently bigger than the original buildings, spread out aggressively, all elbows and asses, too big for the lots they're on. Next to the Vaižgantas house an especially pretentious edifice has sprouted up,

15

apparently wanting to emulate, or even surpass, its old neighbor. On the old Fričas' brothers property the new house barely fits, cramped across and along the lot. In the old days, the two Fričas wives grew various vegetables on their land and sold them to their neighbors right out of their gardens. There were two gardens—one snug up against Vaižgantas Street, the other in terraces stepping down the hill. The fatter Fričas wife was probably the only one in the neighborhood who kept a dog, but no one was afraid of it. No *Beware of the Dog* sign was posted. Dogs, whether angry or gentle, were not used to scare people off. Perhaps fewer thieves were around then?

Now, walking along, I read: "Vicious Dog," "Vicious Dog," "Vicious Dog"—signs on walls and fences trying to frighten passers-by. Someone has even drawn a portrait of a terrifying dog on a board above their gate. Just you dare open the gate, and you'll get it! What are these dogs protecting? Vicious masters and mistresses? On the trampled slope at the top of Būgos Steps, what is that great wolfhound guarding? Perhaps that little outhouse—just like the one we used to have in our village—is listed on the "historical register"?

Many people know the Purickis' house near the radio station—one of the very few five-storey buildings in Kaunas. The building is home to many intellectuals. Just recently, Vincas Mykolaitis-Putinas, the "ex-priest writer" (how piquant that sounded then) moved out, he who had shocked the public with his novel *Altorių šešėly (In the Altar's Shadow)*.

The prominent public figure and doctor of philology Ignas Skrupskelis, who is later to perish in a Siberian camp, lives in the building. With his brother's family, the future famous sculptor Vytautas Kašuba, who in 1944 had to leave Lithuania never to return, also lives in the building. No, he did return. He returned through his talented creations, donated to Lithuania, especially the Grand Duke Gediminas' monument in the Cathedral Square in Vilnius. Also residing here is the ex-cleric physician Juozas Markulis, recently married. Undoubtedly, he is the most handsome man in the building. Later he is to become a famous specialist in forensic medicine. However, there'll never be a memorial plaque for him. Even though he walked with his head held high until the very end, Juozas Markulis was a collaborator and KGB agent, who informed on Lithuanian partisan cells after the war. In apartment number seven the well-known engineer and manager Vytautas Graičiūnas and his wife Unė Babickaitė-Bay, film

16

and theater actress and director, have set themselves up after repatriating from America. For them too, not much time is left to enjoy life. It's good they don't know that.

The Purickis apartment on Vaižganto Street

Destiny's glass is filling for us all. The war has yet to begin. Only perceptive people and intellectuals are taking note of the Nazi threat from the west. To the east, Stalin is already rubbing his hands together waiting for the Second World War, and through it, the dominion of the world proletariat. He's engaged in a secret race with Hitler—who will attack first?

...My mother, already divorced, is discontented with her mediocre apartment on Aušros Street. She wants more space and beauty, and so looks to rent on Vaižgantas Street. Here the apartments are big, not entirely suited to her purse. No matter. She's ready to rent a one or two-room apartment. On the fifth floor there's a four-room apartment with a large kitchen and a small room for a maid. Two spacious balconies, with the best views of Kaunas. You can see the whole city, from the confluence of the Nemunas and Neris to the railroad station... Temporarily, the young, handsome Count Zubovas lives there, intending to marry M. K. Čiurlionis' daughter, Danute.

Mama really wants this apartment. We come to look it over. The young count asks the three of us to be seated—Mama, her friend, and me. He speaks:

17

—Ladies, this morning I ate some garlic, but tonight I'm going on a date. What should I do, how do I get rid of this smell?

The ladies are eager to help out the Count and advise him to drink some milk.

—How much—asks the Count.—A liter, two?

—A cup—say the ladies—better if it's warm.

The Count excuses himself, saying he'll return right away and show us through the apartment.

—He's gone off to heat himself some milk,—determine the ladies.

We wait a long time. We marvel at the town's panorama. Over there, the Freda and Aleksotas slopes, the huge grain elevator, and there, on Vytautas Avenue the "Lietūkis" cooperative offices. More to the right—the Soboras' cupola. And further west—the confluence of the two rivers, the church towers of the old town, the sparkling flow of the Nemunas.

An hour goes by, maybe an hour and a half. The ladies are seriously concerned. Maybe the Count has had a heart attack? Maybe he's lying there dead, and since we're here by chance, what's it to do with us? The ladies make a determination. What will be, will be—they will go and look for the vanished Count. They go through the rooms and finally find him. The host is lying on the sofa, snoring his head off. The ladies, not used to this kind of a reception, leave, slamming the door shut from the outside (thank goodness for the new French lock).

Nonetheless, soon the apartment is ours.

Mama is afraid of the philistine interiors as much as she's afraid of fire; that's why there's nothing in the apartment that would testify to that kind of taste. We have no étagère for bric-a-brac, no paper flowers, no ficuses, nor seven-elephant figurines, each one following the other in descending size. Needless to say, we have no dark tapestry on the wall with its antlered elk peering out from forest depths. In the new apartment's kitchen Mama forbids the hanging of the then popular hand crafted items—dish cloths embroidered with red or blue threads. You used to be able to buy them at the Carmelite's market—already embroidered, or just as patterns drawn on paper. "Bon Appetite" said the scripted, sewn-in red letters underneath the plump cook. She, with her cook's hat, is bent over a red pot on a red stove. The pot is releasing bold red curlicues—steam, we're to understand. "Good Night" says the puffy feathered duvet, trimmed with blue swirls. Blunt-edged

18

stars float on the white cotton sky in the blue-trimmed window frame.

I believe, those naïve embroideries would be more beautiful to me if I could see them today...

I have my own room. Not very big or spacious, but my own. In it stands a wardrobe, a cabinet with a mirror (I'm pleased to still possess them) and my little bed. The bed is of yellow wood, with a slatted side that can be lowered. Next to my bed, an embroidered tapestry on the wall, Mama's handicraft. It depicts a band of happily singing girls in a flowered field. The only boy, wearing a white hat and short pants, flies above them carried by variously colored balloons. A lot of art there isn't in this composition. But how much space for imagination... It's sewn masterfully, like all of Mama's youthful embroideries—with colored silk threads in various hues. The birch tree alone has leaves of at least six shades. The faces of the children are detailed in oil paint, their hair made from a special fiber.

Now, after many years, the colors of those threads are still like new. But the children's heads are bald, the fibered hair long ago crumbled away. My little granddaughter, Vaidilė, generously clips some of her own hair off and asks to have it glued onto those time-ravaged heads. She gently strokes the little kids' faces with her sunburnt hand and asks for their names. Alas, I can't pull them out of that other time. I have to invent new ones.

A wicker table and chair also stand in my room. And that's it. No, that's not everything. A huge window and a balcony beyond it runs the length of the apartment. The entry to the balcony is through the window, since my room hasn't a door to it. No problem. The window's wide and the sill's not very high, and I can ride my scooter, called a *roleris*, at will on the balcony. Even now my heart longs for that *roleris*. In what dump did it rot? In those days scooters were wooden.

—Buy me a scooter,—I say to my husband after sixty odd years.

He looks at me with surprise, even alarm—am I checking out mentally? But he buys me one. And after a few days says:

—You'll have to let me ride on it, too. But please, not in Vilnius, in Palanga, by the seaside.

And still that's not quite all there is in that room of mine. Most interesting of all are the stairs. Wide, wooden, painted—they begin in the corner and lead to the door; behind it they climb up to a higher door. On hot days it's cool on the stairs, in winter moderately cold. The stairs serve as our refrigerator, as we didn't have one, nor even knew of the existence of such a thing. That's why something was always placed on each step—on the first a pot of soup, on the second a basket of eggs, on the third a sack of potatoes, on the fourth the box of chestnuts I'd gathered last year, on the fifth glass jars of preserved berries, and so on up to the very top. The stairs were tall, like the rooms. At the top the door was always locked. What's behind that door?

Behind that door—an entirely different world. First of all, a delicious smell of timber. The tin roof is held up by wooden beams. They're vertical, horizontal, and diagonal. Lots of partitions, empty wall cabinets, and various nooks and crannies. A few small windows under the roof itself. Not much of anything else, except a rope or two hung here and there for drying the washing. During the day it's fairly light and dry there—on a sunny day, even a little stuffy. Most interesting of all, instead of a floor, there's sand. Really, real sand. Like the beach at *Panemunė*.

But the loft remains empty. No visitor ever goes here. It could be a good hiding place. But for whom? Who needs to hide, and from whom? The future victims of the war slept, ate, conducted business, walked to their jobs, raised children, studied, read books. Probably the future aggressors did the same. But not only that. They already knew what was to happen. But why were their victims so short-sighted? Did they lack information? Resolve? Strength? How many answers have been put forward over the years even to this very day? My cousin Emanuel says:

—A sane person couldn't have expected what we got from the cultured German nation.

I think he's in error.

Probably, only after we've learned how to move faster than the speed of light, will we be able to return to that past, as the scholars say, and take a look at the present of that time through the eyes of our own present.

The distant past of ancient Egypt was studied by a Kaunas University professor, Marija Rudzinskaitė-Arcimavičienė. We subletted her the corner room with one of the balconies. My baby-sitter, Janė, and I used to call her "Arcimuvka." We knew she was Lithuania's most renowned Egyptologist. She'd written a number of books about ancient Egyptian hieroglyphics, Tutankhamun's tomb, and the monuments at Thebes. For a long time after the war I kept those orange-covered books, until another—self-taught—Egyptologist cadged them from me. Arcimuvka had been to Egypt and Palestine a number of times; the mummy and other ancient artifacts she brought back are kept today in Kaunas' M. K. Čiurlionis' art museum.

I'm about six years old, Janė is 10 years older, and to both of us, Arcimuvka, at about fifty, seems hopelessly old. She wears heretofore unseen Egyptian scarves and a strangely disheveled hairstyle—unlike any other woman's. In her room you can't see the table, cabinet, or sofa—laid out everywhere are cloths, scarves, and dresses with oriental patterns. There are unusual bronze vases and ceramic figurines. I enter that room as if into the fairytale world, as if into "A Thousand and One Nights." Arcimuvka loves me and often invites me in:

—Come on, Ditele. Today you can be Princess Anchesenamona,—she says and dresses me up in silks from distant lands, wraps me in thin linen mantles with exotic ornaments, and decks me out with gold bangles inscribed with secret hieroglyphics.

She takes delight in dressing up a little girl like this, as if she herself had breathed the spirit into some pharaoh's mummified daughter.

Arcimuvka, like a proper scholar, was absent-minded and impractical. She was capable of covering her chamber pot with a towel and then using that same towel in place of a tablecloth when offering a guest some Eastern-style coffee. In fact, one guest accidently kicked over the chamber pot under the sofa, and the scholar quickly wiped up its contents with a towel pulled from the table. But that's not of most importance.

In her room, unearthly odors fill the space from never-before seen incense sticks standing in special incense boxes. Bronze dishes shine dimly as do glazed vases. On the table, ears alert, sits a stone pharaoh's dog. Not understanding much, I'm charmed by her Egyptian art reproductions, but I can't help noticing how those ignoramus Egyptians can't properly draw a human being. Both men and women are drawn the same way: head turned to the side, chest forward, legs and feet also to the side. Just you try standing that way! From the scholar's lips I first heard of the pyramids, Tutankhamun, Echnaton and Nefertiti...about the Bedouins and Berbers, the Nile and its delta... Such was my first exposure to ancient Egypt with its art infused with the fragrance of eternity. At that point, I didn't yet know about other great cultures.

When she found out that the scholar was sick with tuberculosis, Mama worried about me, and Arcimuvka had to move out. The war began. Our scholar died in Vilnius in 1941 at the beginning of May.

Mama moves into the scholar's room. No smell of incense remains, no garments with strange ornaments and hieroglyphics, no ancient Egyptian secrets. The room is now clean and quite empty. The long balcony is empty too and no longer snug. I'm forbidden to stand on anything and lean over the balcony wall. How can I not lean over? One has to water the petunias swooning in the summer heat. And find out how the excess water flows through the water pipes on the side. I climb up on a wooden box and lean over. Carefully, of course. After all, it is the fifth floor.

—If you fall—Amen. We won't be able to gather up your bones—Mama had already warned me.

On the level below, another balcony. And there, in a patch of sunlight on a mattress lies a woman—naked as a jaybird. Ach, for shame! I quickly run to the bathroom and fill up a pot with water, climb back on the box, and sploosh!...right onto the heated-up lady, and then I hide.

It turns out the nude lady is the actress, Unė Babickaitė-Graičiūnienė. The lady's in her forties, so, for me, she's ancient. But I must confess she is a real beauty. At that time I'm a very pious, practicing Catholic, and I want to do battle against all sorts of indecencies. However, for my upstanding moral behavior I end up getting a good whipping, just as soon as the lady complains to my mother.

From that time on, I didn't like my beautiful neighbor. Nor she me. Going up or down the stairs past her apartment, I ring her bell and run off. But now I'm a little more clever and don't admit my actions to a living soul. Up until 1961, when she died, I could have met her and pleased her with an apology, even if belated. Alas. There's a lot we end up not doing or saying to the living. But when they're dead, we try to commune with them mystically, lighting candles on their graves, and metaphysically offering them our love and remorse. But then it's all too late. Too late.

...The small garden of the Purickis house is blooming. In it are benches, a sand box, and neatly tended flowerbeds. The trees offer shade from the sun. Bushes where you can play hide and seek. A path made of boards runs from the gate to the garbage cans. In her flowerbeds Mama has planted snowdrops, blue phloxes, peonies. From the garden by the Volfas villa, she has transported a small lilac tree. She had gotten that tree as a gift on the occasion of my birth. In the flowerbeds of the Purickis garden the lilac tree happily takes strong root, and every spring spills over with large, firm clusters of flowers. The flowers are white and double-petalled. Among them you don't have to look for fortunate ones. To the very last one, they're all fortunate.

Today, in place of the blooming garden, a trampled down rocky plot. One apple tree remains. No sign of the fence and gate. Sand—not a grain. Board path—not a plank. As if there wasn't a single child in the building. There are no more flowerbeds. On the other side of the street, where the radio station's property was, stands a huge trash container. It stands on raised ground like some sort of monument. A human creature with a blue face bends over, says something into the container's opening.

—A lunatic,—I think to myself fearfully.

Not at all. He is simply talking to another human being who is already inside the half empty container. They must be looking for empty bottles to sell. But it seems people are in no hurry to litter. Or drink the bottles empty. Maybe even eat. It reminds me of a cartoon I once saw: a spider web on a naked rear end. And that's better than a spider web on the lips.[1] But let's put sentiments aside.

We're sitting now in front of our TVs and computers.

—Lithuanians—a nation of kings,—said a female politician on the radio recently.

Is that what we used to be? Or are we yet to be?

Then I saw and considered it;
I looked and received instruction.

Proverbs 24: 32

A wise man is mightier than a strong man,
and a man of knowledge than he who has strength.

Proverbs 24: 5

---

[1] When a person has nothing to eat, there's no need to go to the bathroom. And when you're afraid to say what you think (i.e., against the Soviets, or any occupying regime), you walk around with a spider web across your lips.

Young Milda

3
This Dear Hand

My first ever phobia springs from a phrase I over-hear my father say. Looking at two old plugs by the electric meter, he declares:

—They ought to be replaced, so the whole apartment doesn't burn down.

Everything he says is vital to me. I awake in the middle of the night and stare at the two little windows in my door and wonder fearfully if there's already a fire burning in the hallway? No, but the blackness in there is suspiciously black. And if there is a fire, what color would it be? Yellow? Orange? Red? Will it crackle as in the kitchen? Or will it glow silently? How will I get to Mama who is sleeping at the other end of the hallway? Since I'm not allowed to cry for Mama unnecessarily, I first chill my feet on the wooden end of the bed before I call for her. With cold feet I have permission to take myself to Mama's bed.

This clever strategy comes to an end, though, when Mama marries for the second time. Still, my guardian angel in the picture on the wall is merciful to me. There's no fire. My guardian angel, thanks to him for everything, never forgets me during all the terrible war and post-war days. But up to what age do the angels protect us? My angel tries very hard but, apparently, can do only so much. He helped grow my body but left my spirit muddled, tangled, knotted up. Only after many years did it straighten itself out and, even then, not completely. But maybe the spirit isn't his area of competence. Whose then? God's?

That childhood fear of fire morphed into a simple dream, the only dream that I still remember from childhood: I'm sitting on the steps in my room, The door to the loft stairs is ajar, with some scary unknown lurking behind it. Suddenly, the door opens wide and from the darkness out leaps a witch—such a classic one, too, with a dark gray cloak, hooded, covering her head and reaching the floor. And that's all. I am terrified in the dream and after I wake up as well. That dreadful gray cloak has remained with me for over sixty years, sometimes shrunk to the size of my palm, sometimes expanded to such great widths that it blankets all my courage, all I know, all I can do.

In those days I was afraid of many things—darkness, fire, war, bombs, soldiers—German soldiers, Russian soldiers—my math teacher, deportation to Siberia, not passing my exams, losing my loved ones, getting sick, and even dying. I feared informers, robbers, traitors, violators. Some things from that list I'm now able to cross out— soldiers, deportation to Siberia, my math teacher, and exams. The rest remain.

In broad daylight, Mama opens the door to the loft.

—Look, there're no witches here, just sand and wood.

Through the loft window a slanting shaft of sunlight stabs into the sandy floor. Thousands of dust motes dance in the sunbeam. Not too long afterwards, I find the same repeated in a poem, *Illuminated Speck of Dust*, by Mykolas Vaitkus:

> In Great Beauty's fresh sunbeam,
> as in the path of a golden dream
> that leads our yearning up to Paradise,
> the dust motes fly.

Only much later did I begin to understand the meaning behind this poem—and what that "speck of dust, enchanted by light" was. At that time I only saw the image, leading towards more abstract ideas. The symbolist poetry of Mykolas Vaitkus, read and enjoyed at an early age, still echoes in my heart with its conception of the human condition:

> ...And so Fate cheated yet another poor one,
> having strewn pearls before him with its
> gracious hand:
> while he hurried to pick up at least one of the
> beads,
> they all rolled off and disappeared into the past...

In the loft it smells nicely of warm air and open space, since no old junk is stored there. Sinking into the loft's sandy floor with her high heels, and leaving small holes instead of footprints, Mama walks towards one of the old wall cabinets and opens it. Yes, it's empty, just as it should be according to the fire-prevention rules—but not entirely empty. On the top shelf there's a cardboard box. Mama can't quite reach it to take it down but can put her hand into it. Suddenly, she jumps back frightened, grabs me by the hand and in a flash we both clatter down the stairs.

Recovering her tongue, Mama insists she felt, between sheets of thin wrapping paper, something like a human nose, and even the hair of eyebrows. Our fellow residents can't believe their ears. After lengthy consideration, and after summoning a few of the more courageous, the box is brought down to the apartment, opened, and thoroughly investigated. Indeed, in the box, wrapped in thin paper is a plaster death mask complete with eyebrow hairs. Further, from among the sheets of paper a plaster hand falls out as from a husk—also with hairs on it. The secret reveals itself from the letters carved into the wrist: "This is the dear hand of Doctor Juozas Purickis," along with a recent date of death.

I bet Mrs. Purickienė, who lived on Vytautas Avenue, didn't have much peace of mind long after that. The entire household and the neighbors, all having heard this story, condemned her for not loving her husband sufficiently enough to honor his memory.

•

Today, I think perhaps the opposite was true. Maybe he didn't love Mrs. Purickienė? Maybe the two of them were like my parents, married, but not in a church?

Young Milda, throwing off the provincial bonds of Marijampolė, comes to the big city of Kaunas. At first she lives with Auntie Černiauskienė in Panemunė with the Fifth Division of the Lithuanian Army, where Černiauskienė's husband is stationed. Later, she rooms with her friend, the actress, Gražina Jakavičiūtė. They remained friends into their old age, parted in the end not even by death but by illness and dementia.

The young Samuelis learns French, getting ready for his studies in Belgium. He has to be a good engineer, so to study in Kaunas would not be sufficient. At least that's the thinking of his father, Moses Subockis, ambitious businessman and owner of a contracting firm.

These two young people meet in Kaunas and fall in love, even though Miss Milda, led by her woman's intuition, says that their marriage will cause not only a lot of discomfort but also irreparably damage their own and their near ones' lives.

26

My father Samuelis is not afraid of life's future uncertainties. He wants to live here and now. He is no milquetoast, having already served in Lithuania's army—later he would become the vice president of the Kaunas chapter of the Union of the Lithuanian Jewish soldiers who fought for Lithuania's independence.

Offering his hand and heart to Miss Milda, Samuelis doesn't immediately get a positive response. Therefore, he uses a tried and true method as old as the earth itself—he asks help from his future descendent. By pure chance thankfully that descendent turned out to be me, and even though I was not there yet, in my name the two of them finally marry—in a neighboring country where civil unions are permitted. So that I could be born legal. My parents didn't know what I would be, male or female. Hearing what I am, Mama sighs with relief:

—Thank the Lord, a girl.

Mom and Dad on Freedom Avenue, early 1930s

Joy, too, from the Christian side of the family. Truly, there won't be anything to snip off of me.

27

Needless to say, I don't remember the first time my father took me in his hands, but I bet I loved it, because his hands are warm, large, with beautiful long fingers, though covered with prominent veins like a working man's. Since the first time I became aware of them, I loved them, and have all my life.

Now, after these many years, I know that my hands are just like his, though smaller. And that my son has the same hands. And that those hands are immortal—they will be repeated many times through my grandfather Moses' descendents—since I have no doubt that grandfather Moses' hands were exactly like mine, only bigger. I also know that father loved me from the start and loved me to his last breath. I know that that last breath was not unlike the sound of my own name, Dita.

Even before the Second World War, when my father and my mother—those two very different worlds—separate, Madame Milda remains unbound by benefit of the matrimonial sacrament. In our Catholic country it's as if she never wed. She's still fairly young, independent, elegant. She's elegant thanks to her dear friend, Zosė, a seamstress, who works in Kaunas' most prestigious dressmaking firm run by Elena Trejienė, called by our local ladies, Madame Treu. She makes a good profit off wealthy clients. Every year she travels to Paris to bring back the latest fashions and patterns. The products of such a salon are clearly too expensive for Mama, but Zosė sews for her out of her own home. She sews the most astonishing and fashionable dresses. Not only dresses, but coats as well. She's even sewn a pink dress and hat for my doll. Zosė sews with truly remarkable skill. Her gowns cling. And so it is that she sews a modern dress for Mama directly from one of the latest of Madame Treu's Parisian patterns. Unfortunately, however, a dress like that has already been sewn and sold at great expense to one of Kaunas' leading ladies, presented to her, of course, as the unique and solely existing exemplar. The second version is made by Zosė for Mama— at home. Draped in this dress, Mama attends the opera...

She looks stunning with her uniquely colored *feuilles mortes* hair and in that dress of black chiffon with black woolen appliques. Black squares with cut-out corners form into four-cornered stars subtly glowing dark red from the red lining.

At the opera house, the lady with the same "unique" dress sees her and turns green with anger, and next morning attacks the owner of the dressmaking firm. This scandal almost causes Zosė to lose her job; however, a savvy businesswoman is not going to let a master crafts-woman go. Zosė keeps her job and also continues to make "underground" clothes for her friend—of course, now somewhat modified to differ from the original patterns.

Zosė Blažienė with her brothers Felix and Adam, Lithuanian soldiers

After the German occupation, and under the new Soviet regime, Zosė lives with her reserve officer husband Leonas Blažys and three small children at his home village. In the city it's difficult to find enough food. But from his ancestral home they get deported to Siberia. After serving ten years, when she returns, she says they had been turned in by a neighbor—because of an axe that someone wouldn't lend someone else. Exiled to the Gulag, Zosė didn't lose her head. She took her Singer sewing machine with her, and that machine fed and clothed her family there. Her reputation as a miracle worker spread for over a hundred kilometers in all directions, as one who can sew any piece of clothing, for anyone, out of anything. The Party functionaries' wives vied among themselves to see who could snag the most "Westernized" clothes. It seems that Zosė had memorized any number of pre-war fashionable dress patterns and was thus able to salvage, at least in part, the flabby figures of the soviet ladies. She was getting enough work, but her own figure was irreparably ruined.

When they returned after many years, we came to meet them at Vilnius railroad station. Zosė was extremely overweight—Leonas, quite the opposite, very thin, malnourished, smelling of cheap tobacco, constantly coughing and clearing his throat. The kids were now grown some and spoke Lithuanian with a Russian accent.

—Thank God, you've all returned safe and sound, and during such a beautiful spring just as the lilac trees are flowering—says Mama, trying to keep a lid on her grief.

—And what are "lilacs"?—asks Audrutė, the oldest of the children.

At this point, Mama can't keep it together anymore and starts to weep. Zosė, too. And they both cry in each other's arms as if trying to release all those years of accumulated suffering.

It was hard for the Blažys family to settle back in Lithuania. But once again, the Singer machine came to the rescue, like a true family member, returned together from the Gulag. Zosė sits in front of it with more work than she can handle. Leonas picks up random odd jobs for which he's overqualified. All of his spare time he spends with his ear up against the radio, listening to Voice of America. That radio station, interfered with by the Soviets, buzzes and hums impossibly, but Leonas is well informed by the broadcasts. And it doesn't seem to damage his hearing. But Zosė in her old age grows almost stone-deaf.

—My dearest friend,—wept Mama two weeks before her own death when Zosė came to visit her. Mama no longer recognized most people, but how could she not know Zosė? And they both wept in an embrace just like the one at the station years ago. Their bodies were much changed by time—honestly, changed much for the worst. Both of them were at the very front of death's list, but their wrinkled hands still hung on to each other as if they were holding on to vanishing life. Their old hands, worked out and worn out, sought warmth and understanding from each other, which they could no longer give.

After two weeks, Mama's hands rested on her golden-colored burial blouse. Her hands were nothing like the plaster copy of Doctor Purickis' well-groomed hand. No need for a material copy that will be forgotten. Let it be gone—but remembered.

Saying good-bye to her, I kissed my mother, not on her cheek, but on her hand, as according to the old custom. I wanted to not only humble myself, but also to ask her forgiveness—for my impatience, lack of openness, insincerity, unmercifulness. Because she, too, was impatient, guarded, insincere, and lacking in mercy towards me. Worst of all, she was intolerant. I still hold tolerance as one of the highest of human values.

Who of us had to make the first move towards change? I guess I started first. But it was too late, since it was already after her death, alas.

Then let us no more pass judgment on one another.

Romans 14: 13

**Grandmother Ona
Žolynienė**

4
Adam and Eve
or, Just Mommy

I'm the only one who calls her Granny because at that time I'm the only grandchild. The extended family, and even strangers, though, have only one name for her—"Mommy."

In the photo, browned by age, stand a young couple in formal wedding gear, Onute Matulevičiūtė of Kumelionis village, who holds the helpful arm of her new husband, Jurgis Radzevičius. Little Ona is only sixteen; Jurgis is older and, according to relatives, is well educated, and works as a scribe. He stands straight and tall, with a medium-sized mustache and a high forehead, and is almost a head taller than his wife. He chose her from the Matulevičius-Matulaitis clan, much spread out from its origins in Marijampolė. That farming family from Suvalkija district numbered among its progeny quite a few shining lights—publicists, physicians, soldiers, priests, and now the beatified bishop Jurgis. He picked a comely bride. She's dressed in a white, gracefully tailored dress, her blonde hair topped by a modest tiara. In her right hand she holds a small bouquet. My heart skips a beat—where have I seen one just like it, held by another slender hand? Yes, in my very own daughter Eglė's hand on her wedding day. And so an invisible thread extends from 1900 to 2000. The little bouquet, after exactly one hundred years, recreates itself again in a great granddaughter's hand.

To lessen the ache in my heart, I begin to play around with my thoughts: in my imagination, I dress my new bride-grandmother in one of today's bikinis, and I see that in the narrowness of her waist and the lift of her breasts she would not lose against today's contestants for beauty's crown. I know that it was from her that we, her female descendents, inherited our erect posture and beautiful legs.

Ona Magdalena Matulevičiūtė and her husband, Jurgis Radzevičius, on their wedding day in 1900

After many years, when Granny was on her deathbed, I saw her legs—white, smooth, completely absent of any swollen veins or knobby knees. I looked at them dumbfounded. They seemed undamaged by life—not by St. Petersburg's cobblestones, nor Brooklyn's asphalt, nor the long years of wading through the stable muck of her Žvirgždaičiai farmstead.

And what about her hands? What were they like? I can feel them— taking my cold feet, warming them until I fall asleep.

Bride Eglė's hand

Back then, at the beginning of the twentieth century, Jurgis took his young wife to St. Petersburg. The years have drowned any memories of that time; she remembered only the name of the neighborhood they lived in— Vasilievsky Ostrov.

After that, fate took them to America. I wrote it as a cliché, yet how much hope, pain, uncertainty, hesitation, and resolve were required for that one step. And again, everything is gone without a trace, irretrievably extinguished in that other time, snuffed out like a spent matchstick.

They settled in Brooklyn, ran a tavern, and gave birth to my mother Matilda (Milda). After some time it became clear that "the climate didn't suit" my grandfather Jurgis—as they used to say in those days. Or were they simply plagued by nostalgia?

"Be, Lithuania, for me that beckoning light!"—wrote Jonas Aistis in 1944 when he was still in France. And later, in 1952, from Brooklyn also:

> *Did you dream, did you believe?*
> *In a childhood dream did you ever see*
> *That our little boat of fortune would be*
> *Wind carried, wave rocked and*
>
> *Dashed against some distant cliff...*
> *Broken for nothing, and on an alien*
> *Shore our prayers would fade*
>   *overcome by louder voices,*
> *The scream extinguished by glassy sky...*

When the American climate started "not suiting" Grandfather Jurgis, these verses were still far from being written. But they were already hovering around Brooklyn, needing only a pen to put them down—and, of course, Aistis' talent.

Before the First World War, their small daughter in tow, the two of them returned to settle in Šunskai. Grandpa Jurgis soon died. Dusty oblivion trod directly onto his grave, and no one knows anything more about him. I don't even know what I inherited from him. He left behind a little daughter and young widow, who opened up a little tavern... from where everything began again.

—Onute, would you like a little pear?—this, offered by Jonas Adomas Žolynas, farmer's son, to the young widow. After mass at the Šunskai parish church he stops by the tavern, not so much to "wet his whistle," but to enjoy taking a look at the tavern's pretty hostess.

Onute didn't say no to the pear. The farmer's son was handsome, fair-haired, with a blonde mustache. Soon love came, then a wedding, and even gossip by Jonas' relatives that the farmer's son took the *šinkorka,* the tavern-keeper, for a wife.

34

The Žolynas Couple

...Another old photograph graces my Aunt Teresė's home: two people in an embrace, a man and a woman—my Granny, no longer a slim sixteen-year old and Jonas, a serious middle-aged man. Jonas and Ona—Adam and Eve. Only Eve didn't offer an apple to Adam; rather Jonas offered Ona a pear. And the Lord God exiled them from their own home in the Garden of Eden, but only at the end of their lives. He exiled them painfully, but at least not too far away, only to Kaunas 70 kilometers away. Kaunas didn't awe my Granny overly much, she having seen more impressive buildings and streets in St. Petersburg and Brooklyn.

—Did you speak American?—my Aunt Prakseda and I would ask her.

—I've forgotten it all,—Granny would say.—Ah, I do remember one thing—"Dem devil"—and she'd add:

—Girls, don't ever repeat that. It's a very ugly curse.

Granny became a farmer and gave birth to five children, who were all given resonant sounding names: Konstantinas, Ričardas, Mikalina, Teresė, and Prakseda, the last one born late when Granny was already forty and Grandpa over fifty.

Withered and old stood the fateful pear tree alongside the farmhouse, the only one on the farmstead. It stood the entire time of the old folks lives there on that plot of earth. No use ever came of that tree; it gave no fruit anymore. But Grandfather, a true Suvalkietis[1], refused to chop it down. Let it be, he'd say; after all, it's not interfering with anyone...

---

[1] inhabitants of Suvalkija region in southwest Lithuania

⋅

Thus, Onute the tavern keeper became a farmer and did all her chores with boundless energy, even with inspiration. I wonder when she ever sits without a task in hand, when she sleeps, when she rises? Look, here she is bringing in full pails of milk. Here she mixes chopped up bits of leftovers with boiled, unpeeled potatoes for the pigs; here she lugs heavy buckets of swill for those eternally hungry swine who, it would seem, would just as soon eat her alive, if she were to fail in bringing those buckets. And really, she carried them not so long ago...and will again. The chomping pigs stick their snouts and forelegs into the troughs and try to push each other out of the way.

Recently, I read that of all the animals, the internal organs of pigs are most similar to humans'. What else is similar, I wonder?

In those times, such parallels didn't exist.

⋅

Like one of those curly pig tails, I try to follow Granny closely everywhere. Granny takes the wool shears and heads for the sheep pen. The folks have an entire flock of sheep. They're all overgrown with thick, dirty white wool. And it's already too hot for them in June. Today the sheep are not grazing in the fields but are penned up. They're caught one by one, turned over, both pairs of legs tied, and are carried out. The still uncaught ones bleat loudly, fearfully drop brown pellets, and crowd together in the farthest corner of the pen. The one being sheared, stretched and held on the ground, cries pitifully, shuddering throughout its entire body. A huge tangled layer of wool rolls off and onto the ground like some thick peel. Granny clips confidently with a skilled hand. Only rarely, when a sheep jerks suddenly, does she snip its hide, and a small streak of blood appears. When she's finished with one side, Granny quickly flips the sheep onto its other side, and she hurries, hurries, feeling sorry for the frightened beast. At last, the sheep has been shorn; its pale pink skin is now covered in a wavy pattern. How it runs with all its might to its own kind in the darkest corner of the pen. All the unshorn sheep greet her with prolonged loud bleats, not immediately recognizing this pink caricature as one of their own. Granny's already grabbing the next one.

Over the fall and winter, the wool quickly grows back. All winter long, Granny knits new sweaters, socks, *rankaukas*. I'll clarify this last: a *rankauka* is a separate short sleeve to be worn on the wrist between a sleeve and a glove. If you have to do something with your fingers exposed, it keeps your wrists from getting cold.

Granny stands solidly on the ground, occasionally amazing everyone with some yet unheard and unseen traits of her personality.

Towards the War's end, when Soviet soldiers enter the farmstead, she speaks remarkably good Russian to them.

When Prakseda and I, newly enthralled with atheism, try to get Granny to buy into ex-priest Jonas Ragauskas' book, *Ite, Missa Est,* and convince her there is no God, she replies:

—If there isn't a God, who does it hurt if I believe anyway, and if there is, well, to Him I pray, so that I won't end up in hell.

One warm summer day, Granny suddenly and un-expectedly suggests this:

—Girls, let's ride over to the Šešupė River for a swim.

Well, alright then! The Šešupė is a bit far away, and all this is so sudden... But Granny is already in the corral harnessing her friskiest mare, "Blackie," who has a reputation for disdaining women and for unpredictable behavior. She's definitely the most beautiful of the four horses, and to have her pulling your cart, well, that's real prestige. Just let everyone see that here comes a real farmer with a fiery black mare in harness.

Mama, Prakseda, and I, having filled up our wicker baskets with snacks, take our seats in the little wagon. Granny doesn't let go of the reins even for a second. Blackie draws the wagon forward, all the while casting her proud head backwards. With her large eloquent eye she observes the females sitting in the wagon.

—Only a bunch of broads,—Blackie snorts with con-tempt.

When she turns back, I see that Blackie's eye is becoming bloodshot. She is angry and contrary, and that's why Granny flicks her slightly with the rarely used whip. This Blackie is totally opposed to, and she slows her pace even more. She's now looking for an excuse to halt completely. Ah, there it is! By the road, a large rock. Blackie raises up on her hind legs, steps sideways and turns the wagon until it's up against the rock and across the road, blocking it completely. Blackie, now calmed down, won't move.

Fortunately, before too long a wagon rolls up with two men, one holding the reins, his friend by his side.

—What's happened—they ask, unable to get by.

37

—We need a man,—says Granny to the stunned new-comers.

One of the men climbs into our wagon and takes the reins, the other pats Blackie on the neck and gently turns her around, back towards Žvirgždaičiai. Well, Blackie does consent to at least take us back home. Granny harnesses Little Bay in place of Blackie, and we're off again. This time without incidents, all the way to the distant Šešupė.

On the bank Granny deftly sheds her outer garments and plunges into the river. Her stout body is white; she tumbles like a dolphin, then lies on her back, then turns on her side, all the while splashing about prodigiously. She's already as far out as the middle of the river. We tramp about on the shore since none of us knows how to swim. And what will we do if Granny starts to sink? Around us only thick bushes and not a living soul.

Where did she, a land-locked dweller, learn how to swim? And why then does she come here to the Šešupė so rarely?

•

Granny sits on a bench by the farmhouse under the wild rose bush. Her knees grip the churn as she churns butter. While the cream is still liquid, the plunger goes up and down easily, up and down.

—Come here, Ditele, help me churn,—she calls.
The cream thickens and I can't lift the plunger anymore, only raising the entire churn as I try.

—Don't worry, you'll grow up—then it will go swimmingly.

•

...The wild rose bush behind her, spilling out rose buds, smells delicious. Beyond the farmhouse in the garden an oriole whistles, calling forth the rain. A flock of geese waddles across the yard. At that time, Granny was younger than I am now. It wasn't until much later, in Kaunas, that I heard her first complaint.

—My organ's gotten weak—she said without the least sense that she should have said "organism" and that the word she used actually means something entirely different. But we all understood and didn't crack a smile.

Granny experienced a lot of suffering, most of it sourced with her own children. Her oldest daughter, Milda, married a non-Christian, and then, later, a divorced man. As if that wasn't enough, another daughter, Mikalina, also married a divorced man. Her daughter Teresė left home at an early age to live in a Simnas nunnery. After a personal tragedy, the youngest, Prakseda, left for Poland. Her son, Ričardas, married, divorced, and married again. Perhaps it's just as well Granny didn't know the fate of her golden haired boy— now under the care of strangers in the Antaviliai old people's home. Only Kostas made her happy when he married a delightful young woman, Ona Hanė Smilgevičiūtė, daughter of a nobleman, Jonas Smilgevičius, signer of the February 16th Declaration of Independence. But...

The house, the fields are gone. The son Kostas and daughter Mikalina are no longer there—Granny herself saw them off to the West. Prakseda will make moves to get to the United States from Poland. Behind her, too, the iron curtain will slam shut.

—To some God gives as He's leaving, to others as He's returning,—Granny used to say.

Who can determine when more is given—leaving or returning. Not possessions, of course, but losses and suffering.

I don't know why, maybe out of envy, but other Lithuanians call the more wealthy stingy. Whenever I hear an anecdote about misers of Suvalkija, right away I remember their exact opposites—Granny, and Uncle Kostas, and especially Aunt Teresė, who was called Teciukė in the family. The Žolynai, by the way, call all their children by gracious diminutive names: Kostas is Kastytis; Mikalina is Mikytė; Teresė is Teciukė; Ričardas is Širdukė.

Aunt Teresė is the only auntie of mine still remaining in Lithuania. She is the very exemplar of kindness and generosity. And now, having reached the venerable age of eighty, she remains loved and respected by family, friends and neighbors, although she's now alone having lost her life-long friend, Vincas—Uncle Vincas, also beloved by all the family. This man, was a true Suvalkietis, whose whole life was also a disproof of those mocking anecdotes.

Leaning on Uncle Vincas' shoulder, Teresė took care of, to their dying breaths, both her father and her mother.

The best of that old couple still live on in their children. Perhaps their shortcomings as well. And in future?

My grandmother died April 17, 1961. In Kaunas at the Petrašiūnai cemetery, three family members rest together— Granddad, Granny, and my mother, who died April 3, 1995.

On the gravestone only one word is inscribed—Žolynai. Around it dark evergreens. Candles on All Souls night. Žolynai[2]. Žolynė (a grassy place). Žolienė (grass soup). Žolinė (grass celebration day[3]). Žolė (grass). Žalia (green). Žemė (earth). May they rest in peace. This earth won't be too hard for them.

> *Some of them have left behind a name*
> *and men recount their praiseworthy deeds;*
> *But of others there is no memory,*
> *for when they ceased, they ceased.*
> *And they are as though they had not lived,*
> *they and their children after them.*
>
> Ecclesiasticus (Sirach) 44: 8-9

---

[2] "Žolynas" refers to a plot of grass, or a kind of grassy herb; the family name, then, could be roughly translated as "Grassly" or "Grass."

[3] Žolinė ("grass day") has been celebrated on August 15 since pagan times. It was later appropriated by Christianity as the Ascension of Mary.

Tėtulis

5
Grandpa

Sheep shears... Our village didn't seem to have any other kinds of scissors. Large, brown, iron—always open until someone closed them with a firm grip. My aunt Prakseda, casting an eye toward her father—known as Tėtulis by us all—as he is getting ready for church, says:

—Come here, Tėtuli, I'll give you a trim. You remind me of a chubby chicken with those puffed-out sideburns.

Feeding chickens

Tėtulis allows himself to be trimmed but forbids any touching of his huge sideburns—his only adornment. Puffed-out chickens truly are walking around the yard, but Tėtulis sees no resemblance between them and himself. Dressed in his one and only home-made grey serge suit, he heads off to church in Šunskai about two kilometers from our homestead. He does this every Sunday without fail, in a wagon or on foot, and not only because the parish priest

41

Vincentas Ambraziejus is his half-brother. In fact, Tėtulis is a very Godly man.

—Holy Fart—Granny mocks him, not happy that Tėtulis takes himself off to church even during the very busiest times at the farm, even if he travels by foot to give the horses their Sunday rest after a hard week. So off goes Tėtulis, alone, to pray for all the family's sins.

In the late blue summer nights, I toss and turn in the old-fashioned bed; its wooden knobbed posts keep watch as I try to fall asleep and ignore the raging fleas under the covers. Alongside, Tėtulis' baritone chants reassuringly. His ancient prayer book open in front of him, he praises the Lord:

Faithful Abiza... giving warmth to David...

These hymns are my introduction to the personages of the Bible.

About the decrepit king David, who even swathed in furs couldn't stay warm. To try to warm him, the beautiful nurse-maid Abishag was assigned to sleep in his embrace. But as I read much later in the Bible, the King "never knew her."

—Give your throat a rest,—Granny chides him through the half-open door,—let the child sleep.

Hushed and humbled, Tėtulis closes his prayer book and rises to leave. Where will he chant his hymns? After all, his holy pictures are all in this room. And I'll be alone with all the fleas, and who knows when I'll fall asleep.

—Tėtulis,—I whisper from under the blankets,—please don't leave, Tėtulis, sing some more.

—S'more?—Tėtulis asks, happy that another seriously God-respecting individual has somehow shown up.

...Whoever wants to serve Mother Mary
and earn her protection
must prayerfully greet her...

—intones Tėtulis' baritone again.

And then it would be the morning.

In the morning Prakseda, the grandparents' youngest daughter jumps into my bed. From her apron she tumbles a bunch of cold sweet apples right on to me. The little apples are wormy, from the old unattended trees, but they're a good deal tastier than those imported oranges wrapped in their tissue papers. Then she sticks her dew-cold feet up against me:

—Warm these up for me, sleepy head.

42

Tètulis is already sitting at the table with a deck of playing cards near at hand. I'm the only person who plays with him—games like a Thousand or Sixty-six. He doesn't even try to get anyone else involved. After all, in his godliness he knows playing cards is a bit of "sin," but who can apply that to playing with a child, really?

—Come, Ditele, and deal the cards,—he invites me at the most inconvenient time when I have other important things to do.

—The old like the very young,—says Granny, but I don't really understand since I'm not aware Tètulis is already old and I'm still a little one.

Everyone on the farm has their own chores. And truth to say, I don't always want to play cards, but Tètulis wheedles me by toting up all the points I've won. I win rarely, actually, but that's not too important to me. It's more fun feeding the chickens. Tètulis will get the chicken feed at midday.

•

...The sun shines with all its might. The good farmhouse's windows are large, and that's why it's now so hot inside. Legions of flies buzz inside, so many you can't even eat in peace. The only weapon against them is a ribbon of sticky fly-paper hanging from the ceiling already covered with dead flies, even though it would seem only the most foolish ones get themselves stuck there. The others boldly reign over the house, leaving their little black dots even on the holy pictures.

At times like this, Tètulis finally declares war. Somewhere by the edge of the garden he's cut himself some goosefoot leaves, nettles, and hemp and tied them all together into a couple of large brooms. The cuttings have just started to dry out and have that heady smell of dying greenery. Tètulis hangs the brooms from the ceiling by their handles, heads downward. They hang far enough down to be at the height of a person's chest. Everyone is ordered outside, except me—I'm allowed to observe how Granddad carefully covers all of the farmhouse's three windows with home-woven lengths of material. The lengths are dark red, thick, making it difficult for the sun to shine through, though it tries very hard. The whole farmhouse fills with a deep red twilight glow. And the flies are tricked into believing the night is coming on. The brooms smell so enticing. They contain so many inviting and cozy little nooks perfect for peaceful sleeping. For a while the brooms shudder and buzz and are then still as the flies swoon into

43

their night's rest. They don't expect what's about to happen. It'll be bad. Worse than during the war. Because they will have nowhere to hide and no hope of survival.

Tètulis makes a sneak attack into the darkened room and with uncanny deftness puts a sack over one of the brooms and ties it on securely. And then the same with the other one. On the floor, the sacks seem to almost rise, full as they are with such sudden activity and uproar. Now the flies know they've fallen into a trap. Every little creature knows the end is near. It wants to be saved. But it's hopeless. Tètulis carries the sacks outside. His face shows no glee at the success of his ruse. Such is the balance of life and death.

—Come, Ditele,—he calls to me.

The tied up sacks have already been well and properly smashed up against the side of the house, and the flies are no longer alive. Granddad unties the sacks and handfuls of dead flies fall to the ground.

—Chook, chook, chook,—I call out to the chickens, but they would have come unbidden from all corners anyway, abandoning even their best hidden nests.

The chickens fall to pecking at such an unexpected feast. It seems a few flies are still alive, having survived the wall-bashing. Too dazed to fly, they try to crawl off, but the chickens are no dummies and pounce on them first. It's the end for this generation of flies. Not to worry, though, some will survive. They will recover, breed and multiply. Like everything alive.

•

...When the war starts, we are inexperienced and don't know what to do, where to go, how to protect ourselves, or what to be afraid of. For our own peace of mind, near the brook, we build ourselves a shelter—that is, we dig a ditch, cover it with planks and cover them with dirt. We'll hide there, if the worst should happen. Tètulis takes no part in digging the ditch and firmly says he won't go "there." Everything's in God's hands: if He doesn't allow it, not even a single hair will fall from your head.

We're eating honey just bought from the neighbors. We're outside, sitting at the wooden table underneath the huge wild rose bush. The entire bush is covered with blossoms, giving off a divinely smelling aura. Of course, in those days, no one knew nor used the word "aura"; nonetheless, it was there, and drew everyone to sit a while on the wide wooden benches at the worn, dark table of indeterminate age. So we're eating honey, when Prakseda points a finger at the clear bright sky:

—Look, there, flying. One...two...three...—and without finishing her count Prakseda jumps up and races off as fast as her legs will carry her toward our shelter. We—the rest of the household—we're right behind her. The planes are already near, coming in low...firing their guns, dropping whistling bombs... We fall into our shelter. The earth trembles and shudders. For a half hour? Or five minutes? Time is entirely different during these kinds of moments— either galloping forward or crawling snail-like. After all's quiet, we return to the house.

We find Tėtulis sitting by the window staring out at the main road. Here and there farmhouses are burning. A column of smoke rises above Šunskai. A wagon pulls into our farmyard from the road, drawn by two white horses. The horses are bloody, the wagon empty...

Only now do I feel the spoon twisting in my hands. The spoon is bent, without any honey on it, but my hands are sticky and sweet. God protected us, especially Granddad. But maybe only this once?

•

...And God looks after Granddad even when we all determine it's too dangerous to be so close to the main road and that it'd be better to move away further. With the front coming closer towards us, we needed to retreat somewhere. That's how people did it in those days, as soon as the news spread that a region was dangerous. People traveled from one place to another, as if urged on by whips. Those living at Point A believed Point B was safer and would journey there, but the residents of Point B were drawn as if by a magnet to Point A. And that's how we started to look for somewhere safer.

Having loaded up our largest wagon with some of our clothes and bedding and having covered it all with one of our dark red blankets, we left for someplace further away. The wagoneer was Grandma herself, since our main farm-hands—Ragažinis and Marė—were left to tend the animals. Tied to the side of the wagon and swinging freely is our cornflower blue tea kettle with its lid...

Tėtulis is walking alongside the wagon—to make it easier for the horses—his hand resting on one of the side rails. We go along this way for about a kilometer when Tėtulis notices that the lid is missing off the blue tea kettle. He tells us not to wait for him and goes back to look for it. He finds it, of course. And, of course, takes it home. And that's

45

where we find them both—Tėtulis and the kettle lid—when we return home after a week of pointless wandering around in that gypsy-red wagon.

Tėtulis didn't blame anyone. He was sitting by the window looking out at the road covered with soft dust. But mostly I remember him another way. I remember him standing to the side of a plowed field, on a narrow path overgrown with yarrow, love grass, and sweet peas. He bends down and from the furrow picks up a good-sized clod of earth and begins to rub it between his fingers. The outside of the clod breaks up easily, letting fall the dry, dusty soil, but soon it's harder as the inside of the clod is damp.

After many years I finally understood—he was rubbing those clods not from some love of the earth or from some romantic mood, but because he needed to know how moist the soil was and if it was ripe for the coming work according to the pre-ordained cycle of nature.

Even later, I understood more—his love was close at hand but undeclared, restrained, matter-of-fact, invisible to the casual eye.

The Žolynases with Ričardas, Milda, and Konstantinas. Mikalina, Teresė, and Prakseda are yet to be born, c. 1919

46

•

...Tėtulis died in Kaunas. He took with him to the Petrašiūnai Cemetery the story of Thumbnail, that he had inherited from his ancestors, who, in their turn, had appropriated it from an ancient myth. The thumbnail, according to Lithuanian mythology, was the tool necessary to ascend, after death, the cosmic hill to God. He often told us this pagan myth, though presenting it as a folktale, because his parents and he himself were already promised to the Christian God and he would never break that promise.

All of us, if we're decent, keep our pledges, and we're unhappy when we break them. But often we're also unhappy if we are sticking to a promise that we have long stopped fulfilling.

Tėtulis rests in the Petrašiūnai Cemetery, far from the fields of his birthplace—but in his homeland, Lithuania. When I read the biographies of people who lived earlier, I always think: fortunate is the one who can take eternal rest in his homeland. Unlike many of those of ours who have been deported or exiled. Rather, like Vincas Krėvė, who even though he died in the United States, in Pennsylvania, had his ashes buried in the Subartonys Cemetery. By the way, every time I hear the word *kapinaitės* (diminutive form of cemetery), I remember Tėtulis. He would not recognize the diminutive form, holding it is a lessening of the dignity of the eternal resting place.

—Say *kapinės,* Ditele. We must respect the dead, he'd instruct me.

•

In my personal lexicon, the word *kapinaitės* can't be found, my good Grandaddy. And I haven't forgotten the road to your house, nor the path to your gravesite.

The Lord is near to the brokenhearted,
and saves the crushed in spirit.

Psalm 34: 18

**The Virgin Mary
of the Seven Swords**

6
"In order that"

From the highway the horses turn by themselves into the short driveway and stop just past the clump of linden trees near the double ends of the farmhouse.

In the Žvirgždaičiai village region all the farmhouses are built out of un-nailed, unpainted, squared logs. The wood keeps its fresh color for only a few years. The weather soon beats it grey; the cracks between the logs are stuffed and filled with moss, which dries and eventually blends with the wood. Throughout the entire region only one farmhouse stands out as at all different—one painted a bright yellow.

—A German lives there; this kind of house painting is their custom—say the locals.

A good German, I think to myself, if he has such a friendly surname—Bruder. It seems he hails from the land of Prussians. For me, the more I age, the more beautiful the silver of that unpainted wood becomes, cracked like old wooden cemetery crosses. Every plank is unique and from each one stares the face of an old *Rūpintojėlis*[1], a "Sorrowful Christ." In the rough-edged voice of old silver the wooden logs tell stories of a green forest, where they used to grow, of our ancestors' hands, which set them into these walls. For a long time now, we've been unable to understand the language of those tales...

From ancient times, farmhouses were built in this way: after the stone hearth, a hallway extends across the width of the farmhouse with a shady section of the garden beyond the window at the end. On the left is the door to the interior single room, three small windows, benches and a table,

---

[1] *Rūpintojėlis* is a folk wooden carving found by the side of a road or path, especially at cross-roads. It depicts a saddened Christ, sitting with his head in hand, sorrowing for human suffering.

a hutch for dishes, a stove, a home-made checkered bedspread on the bed. Nothing more is needed. Oh yes, and two more sets of tools for indoor work: for women, a spinning wheel; for men, a machine for twisting fibers into rope.

On top of the stove sit a variety of pots of different sizes, and a frying pan. You cook and feed the family—larger in the summer, smaller in the winter—and off you go to other chores. The wall near the stove is full of little cockroaches called *bambatieriai,* merrymakers. Who knows how that word of French origins—*bambocheur*—found its way to these remote fields. And also these little bugs are still honored as *prūsokai* after Teutonic knights and invaders of later centuries from the Prussian side. The new invaders have not yet arrived—it's still the end of the Thirties. It's not certain what kind of pests we'll name those who might defeat us. The Yatvingian descendents eat their own baked bread, their own raised pork bacon—the more wealthy ones, their own whipped butter. At fairs they buy their children little oblong sweets. For me it's all good, I'm a city girl, I'm only a summer guest, I know what chocolate is, ice cream, a water closet, a primus stove. Today, my little granddaughter listens to my words, her mouth agape, of how even in the most citified town of Kaunas there was no television, no audio or video cassettes, no trolleybus, no mobile phone, no microwave oven, felt-tip pen, refrigerator... to say nothing of computers. She marvels that villagers had never heard that hay stacks could be protected from rain by covering them with plastic sheets.

Now it's my turn to drop my jaw, since only sixty years have passed since those times. My three-year-old grandson sits down in front of the computer, puts his hand on the mouse, and asks no one but himself:

—Where's that Microsoft Word? Where's that link?

His grandfather, sitting mesmerized day and night in front of the miraculous computer screen, tries with all his might not to be left behind. But, of course, he will be left behind. It can't be otherwise.

And how amazing it was when Tėtulis' son, Kostas, as a high school student in Marijampolė, built himself a radio with headphones and was able to hear—through the crackling static—the voices of European capitals.

•

...Beyond the farmhouse's last window the darkness sighs with goosefoot, nettles, wormwood, the wild untended garden. Through the two side windows shines the happily

49

tended garden full of rue, nasturtiums, pansies, dahlias, amaranths, gilly-flowers. But most beautiful of all, nestled up against the farmhouse wall, are the dark red hollyhocks. Of all garden flowers, they're the ones I love the most, even to this very day. There I am next to them in my white blouse, blue-spotted skirt; I'm suntanned brown—and undoubtedly happy.

Hollyhocks

The other end of the farmhouse is new, still smelling of fresh cut wood. In it stands an old-fashioned table with carved legs, covered with a homemade tablecloth, black-netted, hooked together delicately and ornamented with flowers crocheted from various colored threads. At night when the dog Pyras has fallen asleep and the garden is bathed in the silver light of stars, when even my guardian angel sleeps hand on cheek, then you can hear a soft ticking. The woodworms have started feasting on the old table, the tastiest item in the entire house. Gently and gradually they eventually drill perfectly round holes into the wood. There's no end of those holes in the table, but the table continues to stand firmly. Probably it's still standing, though, pity, I have no idea where.

The bed has bedknobs at both ends and huge pillows. And wedged in the corner a three-sided, double-tiered shelf—probably the most important piece of furniture in the farmhouse, maybe even in the entire farmstead. We call it *kampinė*, the "cornerpiece." It's amazing how many necessary items fit on this cornerpiece. No matter what you're looking for, the standard answer is almost always on the *kampinė*, "on the cornerpiece." There you'll find a small nail file, a jar of Nivea cream, a bottle of iodine, combs, a small mirror, a box of coloring pencils, a prayer book with holy pictures, various household documents.

On the wall at the end hang all the framed holy pictures along with their written maxims. Among all those words,

50

which I don't remember too well since I never really understood them, is one which is the most mysterious and secretive, and therefore full of never-explained meaning and somehow symbolizing the whole household, the entire way of life of those folks...*IDANT*, "in order that."

The handsome, long-faced and long-haired Jesus Christ shows us his open heart...*IDANT*. "in order that." The Blessed Virgin, dressed in blue and white Hebrew robes, also opens her heart to us, only hers is pierced by seven swords. In the midst of that suffering her face remains serenely glowing—*IDANT, IDANT*—such are permanence, invulnerability and the eternal.

A section of the farmhouse is taken up by a brick stove—called *mašina*, "the machine." It is like a warm sofa to sit on during cold winter nights. The stove is fired up and stoked from the adjoining room. From there, though, it's obvious that the stove's primary purpose is as a bread oven. My Granny, with her strong white hands, slides the sweetly smelling rye loaves, still with her fingerprints pressed into the sides, into the oven. For me, a city dweller watching the preparing and baking of such bread remains a lesson for the rest of my life—a lesson about the very nature of bread. The loaves of dough lie side by side, on a bed of sweet flag leaves. Oh, how long we must wait for the last one to be done baking....

Only last night, my granny, sleeves rolled up, kneaded the dough in her wooden bread pail. During the night the sweet smelling rye dough rose up as if trying to climb out of the pail.

Who can now duplicate the smell and taste of bread like that just removed from such an oven?

From your own soil's grain, from your own well water, your own sweet-smelling sweet flag, your own sweat sprinkled into the dough. And granny's slicing is done so beautifully. She takes a loaf as if it's some kind of a live thing, presses it against her breast, and saws off slice after slice. That bread, tastier than today's cakes, sufficed for everyone—even for the occasional beggar who happened by the farmstead.

Prakseda, her fingers flowing with cherry juice, picks out stones from each cherry and then sprinkles the torn cherries onto a large breadcrumb-scattered saucer, and then pours milk over it all. And there you have it, a "beggar's meal." You have to eat this quickly, since the cherry juice quickly curdles the milk into little white curds. But then, we just add more milk and continue to eat, all from the same saucer. And the saucer is no ordinary one;

it's one Granny brought back from America, painted with large unfamiliar flowers.

—It's the last one—, says Granny,—all the others have been smashed.

And she starts looking for the last teacup she's brought over so that I can see how America takes care of its be-whiskered tea drinkers—the cup's equipped with a special mustache guard to protect it from the hot water! Granny doesn't find the cup though—apparently it, too, is among the broken and lost. But it is minutely described to me, especially the fact of its beautiful flowers. And today I feel like I actually saw it then. Maybe I can even say that I did see it. And on the table in a clay pitcher, a bunch of wild flowers. Chamomiles, blue cornflowers, plain weeds.

In midsummer, night comes on very late. It's not very dark, but I'm already lying in my wooden bed with its bedknobs. I'm looking at the graying window's rectangle, I see the dark maple trunks, hear the creaking well handle and someone's muted voice. In the branches of the large birch behind the barn a star shines already, or is it a planet whose name I don't know? In the birch there's an old wagon wheel. It safely holds a nest in which storks sleep— another one of the features of farmsteads in this region of level fields. In these parts, for some reason, a farm was referred to as "she," perhaps to emphasize the feminine roots of a household.

Things in the room have now lost their contours to the growing dark, but I visualize where everything is. On the wall hangs something very important that the householders glance at more frequently than at the clock. It's a barometer, here respectfully called *bulius*, "the bull." The bull is surrounded by an elegant wooden frame with ornamented pictures of what field work can be done according to atmospheric conditions. In the city such an item is hardly necessary, but even now I look at it every day. Not at that same one, alas, but at its brother, or cousin—the one I brought back from Palanga after my father-in-law's death. I don't know why, but I find that barometer somehow very necessary.

In the corner sits a tall cabinet, almost reaching the ceiling, in which a clock with heavy weights ticks. Every half hour the clock murmurs indistinctly—meaning that it will soon strike the hour or half. Every day the weights have to be pulled up. They hang on copper chains, and throughout the day, link by link, they lower themselves down.

On the four-cornered clock face adorned with large Roman numerals, drawings of the same jockey and his mount are rendered four different ways. He's dressed up in his black jockey's cap, short red jacket, white riding breeches, and narrow black boots. In one of the corners of the clock face, on foot, he leads the horse by the reins; in the next one, he rides; in the third, he gallops at full speed; and in the fourth, he lies on the ground, tumbled from his steed, perhaps even dead. I always had hopes that as the hands swept around and up the clock face, the jockey would stand up again, take his mount by the reins, and again speed on through the minutes and hours. In those days, and for years after, I didn't understand the meaning of that clock face. An eternally turning circle? A warning? A statement about inevitable endings? A conception of time itself? *IDANT*, "in order that" I would return here after fifty years? And again in a hundred? A thousand? Then I wasn't aware that life holds many more questions than answers. But you'd think it should be equal—so that the axle of the Universe wouldn't veer off its center. *IDANT*, "in order that."

"Let us wish each other peace,"—says the priest in his sermon.

"Leave me in peace,"—we say to a loved one as we wrestle with some difficult problem.

"Peace be with you,"—says the risen Jesus to his terrified apostles.

IDANT—that unfathomable word rang in my ear. But its secret meaning did not rescue us from War's gaping maw, which readied itself to swallow us entirely with all our holy pictures, bread and cherries, our unfinished cattle shed, and all our sweet apples.

And you will hear of wars and rumors of wars;
see that you are not alarmed; for this must take place.

Matthew 24: 6

53

7
Road Dust

The farmhouse at
Žvirgždaičiai

I could also add, "under the red sunset," but that wouldn't be my own, rather the title of a novel by Vincas Ramonas, the Marijampolė-born author. The fragments of the novel were serialised during the last years of the German occupation as extra sections of a local newspaper. I used to enjoy them a lot as they smelled of the dust of our country road, my people, my beloved village.

Beyond the forest—near the Marijampolė-Vilkaviškis border on the Vilkaviškis side—was the little village of Žvirgždaičiai, affectionately called by old-timers *Lašinukai*, Little Bacon Strips. A simple farm village, like all the ones in Suvalkija. From my childhood up to this very day, the beautiful names of those villages and small towns, ringing from the lips of their dwellers, remain with me as if expressions of fabled secrets—*Ūdrija* (Otter Village), *Bagotoji* (Money Bags), *Višakio Rūda* (Višakis Ore), *Salemos Būda* (Failure's Cabin). But other names were not so beautiful—*Puskelniai* (Half-Pants), *Utėlinė* (Louse House), *Pilviškiai* (Big Bellies).[1]

The homestead mounds rise up from the level fields with spacious barns in the shade of huge lindens and maples, sturdy barns, along with already renewed or soon to be renewed farmhouses. Here the estates of Šniokis, here Šnirpūnas, and there Karužis (a former grand duke's

---

[1] *Translator's note*: the translations of these village names are inexact, only meant to suggest the charm and humor of the originals.

standard bearer). Here--a windmill, turning its four arms in the wind, proudly standing apart from any other farm buildings. A dark silver-colored unique hermit, unbeholden to anyone except the wind freely flying through the level fields of Suvalkija. You travel a kilometer—and there's another one with its wooden arms reaching for the wind. Again the wooden cap, the silver torso—a fortress, a castle of these regions, a guarantor of future bread.

Only from stories did I learn where the old folks' windmill stood, where the smithy used to be. Now neither the windmill nor the forge remains, not even the faintest sign. Only long cucumber furrows, only the sky-thrusting larch, a rarity in these parts. I remember when our larch sailed off to sea. Literally sailed, actually—our larch of the level fields was destined to be a ship's mast. For that purpose strangers came one day, chopped it down and carted it off. My Grandparents needed money to finish building a new stable.

The old folks' yard was big, cut in half by a path to the peat bog.

In the yard geese honk and soil the green grass. Well, too bad, want to or not, at the end of the day you need to wash your feet.

—Only not in the trough near the well,—warns Granny.

After the day's work, the horses return and sniff the water suspiciously with quivering nostrils. They will not drink unclean water. Even if you'd only dipped in your feet, which you'd already just cleaned of goose shit ... Then the trough, carved out of a log, has to be tipped on its side and the water poured out so not even a drop remains. And just how are you supposed to clean those dirty feet when, just the other day, one of the pigs ate that aromatic bar of soap specially brought back from Kaunas.

—Woe, woe is me,—complains the wooden well sweep as it raises the cold, cold water from the well, water so cold that your washed feet burn for a long time after. The well is the absolute celebrity of the old folks' yard. The well is covered by a small wooden "house" with a peaked roof and two "doors." Deep down in the dark green water a patch of sky reflects back. Since that time I've never seen another well like it. Why is it so wide? Who ever dug it out and when? Square, its four sides are built of stacked stones. The stones are rounded and strong, like the heads of ancient giants. Grown over with moss, they stick their crowns out, backs of their heads nestled together; they descend lower and lower into the earth.

—Don't lean into the well, darling Dita; the crocodile will pull you in—say the householders sternly.

Today I can't understand at all why they frightened us with crocodiles in Suvalkija. Why not some kind of devil from the swamps or one of Grandaddy's Thumbnail characters from his folktales?

I'm afraid not so much of the crocodiles, whose existence I half believed in and half not, but the mossy darkness in the depths of the well even on a sunny day. Summer's sunbeams play diagonally along that dark-ness but fade out before they plumb the depths.

—Come here, I'll show you something,—beckons Prakseda.

She fills her mouth with water and with all her might spurts it into the well, there where the sunbeams struggle with the dark depths. Oh, miracle! In the well's bottom instantly flashes forth the most perfect, pure, and colorful rainbow. This vision lasts for no more than a few seconds. So why have I remembered it all my life?

—Again!—I say, fascinated by the bright apparition.

Prakselė, again with full mouth, prepares to repeat the rainbow miracle, but...

—You mustn't spit into the water,—says Grandaddy.

This proverb about not spitting into the water has been around a long time, of course, a typical instance of folk wisdom, but Grandaddy finds it anew, and returns it to its original concrete meaning.

—Later, you'll have to drink that water yourself,—he adds, pointedly.

•

...Everything I touched during those country summers would be referred to these days as my origins or "roots." Here lived our Yatvingian ancestors, and the ancestors of their ancestors, all the way back to the beginnings when people first started living in these parts. Here I learned how to tell the difference between rye and wheat, learned how bread is baked, how sheep are sheared, how a new chick breaks out of its shell—and I didn't trouble my head with the question of which came first, the chicken or the egg.

•

...During blue summer evenings, filled with the inevitable sounds of distant accordions, we awaited the first star to appear in the darkening sky. I wanted to be tall and beautiful like my aunt Prakseda. She was always the first to spot that star. Soon more stars spilled into the sky like

56

grains of wheat from a torn bag. One of them, stuck in the birch tree above the barn, changed colors as it shone, from red to blue, and then back to gold. Perhaps it was a planet—Venus or Mars. I wrote a poem about it once. In those days I'd already begun writing verses and had created over a hundred already. Later I tore up the black-covered notebook and threw the pages away one by one into the peculiar vase-shaped trash bins of soviet-occupied Vilnius. One page at a time, so no one would ever be able to collect them back together again. That's how my youthful "soul's creations" died into Vilnius' trash removal system...

•

During the day, the sky's luxuriant sunflower, lovingly shines down on the flax and potatoes growing in the fields. The mid-day weather whirls around with a hot and vibrating odor, raising the crops higher. How many songs we have about blue flax blossoms... But who has sung of the potato flower? "Who needs flowers, if the potato grows,"—used to say the hungry townsfolk after the war as they waited impatiently for the next potato crop. Just take a little potato flower in hand, white or pale violet... Take a closer look, let it enlarge in your mind. It's truly regal in its beauty, a miniature star shining against the black earth of Suvalkija. But who will praise the potato blossom today? Perhaps only those who advertise the potato's many advantages.

And the corn-cockle—is it not as beautiful as a corn-flower? Both were parasites in our corn fields. The practical folk of Suvalkija used to affectionately call the corn-cockle *kūkalė*. Cornflowers are now domesticated, but corn-cockle has probably been eradicated by now.

On such a lazy day my aunt and I were captured by our folding "Agfa" camera. The two of us stand together between fields of swaying flax and blossoming potatoes.

Dark clouds gather in the distance. We hear no thunder yet. My aunt leads me down the road to the pond, called by all of us the *čioželka*, the frozen pond. That road divides the old folks' property in two. Before the war few people traveled the road, only locals going from Šunskai to Gižai. And the clay surface of the road, transformed into fine dust, soft and warm in the sun, irresistibly invites you to tread deeply into it barefooted to let that unbelievable gentleness between your toes. What can I compare it to now? Maybe to the hands of my three-year old grandson Gerimantas? Perhaps to his quietly uttered words:

—I very, very much strongly love you.

After many years when my son drove us back here in his powerful BMW, my much-praised road was unpassable. Half-meter pot holes yawned from it. Everything's different here now. Only the stone walls of the well are the same, older by half a century the crowns of those ancient giants' heads.

The road to Žvirgždaičiai

What a pity that my children's bare feet never stood in that warm, softest of all clay dust. A pity, too, that the grandchildren will never see bread kneaded by bare hands. Above their heads there's no flash of the upraised battle axe. Above our heads in those times it did flash, and every time, the metaphor turned into a real struggle between life and death.

•

...Like a series of film shots, scenes unroll in my mind— Mama and I are running through a field of oats. We don't know where we're running. Probably to avoid death. Or maybe towards eternity. The road is full of wagons, among them our own covered with a dark red blanket. In that black and white world the red blanket was the only thing of color. A fine target along the black and white road. That's why Mama and I are running across the oat field, with Aunt Prakseda galloping ahead of us. Try running across oats— it's harder than if it were happening in a dream. But we aren't dreaming. Over our heads, flying low, planes spray bullets into that field at two women and a girl, pale with fear, who don't understand that they should now fall down dead, spread-eagled and flat against the earth. But we were alive, and somehow remained alive. We returned to the highway and joined up with Granny again. Granny ran nowhere. She lay under the wagon, never letting go of the reins. Our mares did not bolt, just stood still frozen in fear, their ears twitching back and forth. Now, I think our guardian angel must have stretched his hand out above that field and kept us safe from the bullets. And from the people who sat in the airplanes? So they wouldn't see who was struggling among those oats in the blanched field below. Maybe it was our gypsy-like wagon with its dark red covering that irritated them? Our blood would have been much lighter. Only after clotting would it be dark. Even more than that ripe cherry-colored covering.

And by the way, about cherries.

•

...A large rectangular garden, separating the main house from the other farm buildings, was surrounded by a trellised fence, densely planted with cherry trees. We can barely keep up, eating and cooking cherries, since the old trees, seeping with resin, produced them in abundance, ripening almost to black. My aunt and I would also snack on the sweet amber-colored resin, scraping it off the crooked branches and off the tree trunk.

On a day during the fullest ripening of the cherries, the men lifted off one of the wide barn doors and carried it to the fields as if it were some sort of funeral plank with a corpse on it on the way to the cemetery. They set the door across a dry ditch—called by us a *grabé*—and covered the top of it with newly mown grass. Underneath, in the ditch, they arranged a place for people to lie. It was very large, almost big enough for the entire family. We took to living there at night, as in some sort of prehistoric human lair.

The very same night our softest road, now farther away from us, was filled with the rumbling machinery of war...

In the morning when we returned to the farmyard, we found our cherry trees full of shortish, weary Soviet soldiers. From a distance they looked like toy tin soldiers—with identical faces, identical stature, identically exhausted and hungry. Another equally identical group were picking through the cucumber rows. They wouldn't let us return to the good end of our farmhouse, explaining to us that for the next few days their commandant would be living there.

•

...I enjoyed spending nights under the barn door—no fleas bothered me, the drying hay smelled enticingly, and the sound of cannon fire didn't rattle the windows. Lying

59

half out from under the covering of our ditch, I looked with bated breath on the night sky as rockets flashed sending up flares, which hung in the air a long time, lighting up the places where the bombs were meant to fall. At that particular time, the place was Vilkaviškis, a small, miserable town on the banks of a shallow river called the Vilkauja. They smashed Vilkaviškis for a few nights until they'd almost leveled it, even though, from the very beginning of the war, much hadn't been left in the town after the Germans had done with it. Both occupants vied for that little town of rubble as if it were a gold purse—both in 1941 and in 1944. In forty-four, I witnessed the burning of the distant town—invisible in daylight—under the lights of flares.

We naively believed that the pine-built old barn door would keep us safe from the world's angry might. But something did protect us—something perhaps more powerful than that door. And it kept our house safe. And Grandaddy with his cat Mickus (Micky). Perhaps because of his trust in Providence. Or maybe Grandaddy thought it would be somewhat undignified for an albeit not-so-wealthy farmer of Sūduva to leave his farmhouse and roll around in the dirt of a *grabė* under the protection of a barn door. The yellow and black striped tiger-cat Micky clearly shared his opinion and never stepped foot outside the farmhouse. But the dog, Pyras, snuggled with us in the ditch—maybe he understood less than Mickus, and for him it was terrifying.

•

The artillery fire receding into the distance and the commandant having left our farmhouse, we "ditch dwellers" returned to our beds. From our farmhouse only two things were missing—a small hand mirror and my box of colored pencils. I mourned the loss of my pencils with tears. In those days, they were a true treasure, simply unavailable for any amount of money. But Mama explained to me—the pencils were necessary for drawing maps, so that the war would end sooner. And for the hand mirror (another rarity then), she explained the soldiers needed it to shave and look good and not frighten us and fight well so the war would end sooner.

The soldiers who fought on the front were not big thieves or cowards. They didn't order us to taste the food first that we offered them. They didn't confiscate, only borrow. And so they borrowed one bicycle, then another. And our wayward mare, Juodė (Blackie) traveled off into the unknown, as did the industrious Bevardė (No Name), and the gelding Sartė (Sorrel). The old folks valued their sweet little work horse, Bėrukė (Bay) most of all.

Until the great move, the old folks were able to hold on to Berukė (Little Bay). Then they had to leave their land, torn from their roots, from their farmhouse, from their peat bogs, plains, from their magical well with its hidden rainbow. It was an exodus with never the possibility of a return.

> *Why is one day better than another,*
> *though the sun gives the same daylight*
> *throughout the year?*
>
> Sirach 33: 7

> *Restore us to thyself, O Lord,*
> *that we may be restored!*
> *Renew our days as of old!*
> *Or hast thou utterly rejected us?*
> *Art thou exceedingly angry with us?*
>
> Lamentations 5: 21-22

8
Fairy Steeds...

The peat bog

*A*lksnynėlis—a type of small alder forest on the old folks' property. You start down a narrow path, you look back, and for a while you can still see the field shining behind you. After you take a few more steps forward, you lose sight of the clearance, but then you can already see the end of the path ahead. The little wood's overgrown with wild raspberries, strawberries, and sour catberries—a plant with little clusters of four or five berries reminiscent of a cat's paw. No mushrooms grow here. On the outskirts of the copse grow toadstools, fungus, and puffballs.

The real forests are far from here, bluing on the distant horizon. Only Šunskai forest is green, meaning it's closer. But we're not allowed to go there—we might get lost or meet up with a wolf.

Beyond the alder forest—an entirely different world. A plain, short grass and moss grow in the fields, barely covering the brown, peaty earth. Further on, neat rectangular plots have been dug out, partially flooded with cloudy, non-transparent water. Or maybe it only seems non-transparent because the bottom is peat, and peat when wet is almost black. Where the plots have been dug recently their edges are perpendicular, and straight as if cut by a knife, but the edges of the older plots are turned down, with a thin edge of earth hanging over, like a tablecloth hanging down from a table.

On the still surface of the water, water spiders skate as if on ice—zooming around in all directions. How is it they don't run into each other? Well, maybe if I just sit here they will? Throughout my entire body, from the crown of my head to the tips of my toes, I can feel their joy. The water is so perfectly level it looks solid. I throw in a pebble to check if it's really liquid. Ripples spread out. And disappear. The skaters wait for the water to calm and then start their never-ending play again. Or perhaps it's work? No, though I've been here for a half hour, they won't make any mistakes and run into each other.

On the wet peat edges unhurriedly water beetles mess about, and on the thick leaves of the bulrushes completely unconscious snooze little snails. My eyes slowly wink closed against the mirror-like flickering water's surface, the barely swaying spatterdock and the fresh coolness ever rising from the water below. The reed-mace have sprouted dense and thick, brown spikes sticking out from among the green leaves. They're straight, velvety, asking to be picked.

Prakseda, having taken a brown spike, bites around it with her beautiful white teeth, and, in an instant, the spike is a baroque decoration. In my hands it transforms into a queen's scepter. A queen who will soon lose all of her realms, all her subjects—torn out by the roots that bind her to this land.

In my subconscious, for years to come, the color brown will remain an attraction—wet peat, drying peat, dry peat, reed-mace spikes, the brown opaque water, the brown shining hard wings of insects...

•

After many years, somewhere in an article in the popular press, I read that people who fancy the color brown are introverts, never showing their inner lives to anyone, never letting outsiders come close. Supposedly, no one comes in or goes out through brown.

Once I brought home such a brown reed-mace spike. From some roadside. I stood it up in a clay vase on the verandah. The spike stood there a long time, never showing any signs of life. Brown, velvety, just like the ones before. One morning I looked and couldn't believe my eyes—a white cloud, maybe ten times thicker than the stem, stood out from the dry reed-mace spike. When I touched it, white fluff scattered all over the verandah. Dust... from dust...

•

...Dragonflies. They've been gifted by God (or nature) with two pairs of blue-green transparent wings. The wings gleam gemlike in the sun. Squinting, I try to see at least one fairy mounted on her dragonfly, her steed. Did I see one that time? I don't recall... But now, though I don't see dragonflies very often, surely each one carries its fairy. And each fairy holds a magic wand in her tiny hand; she wears blue and green luminous clothes; above her forehead shines a bright star, much like a miniscule version of our own sun.

Drying peat

Above my world of peat bogs the sun pours down, growing exuberant shadows. The stifling smell of Marsh Tea, the dense sphagnum turning into peat—I can feel it all as I lie on the warm peat bog, in the shade of a pyramid of drying peat sods. These pyramids—stacked as high as a person—are already the third stage of drying the sods. The second stage sods are stacked in smaller cones, about my height. And the first, quite a small heap barely reaching my knees, were called in those days "little Jews." It takes three stages of stacking and drying before the peat is ready to be used as fuel. Even before that, in the very beginning of the process, a kind of peat pulp dries as its spread out in long beds on the ground. Those beds are cut across using a kind of knife-like spade with a long handle. And even before that, the dug up mass of peat is thoroughly trod down by both horses and farmers.

Granddaddy makes some money by renting out parts of the peat bog for digging up or by selling the dried peat. But expenses are endless—he pays for all six of his children to get schooling, from elementary to high school, and later, for those who want it, university.

—Never did daddy ever treat me in any other way—my mother, Matilda, who was my Grandaddy's step-daughter, used to say—than as his own, his blood daughter.

And I never felt I was anything less than his true grand-daughter.

Only now, after many years, the relatives have taken a mind to reclaim that ancestral land, long since farmed and worked by others. Or to put it frankly, in order to profit from renting or selling it. But neither my mother nor I have been included in the list of legitimate descendents. Maybe that's just as well... Since wouldn't that money burn my hands, just as once before, lost in the forest, the nettles burned my feet?

Truth to say, my grandparents' Ona and Jonas Žolynas' great-great-grandchildren are the only ones still in Lithuania. My son Žilvinas' children, Vaidilė and Gerimantas, are Milda's daughter's progeny. The older Žolynas' son Ričardas' daughter, Rasa, hasn't had nor will have any children; the daughters Teresė and Prakseda were childless; daughter Mikalina's children are also without children; Kostas' son Algis has no children, and though Kostas' daughter, Rūta, has two boys, they'll not be Lithuanians. They'd hardly know in what little corner of the world the village of Žvirgždaičiai could be found. And how, not knowing the language, could they even pronounce such a name?

—Ditele,— my aunties call out,—let's go to Little Lake.

Little Lake is hardly a lake at all. A marsh stretches as far as the eye can see covered with white cotton grass. The little mounds around the grass tussocks look dry, but once you tread in them your footprint fills up with water. The aunts have been sternly warned to hold me by the hand. So I don't slip down some kind of quagmire. I'm not bothered at all by the wet turf's sucking at my feet; in fact, I like it.

Here for the first time I see a carnivorous plant. Named beautifully as a sundew, nonetheless, the flower is apparently a stealthy flesh-eating predator. Before my very eyes that little flower ate up an ant after first trapping it in its sticky secretions.

Then, I didn't yet understand that in nature there was an unceasing devouring of one by another—the bigger eating the smaller, the smaller the even smaller, and so on without end... The large are devoured by the even larger—larger or stronger.

Humans are swallowed—excuse me—eaten by, or attempted to be eaten by, fellow humans. Not necessarily by those larger or stronger, but maybe by those with sharper teeth and more aggressiveness. Those who don't prefer human flesh, those less assertive, most often become the victims. Sometimes they themselves don't even know it and live their entire lives digested by others.

•

...I walk with my aunt along a narrow path between tall walls of rye grass. Maybe the rye wasn't that fertile then, but the stalks were tall, almost head high. Nearby a small house. In it lives a family with ten kids, along with the recent arrival of an eleventh, who doesn't walk yet.

—Let's go see,—says Praksele. And the two of us head off toward the dilapidated grey farmhut.

The children are plentiful as peas here. Like timid mice, they immediately hide themselves in nooks and crannies. They hide themselves, but in a way that they can still observe what the two young ladies will do (apparently we were not shabby looking). They—fair-skinned, blue-eyed—may have never seen a dark-skinned type like me before. Good thing that at least Prakseda is more like them in coloring.

—Where's your little baby?—asks Praksele.

The kids, as if by command, all point with their thin fingers towards a wooden cradle. In that cradle lies the infant. Prakseda pulls back the mottled, soiled rags, and I see the unexpected emaciated body, large head, and large bright blue eyes. The eyes are wide open... and never before nor after have I seen such eyes.

In the cradle where you'd expect it to be damp, it is. But among the dark and wet rags I suddenly see writhing white worms. Undoubtedly Prakseda sees them, too—she quickly returns the rag covers as they were, over the worms, over that thin body and those blue eyes. She grabs my hand and we flee back homeward along the ditch banks. We say nothing to each other. The sun continues to shine as before, but no longer so happily. The daisies along the path sway their white and yellow heads, but I don't look at them. Something has broken in my heart...

Though I soon forgot that impression, the scar remained, and over the long years it seemed to come back up. More than once I would remember that bewildering mix of emotions—pity, disgust, astonishment, and hope that the little child would stand up and climb out of those ugly rags... and be like the rest of us.

Today, as I write these lines, after all those decades it strikes me that perhaps that baby was dead. God, please let me be wrong. It would only be right if today he were walking around somewhere, handsome, grey-headed, in his sixties, with grandkids who in their most horrible nightmares would not see what I once saw in reality.

After the war the local authorities transferred that family of many children to another farmer's property not too far away. The governing soviets shipped that farmer and his family by train off to Siberia in cattle cars. After a few months, the partisans shot the mother of all those children. Apparently it was she who had ratted out the farmer. Who knows. It's also unknown how her blond-haired, blue-eyed ones fared without their mother. What became of them? Communist secretaries? Dissidents? Priests? KGB agents?

•

...My aunt leads me home along the ditches. In mid-summer, the ditches are almost empty of water and thus overgrown with tall bulrushes with dry blue-green leaves. I drag behind her, my head down; no blue-green dragonfly carries its fairy. Only a blue-green sadness dogs my steps... I didn't know that sadness of that very color is the most persistent. That sadness visits again after many years, especially during completely unexpected occasions: at a drunken party, suddenly hearing Čiurlionis' "Miške" (In the Forest). Or in the cacophony of a piece of contemporary music, I hear the quiet voice of Jonas Aistis, verses from his poem "Mal du pays" (Longing for the Homeland):

> ...You're walking along pleasantly,
> > full moon in hand,
> Carrying the ashy North's coolness—
> The vault of heaven trembles,
> > stars lose their balance,
> As if the axis of the universe just tilted...
> . . . .
>
> I see from afar,
> > and how beautiful you are from afar—
> I've seen nothing like you ever!
> A tear springs up, laughter of evening,
> > streams, caves—
> The full moon slips from your hand.

...The sun continues to shine. Auntie Prakseda sits on the side of the ditch and with six rush stalks held in her teeth, she weaves a beautiful tiny sash. The sash will dry out, turning from green to brown, and will become a bookmark. I sit next to her, my feet sinking in the soft tangle of bloodwort and the pink cuckoo-flowers. Bumblebees whirl around us. Beyond the ditch blooms a field of red clover, truly the bumblebees' paradise. Who but I will remember all this? Prakseda has been long dead, and I've understood I won't be a guest here for much longer. Others, too, will have their own experiences.

The eye is not satisfied with seeing.
nor the ear filled with hearing.

Ecclesiastes 1: 8

Mama

9
Idylls of Occupation

Don't show me this revolting stuff,—says my mother at the very end of the twentieth century, pushing aside her plate of Ukrainian water melon.

The water melon is mottled, green; a sweet rose-colored liquid percolates from where it's been slit. Its flesh seems to be made of microscopic shining suns.

—A cucumber with honey is much tastier,—she explains.

I know why Mother has abhorred water melons all her life, as if they were somehow to blame for all our misfortunes. I remember how during the Soviet occupation, trainloads of those water melons labeled "For the Starving Lithuanians" would arrive after rolling through miles of Russia. In the Kaunas train station those signs immediately disappeared from the wagons. So folks wouldn't laugh. So they wouldn't be incensed.

Indeed, some laughed, others got angry. Why did so many Jews meet the Soviets with flowers and smiles? No one has satisfactorily answered that painful question until now. Why so many Lithuanians did so—I could explain. Why poverty-sticken Jews did so is understandable. But why did wealthy Slavinas, while entertaining the officials of Smetonas' Lithuanian government in his living room, also let in members of the Bolshevik underground through the back door into his kitchen? Why did both his sons turn into fierce KGB agents? And not only his. Many sons and daughters of the wealthy collaborated. Why?

Humans should seek the truth within themselves. First and foremost in themselves. And not be beholden to another's viewpoint. The intruders made "proper human beings" from people according to their social status or occupation. They tried to make a "proper human being" of our janitor too.

Not long ago I read a Soviet woman's memoirs in which traitorous janitors were condemned. Apparently, when the Germans came, the janitors showed them which apartments were lived in by Jews, which by communists. "Dear Madam, or Comrade," I'd like to say to her, "didn't the Soviet state itself set an ordinary, unpretentious person on such a path, from which he could not deviate?"

Our own janitor's daughter, four-year-old Laimutė, who plays in the yard all day, starts wearing beautiful blue and rose silk panties—instead of the typical white cotton ones. After soiling them, Laimutė climbs out of her panties and abandons them on the ground without a glance backward. In the evening, the janitor's wife, cursing the bourgeoisie, gathers up those gifts of her new life and takes them off for laundering.

The new regime finds out from janitors who lives where, how large their apartments, how many rooms, who has already left. It's now necessary to find housing for the flood of officers arriving in Kaunas, and their families. One day, a uniformed officer, accompanied by another military man and the janitor, looks over one of the rooms in our apartment remarking that it's too bad it has no furniture and further explains:

—Tomorrow, this citizen will take up residence here. He'll bring his family as well.

The citizen says not a word but is of such a cruel-looking face that Mama decides we just won't let him in. The soldier seems to her the essence of terror, one who would devour children. The next day, after ordering us all not to let out even a squeak, Mama hangs the little chain on the front door and double locks the kitchen door. Looking back on it now, I think to myself what holy naiveté—states and nations were crumbling, and we are protecting ourselves with a little chain on the door.

The trembling apartment dwellers held out against the long attack of pounding on the door—three times throughout the day, morning, lunch time, and in the evening. It was the very beginning of the occupation, so breaking down doors was not yet popular. Our door holds, and the cruel-faced one retreats, defeated. And without any consequences, apparently. Nonetheless, before too long it happens that we have to let an Air Force officer into that room, a real contrast to Horrible-face. He is handsome, young, pleasant, and polite. At this point, we're no longer opposed, as we've been advised not to pull the lion's whiskers. Soon the officer brings in a variety of boxes of all sizes, which properly arranged soon transform into tables, cupboards, wardrobes, and beds. The officer's wife, a quiet young woman, covers the boxes with white laces. In one of the boxes she beds down a baby. Slavik—I remember his name, since the intruders' children were the only ones we ever called by name. Any grown man, we called a *rusas* (Russian), and their women we called "Katyushas" after the popular song that had been imported then.

> ... *Flowers bloomed on apple and pear trees,*
> *Mist upon the river floated wide.*
> *Young Katyusha strolled along the cliffside,*
> *down along the bank so steep and high.*

Who knows what fate befell the unknown translator of this song into Lithuanian—did he or she find themselves under the branches of blossoming pear trees along the Lena River in Siberia, or on the cliffs above the Hudson, or did they approach eternity on the banks of the Nemunas?

At that time, the lauded Katyushas, having arrived in Kaunas following their husbands, are speechless with surprise. The stores are still laden with European goods never seen in Soviet Russia. The Katyushas wobble around in high-heeled, sand-colored shoes worn with short white socks unknown to Kaunites. The Katyushas, whose husbands by the standards of the day, make decent money, fall all over themselves to purchase supplies from the fashionable "Batia" store—leather shoes, silk stockings, French perfume. A good portion of these "miraculous wares" are sent back to Russia.

—What are you cooking there?—asks our own particular Katyusha, having wandered into the kitchen.

—Meatballs—replies our maid Janė.—If you want, I'll teach you how to make them.

All week long, Katyusha fries meatballs and praises their tastiness.

—And what are you cooking there?—she asks again, of course in Russian.

—*Cepelinai* (dumplings),—replies Janė in Lithuanian.—If you want, I'll teach you how.

The two of them manage to communicate quite well. Janė feels sorry for poor little Slavik rolling around in grey, black and, oh horrors, red diapers. His diapers are fraying at the edges and not of the same size... She talks Katyusha into buying a large swath of white calico, cutting it up into rectangles, nicely hemming the edges.

Now Slavik is like a little prince—in white diapers and little white cambric shirt. The pilot is charmed by his wife's ingenuity and culinary talents. Their room starts filling up. From a distant Russian village arrives a "babushka," and soon after Mrs. Pilot's niece, and other female relatives.

They all buy and carry back bagfuls of the still remaining goods.

One afternoon, Mrs. Pilot, all aglow, opens the kitchen door.

—How now,—says Janė,—are you off to bed?

—I'm going to a party,—says Mrs. Pilot.

—In your nightgown?—says Janė, jaw dropping.

Now Mrs. Pilot is agape. She's bought herself a lacy, blue-green French dress. Floor length, expensive, since the cheap ones are all gone.

—Oh Jesus, Jesus.—says Janė, caressing Mrs. Pilot whose eyes have filled with tears—I'm sorry, I should have kept my mouth shut.

•

Russians show up everywhere, even in my classroom. One boy, pale and with unhealthy-looking crooked fingers, is called Kruglov. He doesn't speak Lithuanian, and right away I make up a nickname for him—Kruglodurovas, since I'm already familiar with Vincas Kudirka's *Satires*[1]. And I don't concern myself at all about who the boy's father might be. Maybe a high-ranking NKVD-er[2], since he's been sent here with his family, maybe some high-ranking army officer. Mama sternly forbids my ever creating and using any nicknames for my classmates.

•

...I learn a new word—"repatriation." The word signifies action—Uncle Kostas, with whom I've made a good friend, will be leaving. Having just finished law school, Kostas marries Hanė, and sets up house in a new apartment on Frykas Street, full of sparkling new furnishings, dishes, vases, curtains. Alas, the fresh new couple's nest is about to be shredded, since the Soviet-sanctioned repatriation will soon end, and the iron curtain will close down with finality.

---

[1] "Kruglodurovas," roughly transliterated suggests someone who is completely stupid. Vincas Kudirka (1858-1899) was of seminal importance in Lithuiania's rebirth as a nation. A physician and writer, he was the author of both the lyrics and music of Lithuania's national anthem.

[2] The NKVD were the Soviet secret police during the war years, progenitors of the KGB.

Jonas Smilgevičius, Kostas' father-in-law, smells a real danger with that and secures documents attesting that his entire family is *volksdeutsche*[3] and that he will take all his relatives with him to Germany. I understood "repatriation" as a life-belt, to which the old wealthy landlord attached my beloved Uncle Kostas. If someone had explained to me that it meant returning to the fatherland, I would not have been able to understand it at all. Since when was Germany, having already released the reins of their military powers, a fatherland for them? Perhaps that's why they didn't try to explain it to me.

With a borrowed wheelbarrow, Uncle Kostas brought a portion of their furniture and dishes to our place on Vaižgantas Street and, across his shoulder, wooden curtain rods and skis.

—Like Christ with his cross...—my mother said pityingly.

They left in a big hurry. We had no news for a long time. Only during the German occupation did we finally receive a letter from Berlin. "We're alive. Working in a couple of firms. It'd be nice to have something fattening. You won't find anything like that here even with a flashlight." All letters were censored during the war, but apparently the censors had no knowledge of Lithuanian bacon and allowed the letter through.

Grandma provides the bacon, Mama packs it up and sends it off. From that remarkable Žvirgždaičiai bacon, ribboned with red meat, Kostas quickly betters not only his own diet but his everyday life too. Even their German landlady's sour expression blooms into a grin upon receipt of such a valuable gift.

Kostas sends me two checkered taffeta ribbons for my hair. He and Hanė have bought one each, having gone into the store separately, since only one ribbon per family is allowed, and, of course, I have two braids.

•

...The first Soviet occupation, though it wiped out the government, did not immediately nor completely transform everyone into Soviet citizens. But Moscow knew how to frighten the disobedient and reform the indecisive.

In the middle of June, first at night and later throughout the day, Russian trucks started arriving, each one with two or three soldiers dressed in muddy-grey coats. Up stuck

---

3 *volksdeutsche:* a term used by the Nazis to specify ethnic Germans living outside the Third Reich.

their pointed caps and rifle-mounted sharp bayonets. Most of the soldiers are of Asiatic ethnicity, completely different in appearance from the ones who paraded just a year ago down Freedom Avenue. These soldiers have lists of names and addresses of the "enemy" who have to be removed wholesale with all their family members and dropped off at the railroad station. These half-literate minions are concerned less with the exact identity of their charges than they are with raw numbers. When they find locked and bolted doors instead of the occupants they're seeking, they grab and cart off the neighbors.

The purely geographical name of Siberia turns into the name of a place of death for at least the next several generations.

Even some Soviet adherents were labeled "enemies of the people" and later had to be plucked out of Siberia by the "president" himself, Justas Paleckis. That wasn't so easy to do. People were lost in that gulag like wood chips in a forest. Terror stalks throughout Kaunas. People try to hide with their neighbors—their neighbors no longer sleep in their homes.

—If they take us away, will I be able to bring my books?—I hear myself asking as if it were today. If nothing ever truly disappears from this world, that question is still hanging in the air somewhere above the corner at Kipras Petrauskas and Tulip Streets.

—Yes, you will be able to,—says Mama who leads me farther away so I won't be able to see a dreadful sight. But I do see it. A parked truck, in it two soldiers with sharp bayonets, peaked caps with red stars. And in the truck bed sit a man and woman, leaning against the cab. The woman is older, the man younger—from their similar features, a mother and son. Both their mouths are tightly closed, down-turned at the corners. They have long Lithuanian noses. Both sit straight up, unslumped. Both stare ahead with severe, identical grey expressions. My inner camera freezes that image for a lifetime. I've forgotten many faces, but those two I remember.

After a few days, on an early Sunday morning, my inner camera clicks again. I see, somewhere in the direction of the grain elevator, just this side of the Nemunas, two large tails of black smoke. Billowing and growing along Freda's green slopes, they move eastward.

—War...—ripples out a sigh of relief.

—War!—cry out our apartment building's residents.

—War,—says our family, thinking it the lesser of two evils.

74

—Maneuvers!—assert the Russians living with our neighbors, realizing that war is a somewhat greater problem for them than their current situation.

•

Kaunas burning, June 1941
(from a newspaper clipping)

...After many years, a former intelligence officer for the Soviets, Viktor Suvorov (Vladimir Rezun), claimed in his book about the Second World War that Stalin was preparing his army for invasion no less than Hitler was. He just wasn't ready first. The author presents many solid and clear arguments. He cites not secret files and documents but ordinary publications of the time. However, in 1941, Vladimir Rezun had not yet been born.

—Maneuvers!—also insists our pilot's wife, indignant at our brightened up indigenous faces. Only this morning, the pilot has set off for the aerodrome. There he finds all the planes bombed out and utterly destroyed by the Germans.

In the afternoon, Mrs. Pilot leaves with all her household in a military vehicle, heading east. She trusts us to look after her boxes and promises to return soon.

Why do all those who leave promise to return soon? And the more they sense they'll never be returning, the more passionately they promise.

The Russian military beats a hasty retreat. For some reason, we're staying the night in a large house on Trakų Street. Perhaps we're afraid of being taken away. In the afternoon we're staring out the window of the empty room— along the sidewalk comes a small platoon of soldiers, heading towards the train station. Silently we look at them, they at us. Clearly the soldiers don't like our physi-

75

ognomies, since they reveal our impatient, unspoken urging: quickly, quickly... leave us—and don't promise to return!

—Shall we toss a grenade?—says one of them, apparently the group's leader.

Holy Jesus! We scramble from the room to the antechamber, from the antechamber to the stairwell, from the stairwell to the cellar, from there to the yard and—into the adjacent house's cellar. With only socks on, I shuffle through puddles on the cement floor.

But no one tries to blow the house up. Early next morning we're standing on the threshold. The men raise our national tri-colors (Lithuanian flag) by the front door. Gunfire rattles our way from the direction of Vytautas Prospect. The men take down the tri-colors. The firing ceases. After a brief consultation, they raise the flag again. We all decide to return home to Vaižgantas Street. Many people mill about on Freedom Avenue, but most of the shops are closed. The three of us,

Mama, Mr. Tadas, and I get two loaves of bread. We carry them unwrapped in our hands. We don't know when or where we'll get others. We head home through Vytautas Park. Near the steps on the slope lie two Red Army soldiers. They're no longer young. They're in mud-colored greatcoats, even though it's unseasonably warm. They don't have those pointy caps.

—You better run to the train station; the Germans will be here soon—Mr. Tadas urges them.

—We're not running anywhere,—they reply, and add,— We'll stay here and die.

We leave them with a loaf of bread and take the other home.

The neighborhood of Žaliakalnis is quiet. And the next day, too. The bolder residents hang out their tri-colors. We're walking along Vydūnas Avenue. I'm in the lead, Mama and Mr. Tadas a few steps behind. Three teenagers with white bands on their sleeves are playing at rebels.

—Jewess?—says one of them pointing his stick at me.

I remain quiet. I don't know what to say. And even if I did, I wouldn't be able to utter a word. The grey witch's robe turns into a solid ball and stops up my mouth.

—No, she's not a Jewess,—says Mr. Tadas stepping up to them—Beat it.

And they beat it. Innocent as I was then, I did not know a rebellion was already going on in Kaunas. I wonder if my mother and my future step-father knew?

Now I understand it was a terrifying time for them. And they weren't the only ones who were terrified.

> *But the earth came to the help of the woman,*
> *and the earth opened its mouth, and swallowed*
> *the river which the dragon had poured from his mouth.*

Revelation 12: 16

Tadas Lomsargis

10
Mr. Tadas

An elegant lady, a divorcee, mother of a young daughter... Of course, such a one attracted the attentions of more than one man. One of those men's attentions turned out to be fateful. That young man, who had finished his schooling in Czechoslovakia, is the artist Tadas Lomsargis, who happens to live in the same Purickis apartment building, in the basement. It's a basement only from the street side; in the back it has as big a window as any of the other apartments.

One fine day lady Milda receives a short letter written in beautiful handwriting on fine quality paper. The letter politely inquires whether the respected lady might not want to meet with the letter's author at a time and place of her own choosing. Lady Milda considers the letter seriously, forbidding the maid, Janė, to smirk at it. It remains unknown, however, how the rest of the household, indeed the entire apartment building, comes to know about the letter. Everyone waits for the barely begun romance to unfold. After a respectful time passes, with the help of her poet friend Kotryna, the elegant lady pens a reserved and feminine reply: she is not accustomed to meeting unknown gentlemen in this manner; however, she does agree to go to Perkūnas (Thunder) Avenue, by the Sports stadium fence, at the time specified herein.

That was in 1939.

Fate itself seemed to put its stamp on these two letters, having brought together two people who by chance lived in the same building—one on the very top floor, the other in the basement. Was it by chance or was it unavoidable? Most likely it was a cruel joke played by someone or something unknown. That "someone" I often imagine as a

78

grand experimenter, who drops human beings onto the Earth like ants, then stands back to observe what they'll do.

The beings right away began clubbing each other. Later they made themselves bows and arrows, invented guns, bombs, even atomic ones. Always for the same purpose—to destroy one another. You really have to be a strong believer in God to not believe that!

Mr. Tadas was a man after my mother's taste—slender build, a subtle, intelligent face, an elegant dresser in fine English suits. He had them made by a well-known tailor, though he wasn't always able to pay for them in time. You see, Mr. Tadas despite his positive outlook was, alas, not very well-off. And that was probably least attractive about him for Mama. However, Mr. Tadas was aflame with a love, which according to his letters, would die only in death, if Mrs. Milda remains indifferent to him. "You are my first and last,"—he wrote. And in another letter: "Only death can be stronger than my love for you."

•

Lady Milda, it seemed, didn't value words so highly, not even those in writing. Like those that had been written not so long before that, four years ago, by my Daddy:

> *... I'm not sleeping well... I feel like I can hear Dita crying, wanting to come into the "big bed." After that I can't fall asleep for a long time, and toss and turn and imagine you all, who are my entire life...*

•

Now, no one can say for sure who she really loved the most. Herself? What did she really want? To be wealthy and independent? Or to be unconditionally loved?

Soon, something takes place that Janė and I strongly resist, though in vain. Mr. Tadas moves from his basement to the top floor, that is, moves in with us. Janė and I fell into an unpleasantness for a while which, however, soon evaporated—seemingly. But only seemingly.

After marrying Mr. Tadas, Mama copied a quotation from Axel Munthe in her leather covered notebook "It is easier to understand a dog than a man and easier to love him." I had come across that quote accidently as I was thumbing through the monogrammed notebook. I've read it many times since. Each time anew. In vain I've tried to grasp its meaning. That statement always wounded me.

79

Mr. Tadas brings up a modest but valuable dowry from downstairs—a big writing desk with a green felt top and many drawers, and a cupboard with glass doors full of books. Among the books there's not a single cheap one, no pulp literature. And into my life, next to the library of children's books bought me by my father, come Rabindranath Tagore's *The Home and the World, The Golden Boat, The Night of Realization*; Guy de Maupassant's *Collected Novels*; Selma Lagerlof's *The Story of Gösta Berling*; Josef Kopta's *The Third Company*; Victor Hugo's *The Man Who Laughs*; Blasco Ibanez's *A Novelist's Tour Of The World*, and many more. Through the years not many of these are still left, but they were all read many times. They taught me, expanded my horizons, and left no place for the poor stuff circulating among my schoolmates. I'd already found other books at home, like Jack London's *White Fang*, Antanas Vaičiulaitis' *Valentina*, Axel Munthe's *Story of San Michele*. In secret I read *White Slaves*, a novel about prostitutes that had been hidden in the sofa—probably from me. It, perhaps, also proved beneficial.

Not yet ten years of age, I held in my hands and slowly read a memoir about M.K. Čiurlionis, as well as Hyppolyte Taine's *The Philosophy of Art*, which later, alas, was lent to someone and never returned.

Mr. Tadas had a wealth of various art collection post-cards. He traded two large collections of Impressionist and Post-impressionist artists for two large black-and-white books of Rembrandt and Rubens. To this day I don't understand why he, a modernist himself, turned away from the art nearest to him. Perhaps he was drawn to what to him seemed ultimately more valuable. Later, after Mr. Tadas had been killed, the former owner of those books asked for them back saying he'd only ever lent them. But Mama knew the truth and didn't give the books back.

In those days, I saw Mr. Tadas as a cold person, someone who didn't love me at all, and maybe didn't even love my mama. Now I see him with different eyes—as someone who was waiting for love and empathy, someone who just wanted to work at what he loved. After many years, Leonas Gudaitis was to write a few articles about him and, even later, a separate study, *Tadas Lomsargis*. The book, written during the Soviet era when Tadas Lomsargis' left-leaning views were in favor, wasn't published until much later during the country's new independence and was abridged by the author himself. The book angered his biological daughter, Liuda, and became the excuse for the final severing of our relationship.

Perhaps the book was imperfect, but Liuda liked nothing in it at all, even though she had read the manuscript some years before and declared it satisfactory. I had also read the manuscript; I liked just about everything in it, and so did not share Liuda's views.

I got to know Liuda in the sixties, but we didn't stay in touch. I called her in 1983 when her mother, Sofija, died. After that, we stayed in touch for a good decade. I helped her publish an article about Sofija Lomsargienė and her underground communist activities, and later L. Gudaitis' book. We grew rather close, introducing ourselves to people as sisters. I took great joy in that, always missing having a sister or brother and felt very close to her as my elder sister. It was nice— sisters—even though we had neither a mother nor father in common. I gave Liuda all her father's hand-bound books, since she had none of his work, except for a leather bound diary. For many years Mama had saved Pearl Buck's *Mother*; a specially hand-bound volume for Milda of F. E. Silanpe's *People of a Summer Night*; Sofija Vaineikienės' *Vaišvila*; a three-volume set of modern art, and other books, among them some from Czechoslovakia. Did I have to give them away? I think so. Tadas was her biological father, even though he was divorced from her mother and never met up with his daughter. In one of Tadas' letters there's even a statement that "everything before 1936 was worse than death."

During my years of dealings with Liuda, her husband Renius Nadieždinas died, and she soon married her childhood sweetheart Rimvydas. I became unnecessary. I had nothing left that could interest her. Even the watercolor of Tadas that had hung on our wall for so long had now been transferred to her apartment wall. Liuda even wanted to make Tadas into "a righteous among the nations"—for having saved me from the Nazis.

But Tadas Lomsargis was woven into my fate only by pure chance. Every honorable person, having stumbled into a similar situation, would not have withdrawn himself. Honor can't be measured in kilograms or meters; it's either there or not. Tadas' honor was above full measure. He had plenty of it without any need from others.

Tadas Lomsargis was killed, as they used to say then, for his leftist views—because of a public utterance during the first Soviet occupation and because of personal intrigues in his new workplace in Vilnius at the Gediminas Castle paper factory. But mostly because of a snitch. More than once I heard the informant's name at home—Šaltenis. As I was already grown up during the second Russian occupation, I tried to track him down. I won't leave him alone, I thought to myself. He'll have to be punished; he'll have to be held responsible. I did find his tracks—but only his tracks. And they led to Siberia. I heard he shunned returning to Lithuania even after the end of the time of accountability had ended. There he died.

"Serves him right," came the spiteful thought.

"God is his judge," I need to think now. I'm glad that I never descended to the level of soap opera, even in sorting out my relationship with Liuda. And just because of that, no relationship remained.

Why was our separation so painful? It was as if I'd buried a real sister. For a long time I grieved over it. Then grief ceased its pain and only a sharp shard remained, eventually rounded off by long years buried in the ground. The only thing left was the scar of disappointment...

Injuries then, during childhood, were many. Only the reasons for them sank in time's dust—why?

... I'm lying in my room in my pale yellow bed. I'm sick with scarlet fever. Why did I get up, dress, and run downstairs to Šiaulių Street where my daddy worked?

—I'm not going home anymore,—I said and sat down, as my fever was causing my legs to buckle and my vision to darken. —I'm going to live with you.

With what words was he able to change my mind? I remember not a one. But he did convince me and brought me home. Mr. Tadas was angry with me. We didn't talk to each other for a long time. Later I had to apologize. I strongly resisted Mama's admonition. But I did apologize. Mr. Tadas didn't upbraid me, didn't moralize, just gave me a kiss.

And again, hour upon hour, he lets me look on while he binds his books... He burns lettering into leather. He fills the letters with gold leaf. He keeps thin sheets of gold in a special book between silken pages. In the corner of the room stands a roll of various bookbinder's goatskins—blue, black, red Moroccan leathers. He also has a large collection of amazing copper tools with sleek wooden handles—for cutting, embossing, decorating the various kinds of leather.

He is an artist growing in fame. Three of his bound books represent Lithuania at a world display in New York. But he's very poor. Is that why he's often scowling, nontalkative? Ultimately, it is insisted that I call him "Dad" rather than "Mister."

Again, I rebel as much as possible.

At last, I decide I have to stop making Mama and my new "daddy" angry. I don't call him "Mister" anymore, but I don't call him anything else either.

Another one of my rebellions was no joke. At the beginning of the Nazi occupation, a danger arises to my very existence. It seems that Mr. Tadas has no choice but to adopt his beloved wife's daughter, since from that sweet girl all of a sudden a death threat looms. My Granddaddy's brother, Vincentas Ambraziejus, the parish priest of Šunskai (may he rest easily in the earth of his churchyard grave), puts together a "somewhat modified" new birth certificate.

•

... Kaunas. Freedom Avenue. Not far from the post office Mr. Tadas has me sit on a bench. Orders me to wait. He goes off to some state bureaucrat's office with my new birth certificate. Waiting, of course, is boring. How long am I expected to patiently wait? For the little girl on the bench, it doesn't come into her head that nearby in some small office a question of life and death is in the balance. My mother's youthful mistake, which called me into this world, now has to transform into an inexorable death sentence or to a conditional tranquility. That conditional tranquility is reflected in Mr. Tadas' face when he comes out of that omnipotent office. I don't yet realize that I now have a different first and last name, a different birth certificate with a different birth year, day and month.

I'm given new school notebooks, and told to write my new name on them. In class, my new name shows up on the list of my classmates. I take a stand against all this. On my notebook, I write the name as I wish and tell the teacher it's my real name. My revolt doesn't last very long— it's quickly explained to me that we're at war and this is required; after the war, "we'll see." They tell me nothing about death, nor about the ghetto in Vilijampolė, nor about mass killings.

The huge catastrophe—the SHOAH, the Holocaust, had already begun.

I was protected from painful stresses the way young children today are protected from sex and narcotics. At that time, among us, these four words were never uttered: Shoah, stress, sex, narcotics. But the death machine wound up by the Nazis didn't take long to swallow up Mr. Tadas as well. Just like my father, who according to Mama's story, "had to leave for Brazil," and whose doorbell ring I awaited for many days after the end of the war.

83

Was I a big rebel? Maybe. But all my rebellions ended in failure. Except for two. One was when they fired our maid, Janė. Allegedly she was not good enough for the newly formed family. I adamantly persisted that Janė should be returned to us. I categorically refused to obey any other new substitute maid. That time I won. Janė returned, but not for long. During the Nazi occupation she was sent to forced labor in Germany. Later no funds were available to pay her. But our acquaintance did not end. I was to meet up with Janė once again.

...The Nazi occupation. Mr. Tadas is fired from his job in Vilnius because of a dispute. He is lying on the sofa reading *Don Quixote*. Summer is leaning towards fall. I'm playing in the large yard of our house. From the balcony comes a voice:

—Ditele, home!

So soon? I don't want to go home yet. Didn't I just go out? No, I'll keep playing.

—Hurry!...—Mama's voice is unusually urgent.

I run across the yard, and up the stairs.

Three people are coming down the steps. Two strangers, the third—Mr. Tadas. He stops, embraces me, kisses me.

—Obey your mother,—he says only.

And they leave. All three.

I don't think anything bad about it.

Upstairs in our apartment, the family is trying its best to revive my fainting mama. She knows people taken away like this don't ever return. Mama is lying on the sofa; she doesn't see me, rivers of tears flow from her eyes. In this case, "rivers of tears" is not a hackneyed metaphor from books, but in reality something that happens to a person at least once in their life.

It was September 23, 1942.

•

After many years, in December of 1984, sending off our son Žilvinas to serve his tour of duty in the Soviet army, I experienced the same feeling of utter loss. An all-powerful alien force takes away your loved one. The person belongs to you, but there's absolutely nothing you can do. You keep a check on yourself in order not to worry him. But after, when he's said his good-byes and can no longer see you, you give free rein to your pain. Your eyes swell up from tears so badly that you can't open them, even the next day. And the rivers keep flowing...

84

Our son has already disappeared behind the iron fence. We're still standing this side—me, his father, his sister. Someone is swearing in Russian, someone else is yelling in a drunken voice. The bright yellow searchlight is blinding us. In the large yard it's as if we're on a theater stage. As if in the painful play of Eimuntas Nekrošius, *The Square*. In the iron cage someone is loudly cudgeling our heads with iron bars. And our heads ring as if made of iron.

The Soviets are at war in Afghanistan. What links my child to that war?

Back then there was also a war. Hitler against Stalin. The Germans are orderly. After many visits to the Gestapo to try to find out about her husband, one fine day a well-fed German presents Mama with Mr. Tadas' rectangular Swiss wristwatch and announces officially:

—Your husband has been shot.

The wristwatch lay like a relic in our Vilnius apartment on Didžioji Street on top of a cupboard until, after a good decade or so, the janitor stole it.

In the archives remained a small German index card with the name of Tadas Lomsargis. The card is filled out in ink but crossed out obliquely with a soft-leaded pencil. Understand: once there was a person—now there is no person. And there's no grave.

...Mama started to change. Bad energy, built up after years of calamities, began to spread, flowing into me as well. My childhood was now over. And so began my hard and contradictory teen years, pressured alas by my mother, who became unfriendly, controlling, angry and ruthless to me. I suffered all that because I thought it had to be that way.

There is a way which seems right to a man,
but its end is the way to death.

Proverbs 16: 25

Any pain rather then a pain
caused by those who never suffer.

Sirach 25: 14

A dedication from Papa

11
Eternal Light

My very earliest memory flashes forward like the earliest star shining in a darkening evening sky.

—Ditele, can you jump over a matchstick?—my father asks me. (I call him by the then popular word "Papa.")

—I can,—I say, ready to demonstrate my ability to do so. I'm three years old, maybe less.

—Don't be so sure,—says Papa slowly drawing out a matchstick from a matchbox. Very carefully, he places the matchstick on the floor, but right up against the wall.—See, you can't.

That was my first lesson that everything in this world is relative.

Another one of my not-clearly-thought-out attempts also ends in failure—I'm left standing in a pot of cranberry preserves, up to my knees. That clay pot, about the size of a bucket, with one broken handle, stands in the ante-room, right under that technological miracle of the time—the wall telephone. I want to reach that miracle, and climb onto the pot double-covered and tied down with wax paper. But the paper doesn't keep me up.

Before the war we live in Kaunas near the train station on Čiurlionis Street. The owner of the beer brewery, Volfas, had built special two-story, double-occupancy homes on his property, then called Volfas' Villas. In one of them the earliest and happiest of my childhood years took place.

The villas were comfortable and simple, surrounded by neat gardens and lilac shrubs, which were covered with white and violet blossoms in the spring. Of those five villas only two now remain. They're miserable, stripped, devoid of greenery, next to the aggressive new factory buildings which swallow the memory. True, one of them has been made to look more contemporary, with a coat of paint and a new roof. A large travel agency sign hangs in front: "Our Odyssey."

—What holy truth, —I think to myself stunned by such a blunt overlap.

Here, truly, my life's odyssey began with all its losses and the knowledge I carry with ever greater difficulty. It's good only that no one will be able to take it from me any more.

Father carries me in his arms along Freedom Avenue. He's moving forward, but I'm looking backward, and I like that very much. Everything we pass, moves farther and farther away from us and becomes smaller and smaller. No one catches up to us or passes us. They just recede. My Daddy is tall; that's why I can see everything around us so clearly. His hands are large and warm, with prominent veins. I especially like those hands. And those veins. You can press them down as much as you like, they always pop back up. I like everything about him—his high forehead, brown eyes, and round eyeglasses with thin black frames. He wears everything well—his grey English suit, his light golf plus-fours and his plaid golf stockings. And his hat, called a derby. He has a fountain pen with the inscription "Lietuva" (Lithuania) on it. On Freedom Avenue he buys me a chocolate "bomb" wrapped in silver paper. Inside the "bomb" I find a small child's ring with a glass stone.

One of the "Volfas Villas" rental houses

...My first milk tooth falls out. My father has a gold ring made for himself, and instead of a precious stone has the

87

tooth mounted in it. If I only knew where that ring had vanished to... Did it end up, alas, in Germany as a trophy, where no one could quite figure out what that strange stone was? Did it end up with a local killer? Or maybe it's lying in the ground here, in our country? In that fatal spot sprouts a tree of tolerance, but it is still so small and fragile.

...Petras Klimas' book *Readings* is full of all sorts of interesting things. Even back then it was an old book, coverless, with yellowed, torn and disintegrating cheap paper pages. It's still the same even now on my table. Also mysterious is the magic lament which issues from the open pages, described in Putinas' strange poem, "The Ring and the Woman":

> *And she hears that night the ring bewail:*
> *Evoe, evoe, evoe...*

Even today I don't understand the poem I didn't understand back then. But abstract lamentations have turned into the concrete cries of that ring.

With my Daddy

Generalizations are created by philosophers and poets. People try to concretize them. They make them concrete then summarize their findings.

•

The Judaic respect for the book, having survived from the most ancient of times, my father tried to pass on to me. Apparently he well knew the injunction of his ancestors to sell your treasure but buy books. Since in them lies indestructible value—wisdom. During those times he buys all the children's books that are published. He requires me to keep them neatly and to treasure them. He cuts up colored, translucent paper and shows me how to make a dust cover for a book. He shows me the same way he learned at school. Back then we had no cellophane covers on books; hard covers were a rarity as well, so books needed to be looked after with care. One of the oldest books I still have, still with its original pale green hand-made dust cover is Albinas Andrulionis' *First Butterflies*. The inscription says that Papa gives it to his "precious little daughter Ditelė" on January 1, 1938. On all the books he gave, he wrote in a beautiful hand his certifications of love to his one and only daughter.

He sends me to a German kindergarten on Vytautas Avenue. So that I'll learn the German language. From the Šančiai neighborhood where many Germans have taken up residence, a *Fräulein* was hired who would spend a few hours every day speaking with me in German.

That language became aversive to me later, when I learned what had happened. Finishing middle-school, I didn't want to continue studying it, even though I knew it fairly well by then. Instead I took up the as-yet-untasted English language. Nonetheless, what I learned in my childhood I could probably recreate without too much effort.

Tired and time-worn—this year they will be more than sixty years old—lie the first and most beautiful love letters written to me.

...Don't think—he writes to Žvirgždaičiai on August 7, 1939—that Papa releases his Little One even for a moment from his thoughts, from his heart. I'm with you at all times, even though from afar. Even though we saw each other not too long ago, I already want to hug and kiss you again.

89

I know, Ditukėle, that it's good for you to be with your grandma and among your own, and I know we're not apart for very long, but still it's very hard for me to say goodbye each time we part. Probably Papa loves you too much, maybe I worry about you too much, but perhaps when you grow up to be older, you'll understand your papa's feelings...

•

For me—among "my own," but for him with strangers? Papa would come to Marijampolė to see me, but not to Žvirgždaičiai. They'd send me to Marijampolė by horse-drawn wagon, and there we'd meet. The boundary of the city of Marijampolė was also the boundary for him. He wouldn't have been comfortable in the farm among the holy pictures and peat-brick pyramids.

At the outskirts of Marijampolė, where the paved streets end and the dusty highway begins, we'd say goodbye to each other. He comes along with me for a few more steps, his hand on the wagon's side-board, but the horses start to trot and he soon falls back from me into the distance. I know that he'll make his way to the train station and return to Kaunas, and he'll be there until I come back again.

...I return to Žvirgždaičiai. All along the roadside ditches, I'm led by the pale blue blossoms of chicory flowers. The blossoms are pale with sorrow. The sadness of childhood might seem relatively light, but it ends up weighing heavily on the soul, stirring up much later on.

My father's cousin lived in Marijampolė. He was a wealthy man—a shoe, iron, and kerosene merchant. When the Soviets came, they confiscated all of his wealth, but they made him a state trade director. Temporarily, probably, until they could find somebody else. Afterwards, the Nazis came and finished off the well-begun disaster.

Thirty years later in a book about the mass killings in Lithuania, I found the following testimony of a Marijampolė resident: "... Subockis, shot through the chest, lying under a covering of dirt, raised up from the dirt on his arms and asked to be finished off, to not be buried alive."[1]

---

[1] *Masinės žudynės Lietuvoje*, 1941-1944. Dokumentų rinkinys, II dalis.— V.: Mintis, 1973. P.163 (*Mass Killings in Lithuania*, 1941-1944, Document collection, Part 2.—V.: Mintis, 1973, p.163.)

"Eternally yours," my father would write. But in one letter he wrote, "Your papa waits for you, who can't live without you." Eternity sneaks up on him, but he doesn't know how close and how soon... He promises to take care of me eternally, but it's already the second half of 1940. Less than a year is left before that word "eternal" will take on its true meaning. In my letter box lies a postcard of a dewy rose and a note: "Since I can't send you a live rose, I send this card," And again, "Eternally yours."

Fate turned out otherwise. I was left without him. Physically, I was protected, spiritually I was "naked among wolves." As soon as he disappears, his name becomes taboo in our household. Nobody mentions him, no stories are told. I question no one. At that time I had it in mind that any questions would be sacrilegious. Later—that the answers to my questions would drown out any remaining specks of memory. Back then, there were many, but today, not many people remember him.

"What was my father like?"—I finally ask after many years in a letter to his cousin Sonia.

"Cheerful,"—she replies.

"I just want you to know," wrote my Uncle Kostas from across the Atlantic after sixty years, "before the end of my journey through this vale of tears, that I remember your daddy very well—he was cultured, intelligent, a man of pleasant and peaceful manner, a true gentleman."

Papa Samuelis Subockis (center) in the Lithuanian army

The light is on, since it's already dark outside. I'm sitting at the kitchen table. We're eating dinner. Next to me Mr. Tadas and Mama. Janė is frying pancakes. Right outside our window one of two radio towers blinks its red lights. We'll darken the windows later, when the Soviet army recovers, stops retreating and sends its planes to bomb the Nazi-occupied lands.

The doorbell rings. Mama goes to answer it, but returning to the kitchen she says nothing. Just orders me to keep eating. A heavy silence descends on the kitchen. I no longer want to eat as a strange unease takes me over. I chew my third pancake reluctantly. Suddenly I lift my eyes to the darkened double-paned glass window at the top of the kitchen door. Instinctively, I feel that someone is watching me through the glass.

And it's true.

Behind the window flit the familiar high forehead and round, black eyeglass frames. It's my daddy, who's missing me, and can't wait for me to finish eating. And it's quite strange that he would come here and at such a time—in the evening. Mama, who has gone through the door, is undoubtedly scolding him and ordering him to wait in his daughter's room. With a constricted throat, I swallow the last bites, quickly wash and run off to where he's waiting for me.

Daddy is sitting by my bed into which I've just jumped. He caresses me with his large warm hand, and then lays it on my stomach.

—You haven't eaten many pancakes,—he says.

Yes, it's true, not many. But how does he know?

—I didn't want anymore.

—I can guess how many,—he continues. Without taking his hand away, he gives my belly a squeeze. —Only three.

—How do you know that?—I ask.

—I just know,—I hear the smile in his voice.

—Sing for me,—I ask, when I grow tired of talking and sleep starts pressing my eyelids down.

Brothers, we're going home, home,
young brothers, home, home...
We'll find Daddy waiting,
holding a belt in his hand...

He carries on with one of his favorite songs. "*Dirželis (belt)...Dalgelis (scythe)...*" Why all that, I think to myself drifting off. "*Namo (home)...namo (home)...*" His voice calms me. I have no will left to ask anything. I fall asleep not knowing that I will never see him again.

No brother is standing behind him, but the goddess of death with her scythe, drawing and dragging him away from my bedside. Of course, he kisses me first. Of course, Daddy straightens my blanket...

—Hurry!—black fire, as black as the darkness itself burns in her dead eye sockets.

—Goodbye, goodbye, goodbye,—footsteps rustle quietly in the hallway, then in the stairwell, and then down Vaižgantas Street. But I slept the deep sleep of childhood. The witch sat huddled on the stairs, upset, wrapped in her grey robe, completely melted into the darkness.

He has gone beyond.

Whatever is taken away from you by force, stays with you forever.

May eternal light shine for him.

The light shines in the darkness,
and the darkness has not overcome it.

John 1: 5

Menorah

12
Star of David

Citation from the Dictionary of Symbols:
Hexagram, Solomon's seal, David's star, a six-pointed star, made from two triangles; found in Judaic, Christian, and Islamic religions; foundational in the Indian Yantra...The star of David is the symbol of Jewish belief, the national emblem of Israel. According to C. G. Jung it is an expression of the individual and universal spheres, or the con-vergence of the masculine and feminine.

Citation from Order #15 from the Kaunas war-time commandant and the mayor of Kaunas, July 10, 1941 (second paragraph):
All persons of Jewish nationality [sic] living in the city of Kaunas, without exception of gender and age, starting on July 12th, are to wear the following symbol on the left side of the chest: a yellow Star of David, 8 – 10 cm in diameter. Jewish nationals themselves are to be responsible for acquiring the stars. Any Jewish national seen without a star will be arrested.

A statement written in blood on the wall of a room in the Kaunas ghetto:
Jews, seek vengeance!

Citation from a 1998 letter written to me by Sonia from Israel:
Your grandfather was shot dead in Kaunas, on Freedom Avenue.

...After nearly sixty years I receive a photograph of my grandfather Moses. Crew-cut graying hair, thick eyebrows, large piercing eyes, spare mustache above a wide mouth. The face is expressive and large featured. On the left lapel of his jacket, on the "left side of the chest," as per the order above—not the Star of David. Not at all. Pinned there is an Order of the Grand Duke of Gediminas. A decoration from the Lithuanian Republic.

Who shot and killed my grandfather? Lithuanians? Had the Germans already arrived? On what June day—22, 23, 24, 25 or later? After all, the order to wear the Star of David had not yet been issued. Would my grandfather have obeyed the order? Or would he have been ashamed of the traditional symbol?

From olden times we're informed by written guides about what Jews were required to wear in various countries: two yellow symbols—one on the hat, one around the neck. A small piece of lead is to be worn as a pendant around the neck. Women had to wear one red and one black shoe, and a bell tied to one of the shoes or around their neck.

Granddad Moses (Moshe) Subockis

That's only the outer form. Over many ages, dispersed throughout the world, Jews respected mostly the powers of the mind and its capacity for wisdom. These strengths opened many doors for them. But they were powerless against people's jealousy and thick-headedness.

My grandparents didn't love me. (Writing this, my hand shakes: I'm slandering them, I realize. They couldn't not love me). That they didn't see me at all was true. The shock of their son's marriage, apparently, never passed, even up to their deaths. They knew that different worlds, different religions, different customs, would not provide a solid

95

foundation for a union. They foresaw the fragility of the relationship and its inevitable tragic separation. No, no, that can't be—they must have thought.

It happened as it always does, when love tramples on thousand-years' traditions, when love doesn't respect beliefs, customs, and long-established order.

Jehova is a stern God. He does not forgive sins. Nor even mistakes. Not individuals, not entire nations.

After many years, I try to understand that God is one.

Then why does he punish those whom he should love the most?

Just before the very beginning of all the calamities of war, my daddy married a second time. He married a woman from his own people and had a son, Mark. He was killed before he began to walk.

Both families lived at opposite ends of the city. Only one day a week, usually Sunday, was set aside for me. It belonged to my father and me. On Sunday mornings Mama takes me to Ugnagesų Street in the old town, goes in with me to the enclosed front yard, and stands apart while I ring the doorbell of a green wooden house. As soon as the door opens, Mama turns and leaves. I don't stay very long at my daddy's place. He dresses, and the two of us leave for the center of town. At nightfall, Daddy drops me off in a similar way at my mama's place.

How wonderful those days were!...

On Sundays, Daddy shows me everything it's possible to see in Kaunas. From the confluence to the zoological gardens. The ruins of the Kaunas castle... The town garden next to the theater... Vytautas Park... the funicular... the Nature Museum, the War Museum, and the garden around it—everything is ours. Everything is explored and explained in great depth. My father even takes me to the "Kaunas audiniai," a new, modern textile factory. I see for the first, and probably the last time, a huge, ceaselessly humming manufacturing plant from the inside.

We both see the film *Snow White and the Seven Dwarves*. The first cartoon in color of Walt Disney's ever shown in Kaunas! Who can describe a child's delight of those times, before the telly, before cartoons, before serials. I've already seen all the black-and-white films of the star Shirley Temple, a little girl of my own age. Maybe those films were sentimental, but how they stuck to my heart. I've already read the story of Heidi, but the film again squeezes out tears over the little girl's hardships.

These days how little we release soul-refreshing tears of sympathy... Not because we'd be ashamed of them. We just

96

don't feel empathy for anyone, thinking that's how it should be, that no one feels empathy for us either.

I read Jonas Biliūnas' "I Struck" (*"Kliudžiau"*)[1] to my little granddaughter. She listens silently. It's already the second half of the short story; already the fatal phrase "I struck" has been read. My granddaughter says:

—If you read any further, I'm going to start to cry.

I am relieved. It seems I, too, have struck.

—Cry,—I say.—Then I'll really know your heart is merciful. Or would you like me to stop reading?

—Read,—she says. And clear drops roll from her eyes.

She takes Biliūnas' book of short stories to school. The teacher reads it to her first grade class and suggests everyone draw a picture of the "happy" ending.

Grant us, Lord, that all our steps come to a happy ending. As in my granddaughter's drawing: a large yellow sun and round flower petals with round, frightened mouths calling out:

—Oh oh!...

And the released arrow whistles by without hurting the kitten.

With Papa, Kaunas

[1] Jonas Biliūnas (1879–1907) was a writer, poet, and literary critic. A sometime socialist and anti-Czarist, he contributed to Lithuania's movement toward independence in the late 19th and early 20th centuries. He died of tuberculosis at the early age of twenty-eight. "Kliudžiau" ("I Struck") is a heart-wrenchingly told children's story of a young boy who kills a kitten with his bow and arrow.

Even before the war, the Soviets, along with their sugary propaganda films, had brought to Kaunas the black and white *Adventures of Pinocchio*. That was the last movie I saw with my Daddy... The last vision etched into my brain before the screen went dark—a large sailboat... sailing to the land of happiness... From that time on, I was fascinated by sailboats, though in fact I'd never seen a real one. Even today, a sailboat seems to me the most beautiful thing made by human hands.

Ah, if only we'd been able to take our life's sailboat beyond the clouds to another shore. Where there are neither communists, nor Nazis, nor murderers, nor angel-faced people with the hearts of wolves!

One morning soon after the beginning of the German occupation, Mama snatches me by the hand and hurries me off to the old town, to the small green house where my father lives. I'm thrilled. It's going to be another lucky day. I'm surprised, though, that she doesn't stand to the side and wait for the door to be opened. Instead, she walks up to the door with me and rings the bell herself. One time, another... impatiently a third... No one opens the door. Mama talks with the next door neighbors. I don't understand about what. The neighbors' faces are dark. They're looking at me sadly. Somehow, I get that they're not only neighbors but relatives also.

...The two of us return slowly home. Only after many years do I learn that my father was detained twice. The first time he escaped. Did he want to hide? Or see me?

—Your father has left for Brazil,—says Mama.

—Why?—I ask, astounded that he wouldn't have said goodbye.

—It would be bad for him here,—says Mama.

—But when will he return?—I ask.

—When the war ends.

Even now, the question still hangs: why did Mama go there that day? Did she want to tell him something? Offer something? Ask for something? I don't dare guess. I'll never know the truth now.

Apparently, the holy lie was necessary. Throughout the entire German occupation, the horrors of the ghetto, all of the killings, were scrupulously kept from me... The ghetto of Vilijampolė is farther from me than that imagined Brazil.

...Occasionally people with yellow Stars of David pass us on the street. Literally, the street. Not the sidewalk. Walking on the sidewalk is forbidden them. The people seem as if from another world, not like Kaunites. Not like our neighbors of yesterday. The Stars are extremely

98

varied—some are handsomely, carefully stitched around their edges. Others are fraying, carelessly cut out of cheap cloth.

I don't know anything else. It doesn't concern me. I study, read books. During the winter, I'm cold in the inadequately heated apartment. I sleep in the small room next to the kitchen where it's warmer. The cold walls sweat and later are covered with slimy mold. The mold sprinkles onto my pillow. Mister Tadas' beloved cactuses are also kept in that room. The cactuses, weakened by their struggle for existence, are covered in white parasites. Later they succumb completely. In the dining room, Mama's long cherished, ceiling-reaching philodendron also dies.

At school it's also cold.

The Germans, having appropriated the biggest and best buildings for their own offices and war hospitals, paint them in terrible brown-green stains so they won't show up at a distance. Some of my school's classes are held in the Institute for the Blind, or in the wooden primary school on Vilijampolė Avenue, later on Kapsų Street, and later somewhere else. Most of the time, we sit in class with overcoats and mittens.

During one class a mitten-clad hand pokes me in the back. It's a note from another row of desks—a doubly-folded sheet of newspaper. It's in Hebrew characters; I don't understand even a single word. I just stare at it like that struck animal who only subliminally senses what the meaning might be.

"*Memento mori!*—that newspaper rustles.—Throw me aside."

From a desk in the other aisle stare the senders' curious eyes and grinning mouths.

But look! My guardian angel has stretched out his hand above my head again. What is it that glimmers so in his hand? The eyes close, blinded by that light, the lips press together and hide the teeth.

—Send it back,—I say calmly, turning to my classmate sitting behind me.—I don't understand this writing.

After the war I learned that on the edge of Žaliakalnis and in Vilijampolė, the residents robbed the belongings left behind by the banished Jews, profiting by exchanging their possessions for food. How did those girls in my class get a Jewish newspaper during the very height of the German occupation?

I have lots of girlfriends. But I'm not very good at playing Squares. And I don't read *The Skull in the Green Suitcase.*[2] During break I don't want to eat my bread-and-butter sandwich. The butter was brought back from Žvirgždaičiai the past summer. So that it won't spoil, it's been rendered down, but it's still pretty rancid. Mama tries to preserve the eggs she's brought back in a peculiar way: she dips each one into boiling water for a few seconds. Nonetheless, a third of the eggs still stink... Mama has nothing else to put on bread, so she sprinkles on sugar. For me, such sandwiches are terribly unappetizing. I bring them home from school and hide them in the distant corner of my drawer. I know I mustn't throw out bread. Later, Mama finds a whole pile of the dried out sandwiches, and she weeps.

In our class, some eat sandwiches with nicely smelling sausage, some eat nothing at all. Much later I learn about social inequality, but even then I begin to understand about poverty of the soul. Accordingly I start to distinguish among people and try to make friends, though I often make mistakes. I understand one other thing, which took a long time to come to its final form—nothing hurts as badly as a friend's betrayal. But no need to grieve if your foe betrays you—you couldn't expect anything different from them.

In Kaunas, Ugniagesių Street no longer exists. After many, many years and after having at last steeled myself and dulled my feelings, I look for the wooden gate and the green house beyond it. The street now is Juozo Gruodžio. No sign of a gate anywhere. The yard is completely different. Open at all sides. The green house is no longer there. In the yard, puddles.

Back in Vilnius I don't want to believe that nothing remains "there" any longer. I travel to Kaunas again, go "there" again—it's really true, nothing remains. Only after visiting the lot for the third time, and looking around at everything, do I fully get it—nothing is there anymore, and it never will be again.

But I'll return some day. Maybe I'll meet up with some shadow. Maybe see a fateful sign.

> *Though the wicked sprout like grass*
> *and all evildoers flourish,*
> *they are doomed to destruction for ever.*

Psalm 92: 7

----

[2] Justas Pilyponis (1907–1947) was a pioneer Lithuanian detective and adventure story writer.

100

Dita's First Communion

13
Litauische Schweine...
Lithuanian Swine

Work, pray, and smile,—wrote the priest Čyvas in his pretty Rococo handwriting on the first page of the prayer book he gave me. I didn't succeed in keeping the book, but I well remember the inscription, though nearly sixty years have gone by. And I suppose that's how I lived—I smiled and even laughed, often for no reason; I prayed, but very little; and I worked much less than I could have. It might have been better if he'd written just one inscription—believe in yourself. I felt the lack of that throughout my entire life. It's strange that no one has ever said: don't hesitate, be decisive, reach and you'll attain. In short—you can do it. Slug them back if they bully you. Don't just imagine it's raining if they are urinating on your head. That's how I turned everything into a psychological complex throughout my life—I'm not beautiful enough, I'm too fat, my shoe size is too big, I won't be able to do the job required of me.

Of course, I didn't reveal any of those complexes to anyone, only carried them within. How surprised I was while working in radio when one of my bosses signed his name to a report I'd written about our listeners' questions and had it published in the newspaper. That boss, now eternally at rest, once claimed:

—Better a bird in the hand than one on the roof.

The efforts of subordinates to explain that he got the wording of the old proverb wrong, and that therefore it was no longer a proverb, just caused him to retort with the unopposable argument:

—Are you saying it's not better?

—Yes, better,—all that was left to say, agreeing with the boss.

101

I'm not saying I've never been praised, complimented, or had good words said about me. Unfortunately, I've never once believed them. And that's a pity, since it would have been better for me if I had.

But, nonetheless, thank you, priest.

Today I open the low, plain doors of the Kaunas Carmelite church...and right away I hear the priest's words:

—He took the bread, blessed it, broke it, and gave it to the apostles saying: take and eat this, since it is my body, which I surrender to you.

At that time, during the uprising, when we heard the church bells ringing, we had no thought at all of raising up our heads. And the biggest sinners beat at their chests with fists asking for forgiveness. Now I do raise my head—among the long rows of pews sit a small number of women, and even fewer men. It's that same Crucified One in the center of eight columns. Higher up—two bright angels with golden wings. One of them, my own, guarded my childhood, but then I left him behind. And now, here I am standing below, looking up, and saying to him:

—Thank you. Forgive me for not visiting you for so long.

—I pray for you always,—he replies so quietly that my daughter standing close by doesn't even hear him.

Angels of Carmelites' Church

Today, the pulpit, just as it was back then, looks made out of chocolate and glazed sugar. It reminds me of a fancy chocolate cake decorated with eight chocolate cherubs. In my mouth, the taste is not of bread but of chocolate and childhood. In my memory I see the two chocolate figures in the window of Konrad's cafe, almost as large as two boys, poised to begin wrestling. I used to believe they were made of pure chocolate. Now the whole church seems to press warmly around me in the fading brown, gold, and white dusk. Why am I not happy then, being able to return here, better late than never at all? Perhaps the chocolate has grown bitter with age and no longer tastes very good?

•

On May 2, 1943, I take my first communion here. That evening I see myself as completely pure, without the smallest sin. For that night only, I'm not afraid of death, that is, hell, since I can step straight into heaven. That same night I sit in our basement along with our neighbors waiting for the air-raid sirens to sound the all-clear. On that day and only that day I fear nothing. The Soviet long-distance bombers, droning frighteningly, have flown off somewhere to the west and should be returning soon. And when they do, the sirens wail in a drawling manner, meaning the danger is over and everyone can go to bed. The planes fly over just about every other night. Immediately, Kaunas Radio goes silent. That's a sign that the bombers are crossing the front lines and that the warning will be given soon. And it's true. The clamor of the sirens' wailing seems to be pulling all of your insides out through your throat. I feel sick and want to throw up, but there's no time. I want to sleep, but they're pulling me out of bed, saying:

—Hurry...

They dress me quickly and lead me down to the basement. There almost all of the residents of the Purickis building are gathered. Only the Graičiūnas family is missing. They are free spirits. No Soviet bombers are going to force them to root around under the ground like some kind of moles. Their neighbors, real Lithuanians that they are, don't pass up a chance to take a bite out of those close by:

—They'd like to meet their end with their treasures.

By the way, Mrs. Unė was perhaps the only lady of all the Kaunas granddames who had a silver fox coat. Back then, owning even one silver fox meant that you had made it, but here she was... Women counted and counted but couldn't agree on how many silver foxes you'd need to make that one coat.

•

From a military perspective, it would seem that Kaunas was an insignificant objective. That's why it was never really bombed, except accidentally. One small bomb is inadvertently dropped on the Miniotas property on

Vaižgantas Street. It leaves a small crater and ruins the stylish fence of the house in front. In that house lives some kind of high German official who immediately orders the sidewalk repaired, the broken fence slats replaced and painted to match the rest of the fence. Our astonishment is without end—the Germans come up with the matching brown paint when none seems available anywhere in Kaunas.

That bomb, even though a small one, scared us all considerably. We no longer hid in our own basement from the death flying under the clouds, but withdrew ourselves to Sixth Fort beyond the zoological gardens. Nine forts, some better preserved than others, have encircled the city since the First World War. Now, looking at a map of Kaunas, I can't get over how we covered such a long distance in such a short time. We were faster than the bombers. Probably we walked as fast as we could, almost ran. At first through the scary, whispering forest of Ąžuolynas (Oak Forest). And then along the fence of the zoological garden, behind which something fidgets and scratches, yelps, squeaks. At last the fort. Damp ditches overgrown with nettles, red brick walls. During nights when the sirens have sounded, hoards of people gather there, infants and all. We don't doubt that the old fortress walls will protect us. Inside the fortress it's cold, spectral, eerie. When we discover that the place is full of ghost-like bats, we find them even scarier than the bombers droning high above. I don't remember our journeys back. I was probably walking in my sleep, both my hands held by the slowly returning family. When would we go to bed? How many hours would we sleep?

Because of those bats in the fort, our night trips became shorter. We started hiding in the cellar of a chemical lab that we called the "gas factory." It's warm there; even the electricity is sometimes on. I sit there listening to a creepy bumping sound—not the bombs exploding, but heavy underground iron doors opening and closing. One, two, three. They're being opened by men who go outside to look around, have a smoke. The air in the cellar thickens, bad smells grow, sleep starts to glue together eyelids, clothes start to scratch and gnaw skin. People speak in whispers; exhausted children sleep; they have no strength left for crying.

—If a bomb hits us here directly, it still won't be able to penetrate the ceiling. The floors above are very strong,— someone says.

104

—But the walls will collapse, and we won't be able to get out,—says another voice.

—They'll dig us out in a few days,—adds a third.

—We'll smother in this hole before they dig us out,—a fourth winds up the discussion.

A terrible crash awakens everyone. The walls and ceilings tremble; somewhere doors left open slam shut. Nothing falls, nothing collapses.

—A bomb!—men announce after running in from outside. —Very close by.

The next day, it becomes clear the bomb has fallen very close to the stadium near the Kaunas Sports Institute. It lands right in the soft earth and hence doesn't cause much damage. But, nonetheless, from the depth of the crater we can see it was a very powerful one. Kaunites are in a rush to have a look at that crater. They're horrified at the thought of what would have happened had the bomb landed on houses. Everyone agrees that the bomb was not specially chosen for Kaunas, just that the pilot had to get rid of it on the way home as he forgot to drop it on the chosen target. Supposedly, all the others had been dropped, and only that one was left. And so it hit the empty stadium, thanks to You, Lord.

—Thanks to You, Lord,—say I, too, in my thoughts, since at that time I was particularly religious. During these night journeys I never let out of my hand the ordinary black cross with its plain aluminum crucifix. That little cross lay for many years in a drawer of the writing desk. It patiently awaited the hour when it would be needed again. And that hour came!

It hangs now above my bed. Modest, unpretentious. It remembers everything, but remains very unobtrusive. It doesn't really want to remind me of anything. It just hangs there.

•

—Tell me about your childhood, —asks my granddaughter as she settles in for the night. —But just not about the war.

I've told her about a few "wartime" episodes. She doesn't want to hurt her heart.

—Write about everything, just don't get into politics,— says my friend Alė, after having read some pages from this memoir of mine.

I don't promise.

How can I not politick, when life itself during those times was political. It was full of politics, dependent upon politics.

Then and now. When we no longer know who's the head of parliament, the name of the government leader, when we no longer care about the ministers' agendas, when the president is nothing more than a nice state symbol, then I'll cease politicking.

•

...What's that hammering? Ah, it's them. Kaunas is full of them. And they're not far from Vytautas Park, Vaižgantas Street, Perkunas Avenue... Handsomely uniformed, stiff, puffed up, their boot leather shiny as mirrors. They try hard not to see the ordinary Lithuanians, who perhaps don't even read newspapers. Papers like *Der Stürmer* or *Das schwarze Korps*[2]. Lithuanians, those earth rooters, who've let in the Jews over the centuries, they have no grasp of what awaits them.

By the way, on the threshold of the third millennium, one particular journalist whose name sounds like a pseudonym, calls Jews in the pages of a national daily newspaper cockroaches. Back then, Germans called Lithuanians something different. Many of them had already brought in their families and set themselves up in the best Kaunas villas. And for a long time, as it seemed to them. Their Reich was supposed to last a thousand years. Why only a thousand?—I wondered then. And what comes later? Will the powerful Reich revert to nothing?

—*Litauische Schweine! Litauische Schweine!*—the children of the new colonists shout at me. Understand, you are a Lithuanian swine.

—Why do they call us that?—I ask rhetorically, not expecting any answer. And Mama doesn't answer. Instead, she asks me:

—I hope you didn't say anything back?

—Are you kidding?—I bristle.—I told them: *Deutschland, Deutschland über alles, zwei Kartoffeln—das ist alles—*Germany, Germany above all, only two potatoes—that's all.

My mother is bewildered. She forbids me any contact with German kids. She orders me to forget that little verse and never, ever say it again.

And there is no contact. No more friendships with the kids of foreign embassy workers in Kaunas. Until recently, we played together even though we didn't speak each other's language. But the Germans did make contacts. With

---

2 Two Nazi anti-semitic newspapers published in Germany.

the local ladies. The beautiful ones, of course. There, rustling like a new banknote walks the high Nazi official up the Būgos Street steps with the wife of a well-known Lithuanian architect. Another one, similarly rustling, is brought home by one of our apartment's residents, Miss Teresė P.

Up until then, Miss Teresė had been dating Mr. Antanas. But he, for some reason, never asked her to marry. Miss Teresė worked at the post office. She was a natural blonde, brimming with health. She was no floozy, but a serious and mature young woman. It was only from that lack of a proposal that she felt any grief. At the post office she meets and gets to know a German officer, one Zyler. Having shown the door to Antanas, she allows that Zyler to step through. Miss is nicely settled into the room where until recently the Russian pilot and his family had reigned. Zyler helps her set up a lovely little nest. He fixes the electrical switch himself. Real switches are no longer available for purchase, so Zyler makes a new one out of an old key and a piece of rubber. What had he been in Germany before the Führer called him into the Wermacht? An engineer? An electrician? An auto mechanic? The romance lasts about a year. Then Zyler disappears as unexpectedly as he first showed up. Not only from Miss Teresė's embrace, but from all of Kaunas.

Teresė bends over a sheet of paper, penning a letter to the now cooled-down Mr. Antanas. My mother helps write the letter, as does her friend the poet, Kotryna, who is especially invited for the task. A poet's sensitive words are particularly needed to appease the hurt feelings of Mr. Antanas. And to get him back. The letter is crafted and sent; however, Mr. Antanas does not show himself again. Teresė's cry from the heart thus remains *vox clamantis in deserto*.

Ona (Hanė)
Smilgevičiūtė,
student

Kostas Žolynas
1937

...Kostas and Hanė return from Berlin. They are to live with us. We meet them at the bus station as they climb down from a red, German postal bus. They're both very thin, almost as if they had shrunk... On their faces is written the life of Berlin. And what is that? The Germans go to bed early in the evening. So that they won't have to eat supper. At night the British bomb the city like mad. Soon the newest Nazi weapon, the V1 rocket, will put an end to Germany's misfortunes. Uncle Kostas, however, does not believe in this last prediction. And he returns to Lithuania not because of that, but because he intends to remain here forever. The Reich requires people to take on German citizenship. If you refuse—you're fired. Then there is really no hope for survival, and not only in Berlin. Kostas doesn't want to be a German. But he does say:

—In Germany even fisherman are cleanly shaven, and here the intelligentsia walks around all scruffy.

That's true. Even our intellectuals can't always buy themselves razors. They're not allowed into stores on whose doors hang signs that say, "*Nur für deutsche*"—"Only for Germans."

Kostas finds a job in Kaunas in his field. He's an attorney. Our lives brighten up. Kostas and Hanė are young thirty-year-olds. They have many friends. They want to have fun and party and hang out with them. And to forget they're living on top of a volcano. They don't want to listen to the more and more sinister rumbles coming from that volcano. Good Lord, after all they were younger then than my own children are now.

•

...A pleasant company gathers in the large living room with its darkened windows. Various sizes of black paper blinds, folded like accordion bellows, are sold in town. If you want to turn your lights on at night, you have to make sure not even the smallest ray escapes through the window. There mustn't be the slightest sign for the enemy planes to orient themselves. The blinds, each with two little ropes woven through, are carefully fixed to every window in the apartment.

Lively young people sit around our old oak table. They get up and dance, they talk about things I don't understand, they laugh frequently, and they don't worry themselves about the mean war-time poverty. They enjoy sipping ersatz barley coffee from our rose-colored cups.

They're not at all offended that the coffee is just a wish-wash and not the "Mokka" for which these delicate cups are meant. They sweeten it with saccharine.

I'm allowed to spend time with them for a while. I'm indifferent to the young men, but there's an older black-beard I just fall for. This blackbeard seems uninterested in the friendly young ladies; he'd rather talk to me about my childhood concerns; he even dances with me. I'm embarrassed at how poorly I dance, but he leads me around with a firm hand. Afterwards we sit close to each other. Behind his glittering pince-nez glasses, his eyes look mysteriously large. I know that he is a general. He is Povilas Plechavičius. I know that he will lead the recently created *Vietinė rinktinė*—the Local Army. He invites Kostas to be his adjutant. Kostas doesn't agree right away, only after some urgent persuasion. But after not too much time has passed... one morning in the headquarters of the *Vietinė rinktinė*, the general will issue this abrupt order to Adjutant Kostas:

—Disappear from here as fast as you can. They're on their way to arrest us.

The General, who was cursed and reviled during the Soviet Lithuanian period, died in Chicago after thirty years. Lithuanian independence was regained exactly a hundred years after his birth. He did not live to see it. In his old age, did he think all of his toil had not been in vain? Did he believe that Lithuania would someday learn of his refusal to kneel before any occupier?

...I lie abed, sick with chickenpox. Horrible watery spots cover my entire body. They itch terribly, then dry out and harden, and eventually fall off. I mustn't scratch them as that will leave scars. I lie still as a log. Beyond the wall there's a racket. It's one of Uncle Kostas' typical parties. From time to time Mama or Hanė come by and bring me a bite of something ersatz. During the German occupation everything that isn't traditional Lithuanian food is ersatz. It tastes bad. I'm nodding off. I hear music from the dining room. The door opens again—a male silhouette appears in the doorway. It's one of the guests, Mr. Š. Without switching the light on, he approaches unsteadily, sits down by me on the bed. His breath reeks of alcohol. The man talks to me, but I don't want to respond so pretend I'm asleep. He sticks his hand under the covers, under my pyjama top, and starts looking for something on my broken-out body. What's he looking for? He's not a doctor, after all. He brushes his hand across my healing scabs...

109

What kind of hand is it? I can't describe it but realize somehow it's lewd. And that the scabs enflame his emotions even more.

—Kęstutis,—his wife suddenly calls him, opening the door. Mr. Š. jumps up as if lashed by a whip and disappears through the door.

Sir, if you're still alive, tell me, did you catch my disease? They say chickenpox is highly contagious. And that it's a particularly hard-suffering disease for adults.

The heart knows its own bitterness,
And no stranger shares its joy.

Proverbs 14: 10

On the road

14
The
Basket weaver,
and
something more

Ragažinis—The Basket Weaver. It's doubtful if anyone knew his surname, but his name was Juozas. He knew how to weave beautiful willow baskets. What else did he know how to do? Everything. Whatever you needed on the farmstead—everything. He would always show up in Marijampolė with two horses harnessed to his wagon to pick up those family members who came by train from Kaunas.

Ragažinis is ageless—his face does not reflect the years of his living and is almost free of wrinkles; it shows only his inner peace and transparency; no matter that he never shaves and his chin sprouts sparse, soft bristles. It seems to me he doesn't have a comb—his thin hair is always tousled. Ragažinis' expression never changes, whatever the cir-cumstances—he is a clear, pure, and reliable person; if not, how would he have been entrusted with transporting my mother, me, and other family members.

Ragažinis transports us with a great sense of re-sponsibility, even though the road to Žvirgždaičiai is fairly safe—only one uphill on the way there, or a downhill on the way out. Seeing an automobile from a half-kilometer away (and in those days the road from Marijampolė to Žvirgždaičiai sometimes had one car, sometimes none at all), Ragažinis would lift me out of the wagon and then help my mother down. Then, heroically bracing himself on the wagon seat, he'd tighten and firmly hold the reins against our two uncivilized mares—and Bėrukė and Juodė are terribly frightened, their nostrils wide open, ready to bolt and carry the wagon straight across the fields, scattering the bones of the passengers. Spouting steam, blowing smoke, the automobile would eventually pass by us, while our mares rolled their eyes in terror, scissored the air with their ears, and trembled all along their bellies and flanks; however, the wagon was never smashed nor knocked to the side of the road. Mama and I would return sitting on the driver's bench. Ragažinis, happy about triumphing in the face of a terrible threat, urges the mares to trot faster.

Only after five or six years, during the German retreat, did the real test come—for Ragažinis, and for the mares, Bėrukė and Juodė. Hitching them up to a long wagon, Ragažinis was sent to Kaunas to bring us back with all our possessions. Us—meaning Uncle Kostas and Hanė, and my mother and me. From our place on Vaižgantas Street, Uncle Kostas carefully and responsibly—as he did every-thing—loaded our things into two huge chests and various suitcases, the largest of which was adult-sized and the smallest suitable for a child. It was necessary to load up almost all we had, except for those things which had to be left behind, if not in God's care, then in our rapidly thinning out neighbors'. Hitler's army was now retreating in a hurry, occasionally still trading ersatz chocolate and eradicating those they had not managed to wipe out on their earlier victorious march forward. After making his way through the military—and civilian—clogged highway from Marijampolė to Kaunas, Ragažinis with his two-horse cart finally rolled up to Vaižgantas Street.

...The highway buzzed day and night. It was no longer one or two automobiles along the way to Žvirgždaičiai. Everything had changed—even the two mares, Bėrukė and Juodė. Humble and hushed, they obediently pulled the long wagon, paying no attention to the sputtering, wood-burning German trucks, as if they understood there was no other way out. Well, getting to Kaunas in an empty wagon is one thing. But the journey back—with two huge chests, a slew of suitcases, boxes of all sizes—that was another thing entirely. Meticulously loading up the wagon, Kostas didn't leave a spot empty. Any remaining space he filled up, at least with shoes. After that, Kostas and Hanė mounted a bicycle and pedaled the sixty kilometers to Marijampolė, and the ten more to Žvirgždaičiai.

They were very sad to leave. They must have felt it, but they didn't yet know that they'd never return again to quiet Vaižgantas Street, to their ordinary life. Or maybe they did know, just didn't want to believe it.

My Mama and I remain under Ragažinis' care. Loaded up since dawn and now quite delayed, the heavily laden wagon waits at the top of Parodos Street. Having determined that it's better to have Mama and me down from the wagon on such a steep hill, Ragažinis starts carefully down the dreadful incline, terribly tense, tightly holding on to the reins. Mama and I hurry behind him so he won't have to wait long for us at the bottom. Half a day has gone by; we have to get moving. We stride down as fast as we can until we approach a turn in the street, and then almost run, as we sense something has happened farther down.

At the bottom, where three streets intersect—Parodos, Donelaitis, and Vytautas Prospect—stand our two mares, heads guiltily lowered, the wagon lying on its side, all its carefully loaded contents lying, for some reason according to their size, across the asphalt: the first item is the largest chest, then Hanė's green dowry trunk, then all the suitcases, some of which are open and have spilled their contents like overfull stomachs that can't keep a recently eaten meal down. And this whole spectacle is finished off with a collection of shoes, in pairs, in threes, singly, scattered over the width of three automobile lanes. Cars are blowing their horns and starting to jam along all three streets, and Ragažinis stands there, all tousled, whip in hand, among all the scolding drivers and the growing circle of gawkers. I close my eyes.

What was left for the road users to do? To fall on all that property and quickly pile it back into the wagon! The Red army was undoubtedly approaching slowly from the east, while the Wehrmacht hysterically and in fits and starts, grabbing on to whatever it came across, was undoubtedly withdrawing to the west.

—Don't blab anything to Kastytis about what happened,—said Mama when the horses with no urging hurried again along the familiar way towards home. Keep quiet, it seems, so as not to cause any shame for Ragažinis.

They say that the Germans had mined the Kaunas tunnel. The residents of the Aukštieji Šančiai neighborhood pooled some of their funds and befriended the hungry Germans with real, fatty food and strong drink. For appearance's sake, the Germans exploded some small mines at the very ends of the tunnel, near the openings. The tunnel itself, and all the residents of Aukštieji Šančiai, remained undamaged.

German soldiers were truly hungry. My aunt Prakseda, then a young woman of eighteen, took me with her on the carrier seat of her bicycle, and we rode around the Gižai region swapping eggs for cigarettes from the retreating young German soldiers. Prakseda gathered eggs from the numerous chicken nests on my grandparents' farm. The chickens desperately wanted to hatch their chicks and would hide their nests in the most unlikely places. With a little seeking, though, they weren't too hard to find, and we'd gather up some thirty or forty eggs. Most importantly, it was a conspiracy. Neither Grandfather, nor Mama—nor anyone was to know of our transgression. I was the only co-conspirator, entrusted to keep the secret. And so, we were always a pair, always together. I accompanied my beloved and most beautiful—in my eyes—aunt and friend down the dusty roads and byways of Suvalkija, not minding my calves grazed by bicycle pedals, my thighs bruised, my seat sore from the baggage carrier.

—We'll be back again, we'll return soon,—said the young and, strangely, fairly happy Germans, gratefully taking the eggs and generously pouring cigarettes into my aunt's open hands. —We're only withdrawing temporarily.

—Let them not return, no one will weep,—Prakseda used to say to me as we rode home. Clearly, she was more informed about the German's activities in the *Ostland* (the Eastlands). That's what they called Lithuania and the neighboring states. Just as we were known as the *Severo-zapadnij kraj* (the northwest land) in the time of the czars. All just depended on from which direction our country was occupied. When Normans or Swedes attacked us, we must have been "southern natives."

The approaching Russians were saviors for some—a horror for others. Even today, the argument goes on about who was the most terrible occupier. We tally up the score of which of them killed the greatest number. As if figures could settle it. To me, my Daddy was the one and only, worth more than a hundred thousand, no matter how egotistical that sounds. My father's cousin Sonia sent me a copy of the family tree and wrote at the bottom: "Now you can see what Hitler did to our large family."

—Milda, let's get out of here—urged her friend, Niuta, while they were still in Kaunas. —You don't know what the Russians are doing with those who were living under the Germans. They're skewering little children on bayonets, and the grown-ups…

Niuta drew bloody, chilling pictures, horrifying Mama, who soon decided to move west as had a lot of other residents of Lithuania. I kept quiet. Like many children, I didn't feel scared by all the horrifying stories. It seems that fear comes to a child when it's placed there by the person closest to the child. Or when the child's touched by actual events. Like the bombings. Or whistling bullets above your head.

Anxiety filled the entire family at the grandparents' place. Staying there were Uncle Kostas with Hanė, my mama Milda and I, and aunt Mikalina with her husband Vladas and their less-than-a-year-old daughter Virginija. We all looked to the east, listening to the nearing cannon fire, still hoping it would quiet down and move back eastward. But no! The cannons drew nearer.

One sunny morning, Grandma hitched up Bėrukė to the small wagon, since not too many items needed to be loaded up, and took Kostas and Hane to Kybartai, near the border. Ragažinis was not entrusted with this.It seems it was too important a job to reliably escort them to the last frontier, to say goodbye to a son at the last possible moment. I doubt any of them thought the goodbye would be forever. Grandma never saw her son Kostas and daughter Mikalina again.

—Let's go, Milduke, together,—Kostas urged my mother. And suddenly, unbelievably to all the household and to myself, I said firmly:

—I'm not going anywhere.

And I added to my speechless mother:

—You can go, but I'm staying here.

There was no time for debate. Kostas and Hanė left. To this day I don't understand what encouraged me in such a not very childlike step. Maybe my guardian angel, who may have protected me from even greater misfortunes? Or was it patriotism, which in our society today is so derided. Perhaps it was simply animal instinct, the urge to live here and now?

One early morning I saw an unusual sight. Traveling west along our highway, were belongings-filled wagons, cattle roped to them. Wagons seemed to move across the fields where no roads existed. That sight was reminiscent of Noah's ark with all the rows of various creatures on their way to safety. Noah's beasts were all two-by-two, all different. Here, they were almost all the same, a repeating pattern: horses-wagons-men-women-children-cattle... And again: horses-wagons-men-women-children-cattle... If it weren't for the cattle, it would be more like a funeral procession. It wasn't too much later when the Soviets drove captured cattle herds from the Koenigsberg lands—called by the Germans *Ostpreussen*—along the same trails. The cattle were lean, tired, bones sticking out, blinded by the dust their own hooves raised. They could barely keep themselves going. It's a wonder if they ever reached their destination.

...Onto that ghostly caravan Mikalina and her husband and daughter attached themselves. Grandma again hitched up Berukė and carted them off to the west. Yet again I refused to go, and the time for weighing decisions was even less. For the rest of her life, my mother regretted not leaving, justifying her decision by saying she didn't want to be a burden on her brother's and sister's families. But I didn't regret it even once, though I wouldn't mind being wealthier like my relatives in the United States. I lived almost my entire life in Soviet Lithuania, where there was more to it than poverty: here I was able to amass an irreplaceable treasure—a husband, children, grand-children, friends...and a home in my own country. I often wonder if the land you belong to is the place where you were born, or the one to which your heart is affixed with a glue of superior quality. In which would you like to be reborn?

...That time we couldn't take our eyes off the highway, waiting for Grandma to return from Kybartai. The next day the roads were empty—seldom did anyone move westward, and from the west to the east, no one moved at all. Grandma with her wagon and Berukė was the only one, returning, as it were, from another world. Around our garden and across the entire plain, a strange emptiness descended. And the next morning, coming towards Vilkaviškis from the Marijampolė road, two tanks showed up. We look at them from a distance, not daring to go any closer. On the third day, the tanks disappear, but two Soviet soldiers, rifles slung on their shoulders, come into the yard.

—*Zdrastvujte*,—they say.—*Fašistov nietu?* (Hello. Are the fascists gone?)

And yet another occupation began.

The strong tower of the wicked comes to ruin,
but the root of the righteous stands firm.

Proverbs 12: 12

116

Poet Kotryna Grigaitytė

15
All Souls Miracle

Saint Venancio and Callixtus,—chant the beggars of Kaunas, squatting near the gates of the cemetery and its main path.

—Pray for Moni-i-i-ika's soul,—replies a screechy female voice.

Today is All Souls.

Today all of Kaunas gathers here.

From Vytautas Hill through our apartment's windows, between Trakų Street and Vytautas Prospect, we can see the large rectangular area stretching out. In the summer it's green with tall trees, but in winter, through the black branches it's clear this is not a park. On one side of that property—two Orthodox chapels and burial plots, on the other side a mosque and the Muslim cemetery. The large middle section is designated for Catholics. Neat paths criss-cross the cemetery and, in the middle—the tomb of the Unknown Soldier surrounded by identical cement crosses on the graves of those who died for Lithuania's independence. Here's the great round mausoleum of Darius and Girėnas. During the occupation the mausoleum is empty— the bodies of Darius and Girėnas hidden somewhere. So that, God forbid, they don't attract the interest of authorities. Nearby other Lithuanian pilots' tombstones are surmounted with crosses made from real propellers.

Right after the war, unmarked mounds of pale earth started appearing near the pilots' graves. Sometimes those mounds would multiply overnight. Still with no writing or markings.

—They're burying partisans here,—whisper folks.

Red Army soldiers come here, dressed in pyjamas. They're from the nearby military hospital. They sit on benches, their bare feet in black slippers resting on the earth mounds. Where there are no benches they sit directly on the mounds. Mounds that have been recently piled up prove particularly comfortable for their backsides. A bottle passes from hand to hand... The pyjama-clad soldiers guffaw, let out incomprehensible shouts, which even adults can't interpret.

—It's necessary for us to learn Pushkin's and Tolstoy's language,—our teachers say. At my school they do not say "Lenin's and Stalin's language" yet. But they will soon.

—Animals. God will punish them!—say some devout women, peeking at them from a safe distance. But their voices don't make it to heaven. Nobody tries to reprimand those soldiers. The invaders are victors, hence in the right.

•

Back when those "in the right" were not there, the cemetery was a peaceful, not a frightening place. Each of the meticulously laid out sections was known as well as my fingertips. Juozas Zikaras' sad sculpture "Grief" is beautiful. I always stop by it on the way home from school with my friends. We gossip among ourselves, trading histories and stories about those who now live here, who are buried here. My heart doesn't hurt in this cemetery at all, as I have no dear ones here. Nor anywhere else. And they won't end up in this place.

Cedar, marble crosses, photographs, roses, an occasional crypt, an occasional neglected grave. On those neglected graves during All Souls burn the most candles. Mothers, including my mother, say to their kids:

—Be sure not a single grave is left without a candle.

•

I hold to that command to this very day.

Every year, Paulius and I perform the sacred ritual—we light the path for those souls who have yet to go their appointed distance. With our granddaughter Vaidilė we light ten or so candles in the Antakalnis cemetery in Vilnius. The cemetery mounds are barely discernible, covered with dried grass and thickly coated with wilted leaves. People are buried here. Most probably soldiers. It's not important of which side. Looking back as we leave, in the distance we see the tiny orange flames twinkling in the early autumn evening... Ten small candles.

—That's not very many,—says Vaidilė.

We decide to save our money and next year buy lots of candles. So that the entire slope will glow. My granddaughter looks at me with trusting eyes. Have those eyes seen the biggest miracle of my childhood? On that All Souls night in Kaunas in Vytautas Prospect cemetery? No, no! How could that be? But maybe among those tens of thousands of genes there is one in which an everlasting light shines? Perhaps it will shine for my children when life is hard. And then be passed on to their children. Like the greatest gift, though unseen and unnameable?

All Souls Night at Antakalnio cemetery

...I'm still very young. Those few lit candles on strangers' graves blend in with candles on other graves. And with the light of white chrysanthemums. It grows so bright that the path beyond is easy to see, not only for all Kaunas' souls, but for all of Lithuania's souls from all times. In Kaunas cemetery, Mama's best friend Kotryna's mother is buried. We would sit for a while on the wooden bench. Kotryna Grigaitytė, the poet, was a fragile, kind, and gentle woman. Her talent most likely came to her through her uncle, her mother's brother, Vincas Kudirka. Her first book of poems was published in 1937. *Eyes Through a Fan.* It was dedicated to her dear mother. Reading from that book until it almost fell to pieces, I long fed on Kotryna's lily-pure verses:

> *The free bird with her wings,*
> *The clouds with their sky,*
> *But for my heart*
> *Neither wings nor sky*
> *Seem ever enough.*

After a number of decades, more than a few of her poetry books and letters reached us from America. To my mother's invitations to come back for a visit, she firmly replied: "Dear Mildute, I'll come only when Lithuania is free, when the Bolsheviks are gone."

She never made it back. What remained were her lyrics, engraved with longing for her homeland, through which Kotryna's ageless, satin-like beauty still shines, though with a tougher voice:

I want to turn into an eternal dust mote
(nothing on this land ever vanishes).
Perhaps the wailing clouds will hear each other
And return me to my own land.

•

...After sitting by Kotryna's mother's grave for a while, we continued to honor other souls. Before and right after the war, people would crowd the cemetery paths. An unbroken stream, body to body, the Kaunites would walk around the entire cemetery, from one quadrangle to another. As if it was a pagan rite endowing the dead with eternal respect and protection. Such a dense flood of people, flowing along from nowhere to nowhere on a cold November night, I never saw before, nor since. The moving force of people carried you along in an unavoidable direction. Don't we all go along like that, every day, every hour? In fact only moving ahead the shortest possible distance.

—The Lithuanian nation is one,—the patriot would say.

—How aware are the Lithuanian citizens,—the politician would say.

—Catholics properly respect their dead,—the priest would say.

—Lithuanians hold to ancient traditions,—would say the ethnographer.

—They come to show themselves off, to look at others,— the skeptic would say.

They'd all be wrong, though each would have a grain of truth.

Now it is easy for me to utter the well-worn sentence:

—PEOPLE JUST WANTED TO BE TOGETHER.

They wanted to be saved from unknown but already sensed misfortunes. From Siberia, from Nazi camps, from DP camps...from the refugee's fate in America or Australia... From departures with no returns.

It's easy to say. Now when everything's seen from hindsight. But then...

In the cemetery it's pleasant and bright as daylight. But the miracle had not yet occurred. When at last we pulled

120

away from the crowd of people and went up the Būgos steps, back to the white-walled Purickis apartment building, then...

...Below our feet lies a rectangular sea of fire. It's made up of thousands of burning eye-like particles. Each one twinkles to its own rhythm, but all together their sparkling outshines all the lights of Kaunas. The dreary and dark autumn sky glows an unearthly, indescribable rose. We go to bed while below us the hope of the living continues to shine and glow in the embers.

In the morning I run to the window—my miracle is gone as if it never happened. Snowflakes. The enchanting cemetery plot is all blurry, a gray view through the cold and bare tree branches. True, here and there a rare weak flame burns. But it doesn't console, nor warm; among the frozen chrysanthemums it looks quite dreary. But I know then: in another year, the miracle will be repeated. At the same time, in the same place.

—Damn it! How long is this going to go on?—say the Bolsheviks in charge of Kaunas. On All Souls day, in the cemetery, around the Unknown Soldier's monument, crowds gather and sing the anthem and hymns:

"Lithuania, our homeland..."

"Lithuania, the precious..."

"Maria, Maria..."

Among the crowds prowl agents of the NKVD, young komsomols[1]... from our high schools, from among us... They try not to stand out. But the sign of Cain is written on them in invisible ink. For some on their raised shoulders, for some on their hats. And for some, even on their foreheads. For now, no one fears them. But the threat is growing. From our classrooms, students begin to disappear quietly. No one offers any explanations to the remaining high schoolers. They pretend not to notice. Simply one day another desk is empty. And that's it.

Fear, like my recently dreamt of witch's grey mantle, begins to settle on us. Near the monument of the Unknown Soldier, I feel a stare fixed on the back of my head. Later, the monument disappears along with the soldiers' graves around it.

The hymn-chanting beggars start to disappear as well. But there's still someone around to give a small handout to and request:

---

[1] Communist youth organization.

121

—Pray for Samuel's soul.

Ultimately, the very cemetery disappears as well.

Nobody took account of the specific time that needed to pass before the cemetery could be destroyed. After many years, Father Stanislovas told me he remembered that after the war, before he was sent off to Siberia, the dead were still being buried here.

Today my miraculous four-cornered plot is a park though not a real park, a garden though not a real garden. It's not a very inviting place. You can see right through as if it were some kind of a ghost—from Vytautas Prospect to Trakų Street. Only some trees that watched over the cemetery still grow here with their greenish black, smooth trunks. They sway above the strange criss-crossing paths. Wanting to go through efficiently, you'd look a little crazy. The Tatar mosque perches as if naked in one corner of the plot, two Russian orthodox churches sink into the earth in the other. The fences around them are destroyed. Not even a tiny fragment of the former mystery remains.

In the third corner—the former German high school. Here, onto Vytautas Prospect, from my once attended kindergarten, two windows looked out. It's odd to look at them now. I see nothing interesting there. Just a bent over, graying woman in a black hat and an old gray coat. It is I.

—Go away,—I say to her,—you ghost you.

On the other side, beyond the trees' bare branches, my first school appears vaguely. Vincas Kudirka's School. To me, it was a ship of white light and love. There, my first teacher, Mrs. Kundrotienė, called all her pupils "kiddies."

...It's already dark. Mama is taking me home from school. My first friend, Algis Matulionis, is walking along with us. I share a school desk with him.

—The cavalier and his damsel cook porridge with coal tar!—teased our know-it-all classmates. It doesn't upset me. I like having a "cavalier," even if he's only eight.

—Will you be unafraid to continue on home by yourself? —my mother asks Algis. His home is not far, but he'll have to go back round the cemetery.

—Me? Afraid? —the little hero is indignant.—I can go right through the cemetery!

Having said it, there was nowhere to hide. And here is the small cemetery gate right before us.

With a dumbfounded stare I follow his light-colored coat, as he goes down the disappearing path across the middle of the cemetery. During daylight, it's not frightening here; that's clear to everyone. But in the dark...

Ah! Probably there's no one in my life who hasn't heard this story! I would have fallen for him. Really. But love's time had not yet arrived.

So teach us to number our days,
that we may apply our hearts unto wisdom...

Make us glad according to the days
          wherein thou hast afflicted us,
and the years wherein we have seen evil.

Psalm 90: 12, 15

Feeding chickens in the yard,
Žvirgždaičiai

16
Leaving

The woman with the royal name of Isabela is the ordinary village seamstress, Zabeliukė. She lives in a small hut on the edge of the bog with her old mother and with the household's most important treasure—a "Singer" sewing machine. Sewing is this small family's bread and butter. The local farmers mostly pay for her work in kind, and so Zabeliukė and her mother don't need to work in the fields much, just around the house. Zabeliukė is a tall, slim, straight-backed brunette. Not from around here, her dark, prominent eyes shine. I wonder if Zabeliukė is a gypsy? But, no matter. What does matter is she knows how to sew. Now she's sewing a rose-colored, white-dotted dress for my auntie, and she will sew for many, many more years, and will remain a spinster. For no young suitor will show up in these parts for a landless woman no longer in her first youth. Zabeliukė always greets her visitors graciously, leading them inside across the even, green grass as if laid out over the yard like velvet. Through the small almost toy-like porch, you enter into a small spic-and-span hut, all wallpapered in newspapers. Some are old and yellowed, some still very new. It seems that after she's read a newspaper, Zabeliukė glues it onto the wall, and by the time the whole hut is done, the papers have gone yellow and it's time to start anew.

Zabeliukė is an educated woman, always pleasant, but not overly sweet. She moves peacefully and gently, but not too slowly. Clothe her in royal robes, set a golden coronet on her head, curl her hair, paint her nails, put some satin slippers on her feet—and is she not a dignified, gracious queen? Alas, though, the story of Cinderella took place elsewhere than on the edges of our bog.

•

...My grandparents' land was never very generous. Spiteful tongues used to whisper that the farm was not

124

Believe in children
Barnardo's

414 Brixton Road
London
SW9 7AV
020 72744165
Vat # : 507477337

Date: 29 November 2023 15:16
Transaction Ref: 272-2311-7448364
Served by : TB

Sales

XBK001	1	£2

Books
Price: Open

TOTAL

SUB TOTAL	£2
VAT	£0
TOTAL	£2

TENDER

Cash	£10
Change	£8

Share your kindness & donate good-quality womenswear, mensu
toys to us today. shop.barnardos.org.uk/donations We hope
ove your purchase, if you need a refund or exchange, please
rn your item along with your receipt within 14 days from th
e of purchase, with original price tickets attached. This c
of affect your statutory rights.

looked after well enough, that Granddad spent too much time praying and not enough time marketing peat and building new barns. However, no hungry people lived on the farm, the children were being educated into decent citizens, and their parents' lives slowly tilted in the direction of eternity. Tėtulis, it seems, knew better than anyone that nothing from here would be taken beyond.

A part of the twenty-nine hectare farm was useless swamp; another section a peat bog from which more could have been extracted; and the remaining parts were of fertile earth, which matured potatoes and sugar beets, pushed rye, wheat, oats, vetch, flax towards the sun.

After the war, that one-hectare-short-of-thirty hectares was a true bit of fortune. If you had property of at least thirty hectares you'd have been designated a *kulak* [1], an oppressor of workers and an enemy of the people, speaking in the proletarian terminology of those times. A prime candidate for deportation to Siberia.

—Who works on the farm?

—Where's son Ričardas? Where's son Konstantinas? Where's daughter Mikalina? Have they joined the bandits? Are they hiding in the forest?

The local authorities are worried. Angrily waving papers from the Soviet government, the proletariat's representatives have become quite a threat to my grandparents' lives. After all, they were not *kulaks* only technically, and were not reliably protected by that one-hectare rule. In the 1986 Soviet Lithuanian Encyclopedia it is written: "In 1949 in the interests of the small landowners, the Soviet government initiated a repression of all *kulaks*, eventually exposing them, isolating them from the peasants and all but eliminating them as a class."[2] By the way, try to translate that into a language understood by everyone today.

Repressions had been initiated earlier, right after the end of the war. During the day, Soviet officials and all sorts of armed agents snooped around the villages; at night partisans would come out of the woods, men called bandits by the officials, but that we called "Žaliukai"—"Greenies," or "Forest Brothers." They weren't strangers—they were the sons and brothers of Suvalkija's farmers and intelligensia.

---

[1] *kulaks*:   peasants who owned more property than others; Soviet derogatory term.

[2] Hidden in this bureaucratic language is the simple and terrible fact that many *kulaks* were shot and killed or carted off to Siberia.

Seeing her parents constantly overworked at their farm, hit hard by grain deliveries to the state, and living in constant fear, my mother determined to save them. In Kaunas she approached a Russian army major she knew, Ivanov, and asked him if he could go to Gižai district and help cool things down there a little. The major agreed to go there (in those days, the officers of the victorious army had considerable power). But he wasn't to go alone; I was chosen to accompany him.

And to this day, I don't understand why me. True, I knew the way to Žvirgždaičiai. I knew that those ten kilometers from Marijampolė could be covered in about two hours, though I'd never walked them myself... How did my mother allow me, a young teenaged girl, to go out at night along a dangerous path? To go along the edges of that same *Šunskagirė*—Šunskai Forest—which not so long ago swarmed with fabled wolves and other dangers? True, during the post-war years people were more afraid of each other than beasts. Well, however it came about, I felt myself at that time to be a very important person indeed. And after the journey, I was a true heroine.

By the time our train arrived in Marijampolė, by the time we dropped by to visit Aunt Julija, and by the time we at last left the outskirts of Marijampolė, the sun was already setting behind the distant forest. On that occasion, Ragažinis didn't come to pick us up—apparently he hadn't gotten the news. The Major had agreed to go on foot, as I had explained to him that the village was not far at all. We went along our way, chatting in Russian as by then I knew the language pretty well.

It was dark even before we approached the first smaller section of forest. The quiet and coolness descended on the fields, grasshoppers chirped loudly, and the newly plowed earth smelled of autumn.

—You know what,—says the Major suddenly,—maybe it's better if the two of us don't talk for a while. Sound travels so well here, and we're both speaking Russian...

So we go along in silence. In the sky, neither a moon, nor stars. The dry road dust muffles the sound of our footsteps. In the forest we hear no grasshoppers. No one travels the road, neither from one direction, nor the other. The Major, regretting not having changed into civilian clothes, draws his pistol and carries it in his hand.

—You know what,—he says after a little while,—you go first, and I'll follow at a distance. If they start shooting, fall into the ditch and wait until morning.

126

I know those ditches, I think to myself, they're full of frogs...

But I don't say that out loud. I go first. The small forest recedes behind us. And then a small glade and again a forest, considerably larger than the previous one. Slowly rising from my feet through my whole body floods a primitive, wild fear. I'm constantly looking back. The Major, most likely having seen worse on the frontline, continues to march forward as if all is normal. I remember that a few months ago the Forest Brothers gunned down a truckload of soviet agents. And that was not at night but in broad daylight. I wonder if the Major knows about that?

—You know what,—he whispers catching up to me.—I'll go first. So it doesn't look like I'm arresting you. And you hang back. And don't forget—at the first shot, into the ditch.

—I'll tell them you're on your way to help out my grandparents,—I reply, also whispering.

—Eh,—the Major waves his hand fatefully, apparently already used to the idea that he might not make it out of this forest.

And we continue to plod along as the forest watches us with invisible eyes. The forest was prepared. Grasshoppers kept silent. Everything that was alive and not alive was silent. Against the grey sky, the even darker grey fir tops stood out. Our footsteps were soundless. If anyone snuck up on us in the forest, then surely we'd hear a branch crack. But there was no cracking.

At long last the forest came to an end. Fear abated. I catch up to the Major and joyfully announce that we are now truly not far from our destination. The Major also sighs with relief and puts his weapon away, as if he's almost ashamed that he was afraid.

We walk along together again. But...look! Ahead there's a person! Coming towards us... We see only the dark silhouette.

—Should we hide?—I whisper, melting out of fear.

—Too late,—says the Major, grabbing his pistol again.— He already sees us.

What will be, will be...

We go along. And the other seems to get nearer to us. Here the path turns toward the left and...

—Oh, my, it's just a bush...

—The Devil knows what's going on here. F...!—curses the Major once that life-sized bush is left behind to our right.

127

...After another half hour it's completely dark, but I'm already rapping on the window of my grandparents' newly built farmhouse. After another half hour I'm in the arms of blessed sleep in the familiar wooden bed with bedknobs, unbothered by the hoards of fleas.

When I awaken, Grandma has already introduced the Major to the local officials. The officials were very impressed by the awards and medals on the Major's chest. That time it helped. But not for long. After about a year it was still necessary to leave the farm.

At that time I studied at the Kaunas girls' high school No 3. Our teachers, already greatly frightened by several occupations, hardly managed to inspire us with Soviet patriotism and "the world's most advanced ideology." Lecturers of various stripes often visited our high school. In the large auditorium where we pupils were corralled, they stuffed our heads with their truths gathered from the "theoretical treasury of Marxism-Leninism"... The lecturers urged us to ask questions, since they had no idea what their listeners were thinking. During a discussion of "Stalin's five-year plans," my "agrarian" question rang out in dissonance.

—Rural people—I said,—have to flee their homes because during the day they're visited by armed "people's defenders" who punish them because the "forest brothers" pay them visits at night. But the unarmed farmers are afraid of both. They're powerless. Of what are they guilty?

The lecturer was unperturbed. He spoke to us city girls at great length and boringly, on something we couldn't understand. But that's how I ended up angering our headmistress, Eleonora Janušauskaitė, known by all as "Gangrene." She was a deputy of the Supreme Council. "Gangrene" took note of me then and never forgot me while I studied at Kaunas. I remembered her too for a long time, even though when I studied in Vilnius, I discovered there were other kinds of headmistresses and headmasters.

•

That stay in the village was the last. Thank God I had no idea that I wouldn't return here again for over fifty years. Back then, Grandma delivered the Major and me back to the Marijampolė train station. I traveled with a heavy heart. Maybe not from a bad feeling, nor from the experienced fear.

I carried the picture of farmhand Marė's last glance as if it were some angry souvenir. Marė was a good woman, but was wrapped up in some sort of strange illness, always

128

bent over, always looking down... I had never seen her eyes before. But that morning, somehow she raised her head sideways, strangely, and with flashing eyes glared at the uniformed Major. What that hateful glance toward a stranger meant I'll never know. The Major didn't notice the look. And the rest of the family paid no attention, holding Marė as somewhat batty.

•

...After a short time, my grandparents realized that, nonetheless, they would have to leave. They looked around their farmstead and saw how many things they wouldn't need in Kaunas, and, in fact, would never need again. So then, to the seamstress Zabeliukė's little hut on the edge of the bog, traveled off the beautiful clock with the rider, the holy pictures with the as-yet uninterpreted word "idant" ("in order that"), the cupboard with the black-and-white-painted stripes, and certainly more... Those sorts of things wanted to stay in the village, where they were used to being, as if they understood that was their place.

If I wrote down everything my grandparents would not need in Kaunas, it's hard to know how many pages the list would take up. I'll note just those things that leapt into my mind first:

> water troughs—not needed;
> wooden tubs—not needed;
> cythes and rakes—not needed;
> long-handled spade and kneading trough
>   —not needed;
> chopping knife—not needed;
> bed with bedknobs—not needed
> sheep and sheep shearers—not needed
> wagons—not needed
> Mickus the cat—not needed
> Pyras the dog—not needed
> churn—not needed
> milk pail—not needed ... No, wait, that will be
> needed. And the cow will be needed, and
> a rope to tie her, and a strainer to filter her milk.

My grandparents tied their cow to the one remaining wagon, hitched up Bėrukė (Bay), their sole remaining horse, and asked Ragažinis to fulfill one more service for them—to drive them to Kaunas and leave them there.

They had heard the Lord Jesus' command to leave. And so they did.

Arise, let us go hence.

John 14: 31

Kaunas seminary for priests

17
Praxedis

Your Prakseda is already a real matron,—declared the Šunskai parish priest, Ambraziejus, one Sunday after seeing his brother's youngest daughter in church.

The family debates for a long time what that might mean—is it good to be compared to a matron or is it bad? They take a good, critical look at their daughter and finally determine that it is good. Prakseda had recently transformed from a bony, angular kid to a rather attractive, graceful teenager with strong facial features, a prominent Roman nose, blue eyes, and straight teeth. On her head—a rick of ripe, straw-colored hair done up in a sophisticated twist.

Her Roman name comes from the earliest Christian times. Legend has it that a Roman senator, a student of one of the apostles, had two daughters. Later they both ended up as saints. One of them was *Praxedis*.

I wonder who encouraged my grandparents to name their youngest daughter with the resonant and unheard of name of Prakseda, affectionately known by all as Praksele.

When I was seven and Praksele was thirteen, she visited us in Kaunas to check out our urban refinements. Certainly Kaunas was a big city then, not like some Marijampole.

What Praksele liked most of all in our apartment was the bathroom, and everything in it. Of most fascination to her was the bathtub.

—It must be pleasant to bathe in such a white trough?—she asked.

—Try it out,—I said and started to run the water.

The water was cold. Heated water was provided from a central source only twice a week. Or you could heat the water yourself in a special copper heater above the bathtub.

131

That would have taken a long time. Clearly, Prakseda didn't want to get into the cold water. Throwing off my clothes, I plopped myself in. So that it wouldn't be too cold, I danced something similar to a tarantella. After all, how would our city miracles look if I chickened out? That same evening I came down with a temperature and had to go to bed, and a few days later Prakseda returned to Šunskai to go to school.

During the Nazi occupation, Prakseda was already studying in Marijampolė and lived with Auntie Julija Černiauskienė. The young woman, having broken out of her adolescent shell, turned out to have soft and colorful feathers, and from the young lads who were at least half of her many friends, she could have easily found her true heart's desire. After all, the time for love to blossom had arrived. Prakseda took her time, though, in selecting someone—time at her age had no value. But Adė, who was farmer Kapteinius' son Adolf, turned out to be the fortunate one upon whom her favors fell. I can only imagine it—in the evening twilight Aunt Julija's little house overgrown with vines, the cozy street by the railway station, the shadows of tall poplars, the drawn-out train whistle...

In the meantime the Eastern front was looming over us...

By whose will did Adė put on the Wehrmacht's uniform?

—I will return, Blue Eyes,—says he as he leaves for the East.

Adė writes beautiful letters about his longing, snow-filled forests, the stars in the heavens... Soon after the War, Prakseda shows me one of Adė's last letters. In a beautiful, even hand, Adė informs her that he's been wounded, but not too seriously. He's lying in a field hospital on the outskirts of a forest. Through the window he can see a rabbit tentatively poking its head out of the woods. He doesn't feel too bad, he says. At this point in the letter, Adė's handwriting starts to break up, the sentences sloping downward, the letters crumbling, eventually stopping altogether. That letter was the last. Someone else's kind hand addressed the envelope and sent it to Prakseda. Adė's parents, the Kapteiniuses, received the news that their son had died heroically *Fürs Vaterland.* For the Fatherland, on the Eastern Front. Who is there now to remember Adė?

In youth, the pain of loss doesn't last as long as it does in maturity. Sadness was overshadowed by the sound of cannon fire—at first in the east and then in the west. And during that time, while the Front's wave rolled over our heads, we took ourselves somewhere else again. "Further away from the highway,"—was the explanation given. Withdrawing from our own highway, we drew closer to another. After all, the whole Suvalkija region was carved with highways. Again we scurry across some muddy marsh from the airplanes overhead; again we crawl into a roadside ditch. We try to avoid whistling bullets from both sides of the road. In the ditch, overgrown with dandelions, sorrel, and forget-me-nots, my eyes widen with fear. From underneath Prakseda lying in front of me out crawls a large frog. I start scrambling out of the ditch. Mama drags me back by the skirt. Grandma, as usual, is lying under the wagon holding firmly onto the reins. Later we find ourselves in someone's huge garden, in which we see a shabby, abandoned peacock walking around.

Our place is only about two kilometers away. Prakseda decides to go there to see how Grandfather is doing. As always, he's refused to join us in our bouncings around the countryside. Prakseda heads straight across the fields in the direction of the farmhouse whose grove of trees we can see in the distance.

The sun is already starting to set, the fields are covered with a thin white fog, but there's no sign of Prakseda. She's not here and that's it, though she'd promised to quickly return. The sky is a deep blue hung with an almost full moon.

—I'm going,—says Grandma,—maybe I'll find her. You all stay here.

Grandma walks off in the same direction where Prakseda had earlier fluttered off to. Not too far away now she can see the huge linden trees jutting up from the garden. And now, even closer, in the gathering darkness a campfire is sparkling. Squatting around it, she can see the figures of Russian soldiers.

—*Temnaya noch', tol'ko puli svistyat [Dark is the night, only bullets are whistling]*...—a popular Russian song at the time, being sung by a beautiful male tenor voice.

Grandma tries to avoid the campfire, but Prakseda's pleasant voice calls to her:

—I'm here, Mommy.

She emerges from the darkness smiling, beautiful, happy.

—Please meet Kolia,—she says.

—Don't be angry, *Mamasha*,—says Captain Kolia in Russian.—Your daughter gave us some potatoes, so we're baking them now.

Grandma returned to our straw-covered wagon and said:

—As soon as it's light, we'll return home.

133

I wonder if Grandma slept a wink that night. In the morning, when we returned home, we found Prakseda still asleep in the new room.

—We're not going to ramble about anymore,—Grandma affirms, unhitching the horses.

The merry Captain Kolia has not only fallen up to his ears in love with Prakseda, but has become the entire family's friend. It was good for us while his unit stayed in the Šunskai area. As the Front rolled westward, Kolia came to see us, each time from farther and farther away. He'd stay for a half-day, sometimes longer. Once while we were all asleep, Kolia heard a particular trembling of the window glass.

—Katiushas[1] ...he uttered.—The attack has begun. And hopping on a bicycle he disappeared into the dark.

And that's the last we ever saw of him and the bicycle.

After some time, a letter arrived from Prussia. And then a second, and a third. Kolia wrote and wrote, but Prakseda replied without enthusiasm, more or less out of politeness.

War-time romance—unconcrete and fragile. We were already in Kaunas when another letter arrived from the completely opposite direction, from Manchuria. The Soviets, having overcome the Germans, were in a hurry to finish off the Japanese. Soon after, the letters stopped suddenly. Had the happy-go-lucky captain laid down his head on Manchuria's hills? Or had he returned home demobilized and crossed out all the memories of the war? I believe he was from Kiev.

Prakseda studied in Kaunas at the Institute for Physical Culture. She tried to make it into the faculty of medicine—but that didn't work out. At that time the two of us became even closer friends. We shared our hearts' secrets as well as all the unfortunate difficulties of the post-war years.

Prakseda's red shoes—probably American-made and actually meant for skiing—I was allowed to wear on special occasions when I needed to dress up. From the manner of our living in those days, I remember constantly wet feet, the stench of kerosene coming from an improved Primus stove called a "kerogas," and long discussions at night when we were already in our beds. What is the universe? What does "boundless" mean? What is the meaning of "without beginning and end"? Is there really no God? But if he exists, where is he? What should a human being on this

---

[1] Katiushas were a new form of Russian rocket-propelled artillery; the Germans dubbed them "Stalin's pipe-organs."

Earth? The questions remained unanswered. Not yet filled, our knowledge-thirsty brains were ferociously channeled in one direction only—towards Marxism-Leninism. God, the nice old man sitting barefooted on his throne of clouds, was fading slowly out of my consciousness. But it was still a long way to the Great Absolute.

•

...That spring the Nemunas river woke especially dramatically from its winter sleep. The melting blocks of ice growled and the water kept rising and rising, flooding the old town, the old market by the President's office, even Kęstutis Street. From the slope of Italų (Italian) Street we looked down on the dirty, muddy water...

Almost every one of us in those post-war years had lost something or someone dear. But us young ones, we looked ahead and were able to adjust ourselves to the life that was given us then.

—Greetings, Sister,—the student-priest Juozas in his distinctive dialect greeted Prakseda one time at a social function somewhere.

•

Prakseda held out her hand and saw from the eyes of the young man that flash shoot out which we normally call Cupid's arrow. That arrow sank so deeply that she could not extract it from there for a long time. For too long of a time.

•

...It was Spring. Violets. Youth. Heart's songs, spilled out in poems.

> *...A pity to pluck such*
> *a short-stalked one,*
> *whose bud has barely opened.*
> *But I do pluck it without pity.*
> *In a week the violets will be everywhere.*
> *Also, for your sake—well, nothing's a pity!*
>
> *Tomorrow you'll be greeted*
> *by those who have blossomed already.*
> *Or maybe not by them, maybe just by me?*
> *Probably just by me, and in a dream...*

Love...it came—wanted or not. The kind that comes only once in a lifetime. With the purity of youth and the fullness of passion. But within Kaunas' city center the secluded

135

walls of the priesthood seminary firmly held the young man and hated to let him go. Was he himself determined not to change his vocation? The love of a young, beautiful woman continued to draw him with strength and hope.

Prakseda

You won't disappear from me
Neither through laughter nor tears,
You can't take back with repentance
What you brought me in the summer...

Joys and disappointments lifted them both above the ground. Nonetheless, Juozas went ahead and took ordination. She visited him at his first parish in Vilijampolė, later in his darkened apartment by the Garrison church. The Roman Catholic Church and the young woman wrestled each other a long time. But the years ran by and the young woman lost the contest. After all, she didn't have very much on her side—only a passionate heart, a bouquet of violets in the spring, and verses shivering with cold, full of frozen sorrow written down in small letters.

With what did you grapple so full of hope?

I'll hide your kisses deep
And don't you return mine back.
I believe that even today you'll come and say
They'll repeat our love forever.

The Catholic Church, instead of punishing the young sinner, who didn't even try to cover his indiscretion, began to promote him to higher and more responsible duties.

136

Today, he's only a few steps from the Pope. The Church won, mockingly looking down from its high steeples. Then comes the revelation:

...I never was meant for you, and never will be
Our paths are too different...

* * *

And the thought floated up in the evening—
forget, forget him!

Juozas

Prakseda leaves for Vilnius. But what's the use of a hundred kilometers. It's necessary to flee further. To America! Except that all exits have been sealed in iron. Prakseda takes the only available path in those days. She makes a marriage of convenience with a much younger Pole of the Vilnius region, Sosnovsky by name, therby gaining the right to move to Poland. For this service, the young Pole requires a motorcycle or, as he said himself:

—Just a "motsotycle."

A collection from the relatives pays for the "motsotycle." And the "groom" gives his surname to the "bride." They both cross the USSR border and, once in Poland, go their separate ways.

...Wroclaw. Prakseda is able to find work in a printing house. She does not know Polish. There's nothing to do but wait until her sister Mikalina can find a way to get her out of there and over to America. You see, Poland is also isolated from the rest of the world, but the seal is not as tight.

Prakseda works. Works and waits. She sits for hours on end in front of the loud and monotonous rotary printing press and waits for her American fortune. To fight boredom and sleep, she spends her time chanting. The noise of the printing press drowns old chants she remembers hearing from Tétulis.

...Who ever wants to serve Mary
And get her intercession...

Soon she's noticed by the printing house manager. He's a man already mature, handsomely gray-haired. Name of Petras. And so begins her last, and it seems, her most true love. And without any need for poems—because mutual, strong, constant. The kind of love that lasts.

Finally, after a few years she received permission to leave for America. Prakseda left. But she ends up not staying there for long. Petras has waited for her faithfully. And they end up again together and happy in Wroclaw. The two of them visit us in Vilnius and we joyfully welcome the new member of the family, who we all affectionately call "Petrulis."

In 1970 my friend and auntie Prakseda dies, eaten up by a heavy illness, until her last breath lovingly and gently cared for by Petrulis.

Traveler, if you happen to come across a grave marker in Wroclaw with the name "Prakseda Sosnowska," please know that the name is not her own, just one she purchased for the cost of a motorcycle during oppressive Soviet times. Know, also, that getting a motorcycle during those times was no easy feat. Know, that for rejected love she was compensated—at least towards the end of her life.

Remember her in your prayers, Bishop, Your Excellency. And forgive me for so frankly bringing to mind such ancient happenings.

Has not man a hard service upon earth
Are not his days like the days of a hireling?

Job 7: 1

Love bears all things, believes all things,
hopes all things, endures all things
Love never ends.

1 Corinthinians 13: 7-8

Samuelis Subockis

18
Where's your Papa?

Really, where is my Papa? The storm of war has now rumbled past, and the second Soviet occupation has begun. I should be able to breathe more easily, but I can't.

Around me no one says the word "orphan," since nowadays there are so many orphans, and what's the point.

—Am I an orphan? No!

That word hurts like a sliver stuck under my nail. Just you wait, I think to myself, when my Papa returns from Brazil, then...

What would happen then I had no idea. Only after the war, step by step, news by news, did it become clear what had happened. And now there's no longer any use in trying to protect me. The bad news falls on me from all sides, frank and terrifying. But I still wait for that one familiar doorbell. Just like the one that rang one evening in late June in 1941 while I was eating pancakes. I thought I'd open the door—and there would be my Papa. Young and handsome as he was then when he held me in his arms. Where are those warm hands that didn't save me from the sinister sting of war?

But there was no doorbell.

Instead, one day on Freedom Avenue a middle-aged man called me by name.

—Dita?

—Yes.

—Do you remember me?

How could I not remember him. Jakobas. Papa's cousin and dear friend, a regular guest from the time when I was still very young and not an orphan. And then he told me that my father was killed. That they were trying to escape to the Soviet Union. Near Rumšiškes they were detained. He, Mr. Rosencrantz, urged him to run. But my papa refused. And that's why he was killed. While Jakobas escaped. And therefore survived though his wife and daughter perished. I chewed on those words for a long time, which perhaps to me alone in our entire family were news. I chewed, ruminated, and finally swallowed it all down, and came to this conclusion—my Papa was and will remain in my heart for ever. He was the noblest of them all because he refused to run, refused to leave behind his second wife Lisa and their baby Mark. I don't remember if it was easy for a pre-teenaged girl to come to such a conclusion. But that conclusion, arrived at completely on my own, was closed off to anyone else, sealed, as they say, in a corner of my heart.

Now I really am an orphan, although pitying glances like pointing fingers don't come my way anymore—what's to pity, after all, orphans are everywhere. It's good that I still have a mother. But Mama has neither a husband nor a job. The Kaunas electrical power station near the War Museum where Mama used to work "in the German time" (during the German occupation) has been reduced to a pile of rubble. Electricity is unavailable. We light our homes with kerosene lamps. Our large apartment in the Purickis building is empty and inhospitable—there's no Kostas, Hane, Miss Terese nor her suitors. They're separated from us by the "Iron Curtain." If they're still alive, of course. In the large building, there's no more Kašuba family, nor the young artist, nor my friend Larisa Steinberg's family, nor little Laima's janitor family, nor the Russians Dunajevs. Our apartment is half dead like an upside-down empty coffin.

Only one apartment in the building remains alive—the Graičiūnas'. The beautiful Unė Baye has aged only slightly and no longer wears her silver fox stole (I wonder whether from fear, or did she exchange it for food?). It's unlikely that she'll do much nude sunbathing on her balcony any more. All civilians in our building have been ordered to leave. Our section of street will be blocked off. Only the military will be allowed through. Whoever won't leave voluntarily will be moved out forcibly. The rumor's out that the displacers covet the hanging chandeliers in those apartments, many of which were brought in from Western Europe before the war, mostly from Germany.

Many years later I'm happy to still have three surviving chandeliers, originally bought by my papa. They're my friends from a happy but short-lived childhood. Maybe this will be a comfortable place for the guardian angel to sit? If, of course, he wants to visit me.

So, chandeliers.

Our "liberators" had already evicted more than a few families along with all their furnishings. All chandeliers were ordered to be left behind. The naive townsfolk, not too much harmed by the first Russian occupation, still believe the propaganda and guarantees of survival; they are not yet aware of the theory and practice of the "Great October." They stand up in the unequal battle for the holy right to property. And, of course, they lose.

The Graičiūnas couple resolve to defend their apartment. They alone (fortunate perhaps because they were US citizens and therefore allies) are allowed to stay in the militarized Purickis building. But after Churchill's speech at Fulton, as soon as Vytautas Graičiūnas visited the ally's embassy in Moscow, that perennially smiling, wellmannered, diligent man, ended up being convicted of spying and anti-Soviet activity and sent to the gulag for ten years. There, in 1952, he hanged himself, unable to endure his forcibly imposed and unprecedented way of life. Oh, noble Unė, you see this is not your America, where you could in the thirties bravely defend the citizenship of the little-known country of Lithuania. For your adulation of bourgeois Lithuania and other similar "horrors," you got five years.

After many years I learned that Vytautas Graičiūnas was a renowned scholar, a specialist in management studies and the pioneer of that discipline in Lithuania. I searched in vain for his name in both Soviet-era Lithuanian encyclopedias. Instead, there was a place, for example, for Yevtey Grebeniuk—both an article and even a photograph. I'm willing to bet there's not a person in Lithuania who knows who Sergeant Grebeniuk was. Maybe only the cemetery caretaker of the village of Bubiai where the aforementioned person was killed during the war. May he rest in peace, but where are the bones of Vytautas Graičiūnas buried? In the Kupiškis district, in Palėvenė, where there are many Graičiūnases and Babickases, a cenotaph has been erected for Vytautas Graičiūnas. And let him also rest in peace somewhere, even though he should be resting in that place. Indeed, in 1961, the beautiful Unė was buried there. Her brother, Petras Babickas, the writer, was exiled in the opposite direction, to the West, living and eventually dying in Brazil. Alas, that's where he's buried. I've always felt sad for those who were born here in a Lithuanian village or city but had to say goodbye to the world somewhere else. A few, though in the form of a handful of ashes, have been able to return to their land. Meanwhile his contemporary, the translator Petras Kupčiūnas, as written up in a Soviet reference book, died on June 26, 1941 in Červenė, not far from Minsk. Nowadays not too many people know anymore what it means to have died in Červenė. Isn't it strange that another translator, Jonas Jablonskis, died there, and the public figure, Kazimieras Bizauskas, and many more. Those deaths are chronicled in the Lithuanian Colonel Jonas Petruitis' book, *How They Executed Us.*

...Evicted, we found another apartment. It was also on a hillside, in a two-story building. Here all the doors had been left wide open, everything had been stolen, cleaned out, not a thing left behind. Except, that is, for a solitary witness that people had lived here not so long ago—left on the floor, a family photo album. I have it still to this very day.

The apartment was beautiful—pale parquet flooring, Swedish windows. Two balconies. The entryway was spacious, in the bathroom a big window, German faucets. In some rooms, and in the hallway and kitchen, wall cupboards. And the view from the window!... Just like the one from the Purickis building. You can see the whole of Kaunas all the way to the confluence, the slopes of Aleksotas and Freda, the railroad station, the bus station, the cemetery, and almost all of the church steeples of Kaunas... And there was even more—the sunset in the evening and a huge unobstructed section of the sky itself.

Our little street was called Frykas, after Edmundas Frykas, a famous architect and engineer. His designs were used in building the Ministry of Justice, the "Neo-Lithuanian" student fraternity building, the railroad stations at Marijampolė and other towns, and many people's homes. At the time I only knew that many of the houses on Frykas Street and nearby were expressions of his original modernist style. These houses had many steps and stairs, numerous large and small doors, various shapes of windows, framed with Art Nouveau-styled ornaments, and were probably not too comfortable to live in. Still, the boldness and imagination of the designer can't help but draw the eye.

One of the houses at the bottom of the Frykas Street stairs is downright intimidating. Its terrace, where the stairs begin, is completely covered by dark green moss. In the dense growth of trees, never touched by the sun, on a tall stone pillar, sits a stone owl. I have no doubt that an old hunchbacked wizard lives there. Only in the evening does he come out to enjoy the dark garden slope. And not through doors, which are more numerous than windows, and which look as if they've never been opened, but through some narrow small window—or even through the chimney itself.

The "cosmopolitan" Frykas, who may have even been a Tatar, was completely redundant as far as the new government of postwar Kaunas was concerned. (In those days "cosmopolitan" was equal to a curse word.) The street was renamed Lermontov Street. At the time, that poet's lines seemed attractive:

> The small golden cloud slept
> On the giant hill's breast...

Or:

> I head out alone on the road
> The Milky Way shines through the mists...

Now, after many years, I know that my much loved poet, emissary of Russian imperialist expansionism in the 19th century killed Chechens just as they're being killed today. "Lermontov took leadership of a small band of soldiers made up of the bravest hunters. In leading his unit, he participated in the march on Little Chechnya, distinguishing himself for his daring and coldblooded heroics...."[1]

> ...So why is it so hard, so painful?
> Am I waiting for someone?
> Do I regret something?

Many years of poetry loving had to pass before I learned that the lyric hero and the author are not one and the same. Today I doubt again if that's really so. So, only the lyric hero suffered. It's time to go back—the events that took place over 160 years ago are being repeated, or are continuing—surely they won't be the same after as many years again?

Even though Lermontov came to me from the East with an entirely unfamiliar culture, I loved him more than the Russian-deified Pushkin. By the way, his name was used to change the beautiful name of Miškas (forest) Street in

---

[1] Michailova, E., quote from the introductory paragraph of *M.Lermontov's Collected Works*, 1941.

Kaunas. What do these two have to do with Kaunas? Later, Count Tolstoy, given recognition by the Soviets, also came to Kaunas' streets and even the proletarian Gorki whom they had finished off themselves. For the new and severe Kaunas administrators after the war, even that wasn't enough: they renamed Vytautas Prospect to Lenin's Prospect, and Savanoriu (Volunteer) Prospect to Red Army Prospect, and the Kaunite-beloved *Laisvės alėja* (Freedom Avenue) they gave to the Father of the People, Stalin.

Dita the student

—Where's your Papa?—inquires the admissions committee of the Pedagogical Institute when I stand before it in 1951 to find out if I'm suited to be a Soviet student.

—He was shot by the Nazis, —I reply.

—Or maybe he ran off with the Germans? Do you have a document? Present it to us.

—I won't present it,—I retort defiantly. —The Nazis didn't give me such a document.

I run from the committee room in tears, but don't forget to slam the door on my way out.

—By the devil!—I think to myself walking home. —I'll get a university education as easily as I'll see my own ears?

A week goes by and I'm admitted without any additional documents.

...But back in 1945, we're in the process of moving in to that emptied apartment on the second story. We've all been trimmed back like overgrown tree branches. Some of us recover and start to grow again. Some—don't. It was as if in some theater scene, a sham sun of the friendship of nations hung above our heads. Just like the circular saw in one of Eimuntas Nekrošius' productions[2].

—Tonight there will be arrests and deportations,—someone whispers.

The rumor spreads at lightning speed. The Kaunites well remember June of '41. Now everything happens during the night. Even so, everyone knows. Again, as before in Žvirgždaičiai when we huddled in ditches during the bombings, we hide ourselves in the garden. We sleep in the bushes on the hillside. The arrests and deportations to Siberia are truly happening but not always at the times specified by the rumors. Not in vain were we aware of the then popular prognostications of Mikalda, ancient Queen of Sheba[3]:

> *The Antichrist will gain great power on the Earth*
> *and will have many under him. Those who refuse*
> *to surrender to him will suffer terribly, much more*
> *than during the early years of Christendom.*

We don't know much about who that Mikalda was, but her predictions seemed to be correct.

•

... We're looking at that sham sun, pretending it's real. We feel like it will always have to be like that. And if so, it's time to settle down. With a lot of effort we load our heaviest possessions onto some borrowed pushcarts and start to move ourselves from Vaižgantas Street to Frykas Street. It's not far, but up until now I can't imagine who dragged all these heavy items—the sideboard, the piano, the sofas. There's no lock on the door, so I have to stay with all the stuff and not leave at all. At night, we push a piece of furniture up against the door, and during the day...

During the day, when I'm looking after our belongings in our echoing new apartment, a soldier opens the door. A Red Army soldier, a Liberator. A Savior. The One Who Need Not Be Feared. The one who defeated the insane Nazis. I don't know how, but I'm able to converse with him a little, even though I don't know much Russian at the time.

---

[2] Eimuntas Nekrošius (1952-2018) is one of Lithuania's most renowned directors, known for his complex and lengthy theatrical productions.

[3] Mikalda, who lived 578 years before Christ, reputedly had a powerful gift for foretelling the future.

I had learned some from the war-time book, *Ruskoye slovo (The Russian Word)* I remember:

Ptitsa vysoko letit,
Ptitsa veselo poyet...
(*A bird is flying high,*
a bird is singing merrily ...)

The soldier says he'd like to take a look at the town through our window. I wave at all the windows—go ahead, I say, look where you want as much as you want. The view is unobstructed since no curtains are up yet. The Red Army soldier gazes for a few minutes at the wide valley of Kaunas town spread before him. And then suddenly, turning around, asks:

—From where will your mother come?

—Through there,—I show him the same door without a lock that he himself just came through.

Suddenly, he grabs me in an embrace. In that instant I see his hands—they're covered in white patches, maybe burn scars or some kind of skin disease. Holding me with one hand, with the other he unbuttons his pants and pulls out that thing which I had already seen in Vytautas Park. There on the lawn by the fence, before the war, the local exhibitionist used to wander around. He, fortunately, was not at all dangerous. Almost modestly, he'd open his coat unveiling his treasure to women passing by, even to very young girls.

Who warned me then that I was facing danger? My guardian angel? Maybe my genes carrying the experiences of my distant ancestors, the daughters of Judea, or maybe of the Baltic tribes in their battles with Vikings and other sword-wielders, who coveted their lands and their women. My own throat saved me. It burst out in a loud, protracted scream, with the blare of an air raid siren. Shocked, the soldier springs back from such a strange being, who has become the scream itself, and stumbling through the door runs off. I shut my mouth, leave everything and hurry off to our old apartment. On Vaižgantas Street I meet my already returning mother. I tell her what happened, but not all of it. I'm embarrased.

—He came,—I say,—and I got scared.

We stand there helpless. A two-time widow and a two-time orphan. We are standing in front of the same building where four years ago the Japanese ambassador Sugihara gave out thousands of visas to Jews trying to escape death. They say the line snaked all the way to the Būgos steps.

My father did not come here. He did not leave for the Promised Land. Nor for Brazil. No. He left on foot. To eternity.

> *You shall not afflict any widow or*
> *orphan. If you do afflict them,*
> *And they cry out to me,*
> *I will surely hear their cry.*

Exodus 22: 22-23

Janė Rinkevičiūtė

Janė, do you remember? We're walking together past the little wooden houses squatting along Žaliakalnio Street. Maybe we're going to the market, or maybe we're returning. I'm around six, you're older by ten or so years. I like being with you since you don't tire of talking with me unlike other adults. Besides I don't see you as a complete adult.

Two girls come our way—stout and chubby. As they pass us, one of them turns to us and snaps at Janė:

—Ugly redhead!

—Ditele, wait here, don't go anywhere,—says Janė and takes off after those girls. Sensing something not good, they start running and quickly disappear behind a wooden fence. I don't know what little Janė might have been able to do to them had she caught them.

—But I'm not even a redhead.—Janė can't get over the untruth of it.—My hair is not red at all, is it, Dituke?

—Not at all, not at all,—I comfort her, hanging around her neck. —You are beautiful, Janusinka. The most beautiful one of all.

Even now I don't understand. Why was she so hurt by the not so offensive words of immature girls? After all, surely she'd heard more hurtful words by then?

Dear Janė, your life was as full of those kinds of untruths as a torn nylon stocking full of onions. As you stuff more onions in, the stocking just expands, but doesn't tear anymore.

My mama brought you, still at a very young age, to work for us from the Baby Jesus orphanage in Kaunas on Žemaičiu Street. There you lived with your sister Marytė, both of you small and gray like two little mice, orphans. Next door to that orphanage, Marytė attended a crafts and home-keeping school and learned to do something useful. But you, Janė, were probably not very gifted. You wrote with many errors, and you never did learn a craft. Perhaps you wanted to escape as quickly as you could from that charitable orphanage. Marytė learned how to sew and without even completing the crafts school got herself married. But unfortunately after a short while, she died, and you were left without a single close relative.

With Janė in Vytautas Park

Meeting you in Vilnius many years later, I embraced and lifted you as easily as a feather, but you struggled and protested:

—You'll rupture yourself, Dituk.

But I was full grown by then and much bigger than you.

Who were those Rinkevičiai parents of yours, and how did you come to be orphaned so early, and how were you and your sister such petite ones, as they say now? But letters to the heavens travel only in one direction, so I won't interrogate you any further.

Do you remember—you told me yourself—how the children of that orphanage, carrying large baskets, would come down to Freedom Avenue to the Metropolis restaurant where they'd fill up their baskets with the evening meal's leftovers. What to truly call those "leftovers"? In those days they were charitable support. Later, during the time of the Bolsheviks, they were known as "rich people's scraps."

149

Before the war, it was the "orphans' shelter." After, the "children's home." I wonder if they were still giving something away from the Metropolis in Soviet times, since there was no shortage of diners even then.

•

After the war, by Stalin's decree, the unfinished Resurrection Church was converted into a factory for making radios. That factory spread over the entire block, sweeping off from the face of the earth the pink and white stone buildings of the orphanage and the crafts school. The Orthodox church also disappeared, along with the kerosene shop and all sorts of other ordinary but essential shops. Resurrection Church is now slowly being restored, as if reluctantly. But for you, surely, it matters not anymore.

Escaped from the orphanage, you began your own independent life. You cleaned our apartment, cooked our lunches, carried out the ashes, hauled up logs from the cellar for our stove, in those days called a "hot plate." You earned some money—undoubtedly not much, but you wore nice tailor-made dresses (not some old second-hand ones). The clothes of strangers wouldn't have suited you anyway, you being so petite. You had a beautiful dark green winter coat with a grey astrakhan collar and matching cap made for you. You styled your dark wavy hair in the currently fashionable style called—"bubikopf"—a bob, a young boy's style. You very much wanted to take photographs. And you not only learned how to, but you bought your own camera; admittedly, it looked like a black box, but it was all your own.

And you had your own bed in the servant's bedroom... You had your "kingdom of dreams"—those moving pictures in the movie theaters of the Forum, the Triumph, or the Capitol that carried you to another world, which looked entirely real and helped you at least for a little while to escape the worries of daily life. Lili Damita, Greta Garbo, Rudolf Valentino...

The Hollywood dream factory carried hundreds of Kaunas' Cinderellas off to similar worlds, dreaming of love-stricken gentlemen, sparkling ballrooms, happy lives in the arms of their beloveds. Cinema was young then, too, and showed no violence, pornography, naked rear ends, and brainless young women with breasts reminiscent of my grandmother's cows' milk-filled udders.

150

•

During the German occupation you were taken to a forced labor camp in Germany. From there, in 1941, you sent us a card with a picture of a beautifully snow-covered Christmas tree: "Dituk, seasons greetings from me to your mommy and all the others..." On the postcard in black Gothic printing was stamped "Zurück. Nicht zugelassen!"— Returned. Not permitted. It seems the Nazi postal system didn't know of the city of Kaunas. Later, someone had added in a meticulous hand "Litauen"—Lithuania. Only then did I receive that card, complete with Hitler's head on a red postage stamp.

•

You were brave and quick-witted; however, life rolled along on even faster wheels. It caught you, passed you by, leaving your assigned good fortune for someone else. Everything developed as in a classic banal poor girl's tale. Only without the happy ending. You fell in love, trusted him, were let down and dumped, gave birth to a girl who soon died, drank down some very strong vinegar from a three-cornered glass bottle. You had to be treated a long time for your damaged throat, but by then you no longer wished to die. But the torment of longing for your little daughter never went away. In your mature years you sheltered and adopted an orphan girl. She quickly grew to twice your height and breadth and became unmanageable. You had a lot of trouble trying to relinquish your luckless foster-mothering.

Your deep-set eyes looked on the world with sadness. You got a job in the Vilnius dairy plant. The fat women of Žvėrynas neighborhood stole sour cream, cream, and butter for themselves and their families and to sell cheaper than in the shops. And you, like all of them, helped yourself to the products as well. Then came the arrest. Not only prosecution loomed but also jail time. In those days the punishment for stealing state property was severe. But then they offered you a chance at freedom, with a condition: if you help the investigators resolve some of the other crimes that were committed. Right there, in the prison, but in another cell. You agreed. And you didn't have to serve time much longer.

In your low hut in Žvėrynas on Lūšių Street you took in a little old man, a Russian cobbler. You needed a friend. Any friend. The old man turned your kitchen into a cobbler's workshop full of the tools of his trade, little wooden nails, scraps of leather. His customers from the

151

nearby streets brought in their worn-down shoes for mending. But a living being sat there on a low stool, it's top made of woven leather strips. Mumbling under your breath, though without anger, you cooked him meals and laundered his clothes.

Around the little hut spread a large orchard, almost too big for you, ripe with endless cherries.

—Pick them, Ditele, as many as you want, cook yourself some jam,—you urge me. And you add with care:—Will you know how to by yourself? Or shall I cook it for you?

To you I still seem a little girl.

For your old man's birthday you throw a cheerful feast. You invite the neighbors. I bring him the gift of a necktie. The cobbler thanks me graciously and says:

—In all my life I've never had such a thing. But even so, thank you very much.

After the old man died you got yourself a wolf of a dog, a huge German shepherd. I was worried he'd eat you out of house and home.

Where is your grave, Janė? Who is there to put a candle on it? We haven't seen each other for years. We should get together again.

Gladness and joy will overtake them,
and sorrow and sighing will flee away.

Isaiah 35: 10

Žilvinas in the Soviet Army

20
The Lame Army

Malpa—says Mrs. Lingvienė, my music teacher not unkindly, tapping me with her pencil on my up-sticking pinkie.

I know I should keep my fingers bent down at the keyboard, but it doesn't work too well for me.

—What does "malpa" mean?—I ask Mama.

Finding out I learned that word from Mrs. Lingvienė, Mama explains:

—It means a girl who hasn't practiced her music lessons.[1]

In my eyes Mrs. Lingvienė is very old; her head shakes, and fingers with long nails are yellowed and wrinkly. But she always looks very together, her salt-and-pepper hair combed into a neat bun. She wears an old-fashioned dress rich in threading and with lots of small buttons. A tall collar hides her neck. Several rows of a long necklace. Gold earrings so old they no longer shine. Mrs. Lingvienė has the air of a real aristocrat.

For those music lessons, Mama pays from the very bottom of her remaining funds. Even Uncle Kostas has pitched in. Beside monthly payments it's necessary to pay her "in kind" every other month—with a chicken, cheese, eggs, sugar, or other edibles. During the German occu-pation every bite costs dearly. You can't buy much of worth with inflated German marks. Especially horrible in those days are the coins—the pfennigs. They're grey, dull, without

---

[1] Actually, *malpa* means *monkey* in Polish.

153

weight. After lying around for a while they get encrusted with a whitish, floury mold.

So I study music, even though I completely lack an ear. Actually, it's not true that I study music: I am taught to play the piano. And I don't care for it much, since by the methods of those days it mostly means hammering at endless scales and drills from Hannon's books. In no way can I understand why that's necessary. I finally learn a not-overly-long piece called Alpenglühen (Alpenglow), a piece so beautiful to me that I continue to play it over and over long after ceasing lessons, chopping away at the keys as if they were logs. The red peaceful, alpine sunset turns into some kind of crackling fire. Fireworks, we'd say now.

Teacher Lingvienė regularly puts on student concerts. Her students, of whom she has at least ten, all gather at her salon to show what they have learned. The salon has been filled with chairs and improvised benches for everyone to sit on, including the parents of her pupils. Mrs. Lingvienė invites each student individually to play a piece they've learned. All of these performances are a knife in the gut to me, so much so that when my turn comes up I sit at the piano, numb, petrified, having forgotten almost everything I have learned.

Piano lesson

At one of those student concerts I'm playing Viktoras Kuprevičius' military march, "Pajūriais, pamariais" (Along the Seaside). I know I'm playing it badly. I'm overcome with such shame that my ears are burning, and all I want is to sink through the floor of the salon and never ever return to this place again. At last, the final notes. I can return to my place and blend in with the others. After every student's piece Mrs. Lingvienė gives a brief description of the pupil's effort, his or her accomplishments or shortcomings. Still

154

filled with fear, I don't much hear what the teacher says about me.

—...But her army was completely lame,—I hear the teacher say as her final words.

Well OK, then. Maybe she won't force me any more to try to learn that incomprehensible and, alas, unloved music.

•

And after a decade, when we're living in Vilnius already, on Didžioji Street, and someone buys our piano, I don't feel sorry at all. It's carted off by a well-to-do Georgian. In those days not a small number of people from the Caucasus come to comparatively impoverished Lithuania and are able to buy up "Western" things at bargain prices. Our piano is black, well kept up, made by the well-known Zimmermann firm of Leipzig. My father bought it before the war. Inside the piano lived a strange secret: having brought it back from the shop and opened it up, my parents noticed on a part of the wooden frame the carved name of my mother, "Matilda." Nobody ever found out how and when it came to be there. And the wealthy Georgian, not aware of any secrets, carted off the piano to Georgia.

Later, when my own kids had grown a little, their grandmother decided they should also take music lessons. We buy another piano from Volfas Vilenskis, together with his apartment in the center of Vilnius. Vilenskis, a former hero of the Soviet Union, a former colonel, worked in Vilnius University after the war. He found himself in some trouble with the Soviet authorities when he rose up and took his entire family off to Israel. From the display-stand dedicated to war heroes in the Museum of History, they took down Vilenskis' photograph, leaving in its place a blank rectangle.

This piano is old and out-of-tune. Without any secrets. My kids also have no ear for music. But grandma finds a teacher, frighteningly reminiscent of Mrs. Lingvienė. She's bedecked in the same exaggerated way with beads and earrings, her graying hair coiffed up into an old-fashioned bun. Except her head doesn't shake, and she doesn't smack people's up-raised fingers. The teaching method is similar, though without "Hannon." But music lives somewhere else. Not near that piano. Somewhere farther away.

But my mother truly loves music, even though, like me, she's tone-deaf. Ten times she listens to the same opera, watches the same ballet. From my youngest days, she'd take me with her to the theater. (A brief insert from my son, Žilvinas: "Grandma took us small kids to the theater also, and was joyfully proud when Eglė, during intermission in the foyer, tried to dance in imitation of the ballerinas.") I know half of all arias by heart, know the names of the singers and dancers. I even can parody several scenes from Mussorgsky's *Boris Godunof.*

> *And that was when the Tatars*
> *conquered our land...*

I belt out in a frightful voice, my stomach stuck out, waddling across the room.

•

That specific Russian opera is staged frequently during the German occupation. Possibly because there's a perfect performer in Kaunas for the Boris character. He's an impressive-looking man and a good basso—Ipolitas Nauragis-Nagrodskis.

From the theater we walk along Freedom Avenue, through Vytautas Park and up the steps. It's already dark. Just the two of us. Nowadays, it's not even safe to walk those steps in daylight—back then, though, no fear at all. Yellow lamps like round soup bowls with metallic reflectors shine cosily. From them, large circles of light fall on the smooth, untouched snow. The snow sparkles gold and silver. As of yet there are no muggers and rapists; they're off somewhere sharpening their claws, practicing to rob and kill. But not here, somewhere else, on the outskirts of Kaunas, far from us.

It's scary only when we reach the top and have to pass by a dark, deep ravine. A few years ago, before the war, they found a young man who'd hanged himself there. What an event! The entire neighborhood was stirred up. Everybody discussed and deliberated on the matter. Passersby shied from that ravine for a long time after. People expected to see a ghost more than a human being.

Right at the beginning of the second Soviet occupation, thieves and robbers arrived in numbers, as if spilling from an untied sack. People melted in fear at any rustling sound outside their doors. In Kaunas, the Black Cat gang started operating, breaking into and burglarizing apartments. Soldiers, now the victors, in broad daylight take people's wristwatches and handbags from them... They call the be-hatted intelligentsia *shliapas* (hats, in Russian) and all others—bourgeoisie or German lackeys. And the military uniform is now quite different from the one they wore in 1941. And the spirit is different. Victory! Freedom! Everything here is ours! On each wrist several watches... And what did *you* do during the German occupation? How come you're still alive?

156

Not so long ago German guards herded captured Red Army soldiers, living shades, off to various jobs. And then later, Soviet guards herded their captive Germans. At first, even though they were half-starved, they still managed to sing "*In der Heide*" and were able to patch up the remnants of their uniforms. But that was later. The Russian prisoners of war were shabby, too exhausted to sing. Undoubtedly, it was forbidden them anyway.

•

After many years my son is also a soldier, and a sick patient. I'm sitting in the army hospital in the Latvian town of Ventspilis. The hospital, a brothel before the war, is situated in a pine forest. The wards are not very big, two beds each. The foyer on the second story is spacious—a wide gallery surrounding it. I've rushed here after I dreamt of black worms on his legs. As soon as I arrive, I discover my son has already been operated on both legs. The Soviet army had presented the eighteen-year-old the gift of trophic ulcers for each leg. The incisions don't heal for a long time, and later flare up again. With his ailing legs, my son completes his remaining year-and-a-half of service, more than six months of it in hospitals.

It's some 200 kilometers from Riga to that town of Ventspilis, which is an old Latvian fishing port. Hardly anyone speaks Latvian there anymore, only Russian. Those few who do are not friendly and seem angry at the whole world. It makes no difference to them if you're from Vilnius or Moscow. I have to travel four hours on the bus from Riga to see my son, and then another four hours back with a weeping heart and wet eyes. And then the night train again from Riga back to Vilnius.

The tank unit in which our son serves stretches through a weather-beaten pine forest along the coast. A long fence, a gate with Russian letters, the entry point. Guarded. We wait outside to see our son all the sooner. We wait an hour, an hour and a half. We stop a colonel returning to the unit. We ask for his help. The colonel drills us with his eyes. Our son shows up in five minutes.

At first I don't recognize that man in a mud-colored overcoat (surely I've seen it somewhere before?). He's tall, the overcoat way too short for him.

—Look, our son's coming,—says Paulius, and darkness takes over my vision.

157

It becomes clear his uniform's trousers are also too short, his shins exposed. It's cold outside. He has no ulcers yet, but they'll appear soon. All from the cold, the poor diet, and filthy conditions. For him, long-legged tank driver, there's not enough room inside the tank. Surely, even a fool should know that tanks should be driven by shorter men. Ventspilis doesn't lack those.

Now my child leans against me with one shoulder, against the radiator with the other. There's no time for talk as he's eating. Up until now, I've never seen that so much food could fit into one slender person. Juice, chocolate, roast pork, conserves, rolls, bread, smoked ham, and a chunk of sausage...

—You'll get sick,—I say fearfully.—You should've taken it with you, for tomorrow, and the day after.

My son looks at me in wonder. Take it with me? Are you so naïve and unknowing—in this army everything is up for theft, and stealing is as natural as eating, sleeping, and pooping.

A squad marches along the road, where alongside the ditch the workers digging it have taken a lunch break, leaving their tools behind. The squad passes by, and shovels disappear as if they'd never been there. Not spontaneously or arbitrarily, but by the command of the one in charge. Every time I visit my son, again and again, I bring him eyeglasses—they're stolen each time. A five-ruble piece, unless you clutch it against your body, will for sure be stolen. The eyeglasses case, in which a few rubles are hidden, is also stolen. Without rubles, you can survive in the army—without glasses, it's very hard. Later, in the town of Pabradė, my son, steering an armored vehicle down the main city street and trying to avoid an accident with a school bus, almost takes down a hundred-year-old poplar tree. Once, when training at night in a snow storm he successfully steers his tank over a narrow bridge. His overjoyed crew mates throw him a wild celebration.

Luckily, eyeglasses then were not as expensive as they are today.

•

...When my son had eaten everything we'd brought for him and for ourselves, in an instant, with his head on my shoulder, he falls asleep. He sleeps sitting up until the last instant when we have to rush to catch the bus to Riga and then the night train to Vilnius. We run around looking for someone who might take us to the bus station. Finally some owner of a private car (a rarity) takes pity on us.

At other times, we're a little more clever and reserve a room in a hotel very near the Unit and stay for longer. Captain Semionov, our son's commander, we befriend with a bottle of vodka. So he grants our kid leave for a couple of days and nights. Our soldier sleeps just about the whole time, waking up only to eat. I determine to wash his gloves in the hotel room's sink. My efforts are in vain. My hands, the soap, the entire sink, are covered in a stinking, oily film. But the gloves remain as they were.

At 5:30 a.m., the soldier has to report to his unit for morning inspection, and then he'll be able to leave again. At five I go with him down the dark, unfamiliar street. When we arrive, my son jumps over the Unit's fence and disappears into the dark. I remain alone in the empty street. I go along—on the left the fence and the houses are without lights, like the blind. Towards the right is the harbor. It's snowing. Through slanting sleet, auras glow around the harbor lights. Somewhere in the distance, iron hammers smash against iron, echoing continuously. Underfoot, the squelch of muddy, thawing snow. The yellow-brown lights of the harbor seem to lower the sky above the earth to the height of a human being. I no longer know where that hotel is, where the army unit is, where the world itself is. Everything has sunk into a wet, cold fog. I walk forward, then back. I'm trapped in a fishbowl with fogged-up glass walls. Except that the water is on the other side of the glass. House-sized fish float in that dark green water. One of them—rusted from head to tail. There's strange writing on its side—*Ruskaja Rava*. At last! That old boat, dry-docked for renovation, I had seen during the day. And here's the hotel. A bare light bulb burns cosily at the front door on the sidewalk. But it's still not dawn.

Although the entire length of the fence around the Unit is easily climbed over by the men, no one is allowed through the fatal "PP" gate without a pass. Neither a military person, nor, even more so, a civilian. Only *Baba Mania,* the old crone, can go straight past all the guards. Whenever and however often she wants to. She wanders around the Unit's entire territory, guiding one, scolding another. She lives quite nearby, in a barrack-shaped house in a clean little room with a carpet on the wall and her son's photograph. Fifteen years ago, that son, brought here from the depths of Russia, served in the tank unit. And he was killed, or perhaps took his own life. Who in those days could have gotten the real story? *Baba Mania* came to bury her son and remained here for good. She wears traditional Russian garb—a large brown angora scarf, a dark grey

159

almost black quilted jacket and flowered calico skirt. Seeing us strangers there, she approaches.

—Where are you from?—she asks.

She doesn't care about who we are, our names, only where we're from.

—We often have a lot here from Lithuania,—says Baba. —The young guys are very cultured.

In those days, "cultured" had the broadest possible meaning of praise. A person called cultured didn't steal, didn't spit on the floor, didn't beat his wife, could read and write not only in Cyrillic, but maybe, Thank God, even in another language.

—*Kto chitayet po latyni?* (Who here can read Latin script?)—asks the doctor's assistant, a half-Russian from Tashkent, who through some foul misdeed has been demoted from his sergeant's ranking.

—I can,—says my son.

—Run,—orders the assistant,—and bring me a bottle that has written on it "*Aqua distillata.*"

•

You could say that we make friends with *Baba Mania.* She explains to us that the rules don't allow soldiers to serve closer than a 100 kilometers from their homes.

—It's nothing, don't worry,—*Baba Mania* waves her hand,—we'll fix it up. But, of course, we'll need something for the Major...

—Good, good,— We're overjoyed that the Major is "on the take," just like in Vincas Kudirka's "Viršininkai" (The Governors)[2].—Just tell us what and how much.

Baba Mania confirms that the Major does accept bribes, but only "in kind"—strong drink particularly; it can be "white" but better if it's "colored"—that is, vodka, but even better, brandy.

We never even lay eyes on the Major. Everything's taken care of by *Baba Mania.* We reward her in cash, and the Major rewards us: he reassigns our son to Pabrade, only fifty kilometers from Vilnius.

—"Lord, bring our children home,"—I once saw written at the Hill of Crosses in Šiauliai.

—Lord, bring my child home,—I pray without words into the atmosphere. Until I understand that all kinds of sufferings can be alleviated only by the Lord.

---

2 Vincas Kudirka, "Viršininkai" (The Governors), a satire about military leaders in the 19th century.

•

A cog in the Soviet propaganda machine, the senior radio program editor, holding an armful of candles, is heading to Aušros Vartai (The Gate of Dawn).[3] Her former bosses (some dead now) would turn over in their graves, if they knew of such foolishness. And the ones still alive would undoubtedly fall over from astonishment. But they wouldn't fire her. Since it's already 1986. The nation's Rebirth is already underway.

—Must I say for why I'm offering candles?—I say timidly to the priest.

—No, you don't have to,—he says, empathetically.

—Lord, bring my child home,—I fly down his street as if on wings. It doesn't even occur to me whether I have a right to ask anything from God. Perhaps instead of asking for anything, I should be scattering ashes on my head and beating my own breast.

In December our son returns home alive and intact. He can get back to his disrupted studies. He didn't have to kill or be killed in Afghanistan. Only the scars on his legs will remain for the rest of his life. He's marked, as if a log ready to be sold. But not lame like the army that marched to the piece I once played on the piano.

•

...I throw out my son's pale green shirt. For two years I had kept it by my pillow, unwashed, so I could continue to smell his scent. Over two years, the odor has pretty much disappeared and only faintly remained up until the minute the bell rang signaling his return. What can be more welcome in life than the ring of the bell of a loved one's return!

> *Ask, and it will be given you;*
> *seek, and you will find;*
> *knock, and it will be opened to you.*
>
> *If you then, who are evil, know how to give*
> *good gifts to your children,*
> *how much more will your Father*
> *who is in heaven give good things*
> *to those who ask him!*

Matthew 7: 7, 11

---

[3] Aušros Vartai (The Gate of Dawn), the best-known Vilnius sanctuary with a miracle-making picture of the Holy Mary.

At the Marijampolė home

Where's my cigarette-holder?—she asks. I can clearly hear the irritation in her voice.

Aunt Julija repeats that phrase several times throughout the day. Everyone in the family, except for her own two kids, calls Aunt Julija Tetukė, Auntie. So, Tetukė. My grandma's sister. But they differ from each other like chalk and cheese. My grandma is a plain villager, head uncovered unless with a kerchief; Julija is a lady, a little hat balanced on the side of her head. Grandma married an ordinary peasant; Julija married an army captain. One lives in the tiny village of Žvirgždaičiai, the other in the town of Marijampolė. Grandma is peaceful and self-contained; Tetukė is bossy and full of energy. Grandma humbly accepts the blows of fate; Tetukė rages and fumes, the cigarette-holder clamped down between her teeth. With a cigarette in it, of course. And after she's had a few puffs, she sets it down right where she's been doing something: on the garden fence, on the bench, on the window sill, on the pot lid, if she's been cooking. She always needs that cigarette-holder suddenly and immediately, and anyone who's home at the moment plunges headlong into looking for it. Whoever finds it first is rewarded with Tetukė's favor.

At that time, during the third summer of the second Soviet occupation, only two of us are left in her house—she and I. And so I alone must bear the burden of the search. But now in my thoughts I go back, further back.

...Tetukė prepares the world's most comfortable and softest bed for me. Throughout my long life, nowhere and never have I slept so sweetly and securely. All of Tetukė's beds are spacious and deep, and especially fragrant, when you come into their presence, they immediately sink you into their drowsy embrace. I'm like a baby in the womb, completely happy never to leave from there again. I'm at a reliably safe distance from the world and don't fear it at all.

Even my own bed these days, which I can make up to suit me, is nowhere near as sweet.

But of all the nice beds, the best is the one next to which hangs my mama's youthful embroidery—woolen threads sewn into head-sized poppy blossoms. The blossoms seem to sway on thin green stems. And those stems are fantastically entwined, bristling with tiny green silk filaments.

All of Grandma's kids have lived in Auntie Julija's home in Marijampolė, for a longer or shorter time, while they attended high school. Julija herself had two children— Albytė and Kęstutis. The handsome dark-haired, blue-eyed young man was admired by half of the girls in the Marijampolė high school. Albytė—with her dark, wrist-thick braids reaching below her waist attracted the attention of more than one young lad's eye.

So what that your house is wooden,
covered in budding vines...

—wrote a local poet, later to sail off to the wider world. Tetukė's house on Stoties Street was indeed covered with vines, and was painted yellow with a glassed-in verandah and a cheerful garden in the front yard. And in the back of the house, in the densely growing garden there, climbing beans hid a small, cozy arbor. All around, as thick as wild grass and as tall as a person, bloomed cosmos, yellow Jerusalem artichokes, and flame-colored dahlias. Aunt Julija had bought that house after she returned from Kaunas, divorced from her captain.

....Don't you wait for me, girl,
sad by the gate. I won't be coming
down the path of lindens anymore...

—wrote the poet peevishly, disappointed by the young miss Albytė's indifference to him, renaming the poplar-planted Stoties Street a path of lindens. Young people were to sing these two songs for a long time, never knowing who the author was, nor the young lady, nor where the house was.

By the way, the house still stands today, though the playful voices of those pre-war young people have all died out. I remember there was a game we played—you'd poke the buttons on someone's sweater and say: "bought, stolen, gifted"... When you named the last button, that's the kind of sweater it was. Fate, too, with its indifferent finger, poked each one of Marijampolė's high-schoolers, assigning

163

them life, death, roles as refugees, exterminators, partisans, collaborators, Siberian prisoners...

—No,—Vytautas would say smiling ironically (we never
knew if he was serious or kidding).—We were young, but we
made conscious choices. It's your own fault if you planted a
rotten potato.

In those days, Albytė truly had a choice of whom to pick,
but fate pushed her to the last one.

—Don't you doze off,—Kęstutis said to his friend from
Prienai, Vytautas Krikščiūnas.—Someone else will snatch
her from under your nose.

All this was told to me many years later by Vytautas
when we were both waiting at the Vilnius airport for
Kęstutis to arrive from America. In the American manner,
Kęstutis had changed his name from Černiauskas to
Cernis; he was now a wealthy man, one of Ford Motor
Company's engineers.

—What did you do?—I asked Vytautas.

—I didn't doze off,—he replied.

... The convivial wedding took place in the little wooden
home. *And I was there, and I drank the mead and I drank
the beer[1]...*

And outside, the Soviet occupation's stench thickened.
The newlyweds rented an apartment in Kaunas. While
transferring their furniture, the huge mirror collapsed into
slivers.

—There'll be bad luck,—said Aunt Julija unhesitatingly.

•

Bad luck didn't wait long.—Vytautas' cousin Jurgis, the
son of Colonel Krikščiūnas, joined the partisan movement.
His *nom de guerre* was Rimvydas. He's supported by
Vytautas and Jurgis, sons of the famous agronomist,
Pranas Krikščiūnas. Secret meetings take place in the
newlyweds' apartment. It doesn't take long before a traitor
turns them in. Vytautas' brother Jurgis, handsome, young,
blond, dies in prison, and Vytautas is sentenced to ten
years in Siberian concentration camps, plus five years of
deportation. Magadan, Tayshet, Vorkuta, the gold mines...
Albytė is also sentenced—two years in the camps because
she knew but didn't report on her young husband

---

[1] *And I was there, and I drank the mead and I drank the beer. (Ir aš ten
buvau, alų midų geriau).* A common rhymed refrain in folktales used to
strengthen the narrator's veracity.

and his friends. At the time we were aghast—was it possible to betray a loved one? Later, we learned about the Soviet hero Pavlik Morozov, for many years a glorified young lad because he had turned in his own father to the Reds. Albytė, who had not betrayed her husband, spent two years in the Velsk Forests in the Archangel region of Russia. They didn't cart her off to Siberia—too far, too short a sentence. They planted her in the forest thickets to guard the tools of the slave-lumberjacks left out at night. There was no shortage of logs there, through the night a fire burned, the eyes of invisible beasts glittered. The creatures of the forest kept a safe distance, observing that strange being—a mother's darling from Lithuania—a city girl who had never heard how the wolf howled at night. Or how the owl hooted. Or how the hares laughed hysterically in the depths of the strange forest.

Aunt Julija did not give up for a moment. From the first day of her daughter and son-in-law's arrest, she made every effort to help them. She wrote letters to various soviet institutions (in vain, of course), stood in long lines by the prison hoping to deliver them at least a few bites of food. But the powerful Soviet legal machinery digested the arrestees in its innards, expelled them like something poisonous, and carted them off to the places of decontamination. Tetukė started sending them food parcels. Where did she get the means? On what did she survive herself?

•

...Through long summer days, book in hand, draped across Aunt Julija's couch, I didn't think about any of that. I read books about the war that had raged and humbly accepted everything that was happening then, since I thought nothing could be more terrible than war. But there was! Look at Aunt Julija's destiny—her son disappeared in the West for many years, her daughter in the forests of Russia, her son-in-law far away in Siberia. Tetukė grabbed not only her cigarette holder more often but also a glass. So she wouldn't have to drink alone like some Meiliuvienė (more about her later), Tetukė would sit up at the table where she'd placed some modest snacks, and sit me beside her. She'd take a little carafe out of the cupboard (not a bottle, God forbid) and two liqueur glasses, pouring her own almost full, mine with just two drops, and say:

—I have to take this. For my health.

165

High schoolers 1923, Milda in front

I'd drink those two disgusting drops with her and fail to understand how they could bring any kind of health.

—You can't have anymore,—Tetukė would say, pouring herself another glass, thereby improving her health even more. Later she'd gather up the dishes and return the carafe to the cupboard. But I noticed that sometimes before returning it she'd pour herself another, quickly downing it as if ashamed of my seeing her. I had enough smarts to pretend I didn't see. I was happy to see that Tetukė's waning health was returning, her eyes brightening.

This little idyll became more complicated when Albytė returned from deportation. Firmly opposed to such a health remedy—a little "fix me up," as Tetukė called it—she declared war against that carafe. Now the carafe stood in the cupboard, demonstrably empty. The health-giving fluid

166

had been transferred to a little bottle, and that bottle hid itself in the most unlikely places, sometime even at Meiliuvienė's place.

Julija Černiauskienė

Returned from Russia, Albytė had to officially divorce "the enemy of the people" (understand, her husband!) and only then could she hope to find work. The courts acted swiftly—and unlucky couples like them were legally split apart. This kind of divorce was almost always only formal, and the ex-prisoners on their return took up residence with their families. So Albytė got herself an unskilled and poorly paid job at a Russian school in Marijampolė. One evening she comes home after work.

—Ditele,—says Tetukė,—don't say anything to Albytė that we two have had a little drop to drink.

—Ditele,—says Albytė, casting a glance at her mother,— has Mommy...

I already know what she's going to ask, and I run outside so I won't anger the one or the other of them. I know that each is unhappy in her own way, but I love them both.

When I come back inside, Albytė is crying, and Tetukė is smoking furiously. By the way, I never saw Aunt Julija cry. She was proud, like many self-reliant people. She was a hard nugget, who believed only in herself, and so often ended up hurting those close to her. And the closest one, most often, was Albytė, her painfully loved daughter. Or Meiliuvienė.

•

So now is the right time to explain what this Meiliuvienė is. She's a small, somber woman of unguessable age. She lives in Tetukė's back garden in a small hut, beyond which the yard ends, not counting one more little hut, with a heart carved in the door. Going to that little outhouse was referred to as "going north." And the path went by Meiliuvienė's two small windows. Meiliuvienė helped Tetukė plant and weed the garden, feed the chickens—and the hog, too, when she wanted to fatten it up. Meiliuvienė cleaned the house, scrubbed the floors, was modest, polite, and humbly suffered her authoritarian mistress' attacks. Auntie especially got herself worked up when some girlfriend of Meiliuvienė's would show up, or, God forbid, several, or even worse, some boyfriend. My Lord! What are they all doing there? Maybe they're slandering her in her absence? Auntie finds a reason then to drop by Meiliuvienė's and after a short while returns relieved. To our questioning looks, she waves her hand:

—Ah, it's just swill.

However, without Meiliuvienė's help, Tetukė would not have been able to get by even for a single day. She gets very nervous when Meiliuvienė goes into town and is gone longer than usual—even though the floors have been scrubbed, the chickens have been fed, and no sounds issue from the satisfied pig in his sty. Tetukė worries, keeping one eye out the window for her return, though right now Tetukė doesn't need her at all.

In those days there was no television, and Tetukė didn't read books, only newspapers. And newspapers were not always available.

—It's already ten to six, Ditele,—she says every day, tossing aside any begun or half-finished chore, and both of us settle in comfortably on the veranda for the daily ritual— the arrival of the train. The Marijampolė train station is nearby, opposite us, just on the other side of a weedy lot. After a brief stop, the slow passenger train steams off, and the two of us wait impatiently until the passengers appear coming out of the station. Edmudas Frykas is the architect

168

of this red-brick station with its steeple, completed in the 1920s. An impressive building, it's a true pride of Marijampolė —like the town's central garden and the sugar factory. Like the grammar schools and gymnasiums, like the long list of Marijampolė's brightminded citizens who, from the 18th century on, lay the foundations of today's Lithuania. The little town on the banks of the Šešupė River was born in the 17th century and was soon called Staropol, and later, joining itself with the buildings of the Marist fathers' monastery, changed its name to Marijampolė. True, the town had to change its name one more time under the Soviets. It became Kapsukas[2]. The ingenious "Kapsukans" immediately and without any respect renamed the town "Kapšiukas" (Little Purse).

People are getting closer from the train station. Aunt Julija knows them all and comments on them in a businesslike manner:

—Behold, the Inspector returns from Kaunas with a green folder, probably with a new set of instructions. Oh my, there's Valaitis on foot, unmet by his wife...well that's a pity, if they've fallen out...see, his hat's pulled down. Oh and look, Fotelis is back from Vilnius...stuffed with who knows what...maybe new textbooks... Look, look, Zinutė has brought the kids to meet their dad...her sweetness! And here's someone I'm seeing for the first time, must be the new Party secretary, since the vice secretary is winding around him like thread on a bobbin...Boy oh boy... Sirutienė bought herself a new coat in Kaunas...

The stream of arrivals is exhausted and the two of us return to our unfinished work.

But I go back further, even further...

I'm four years old, still unbaptized. The Christian half of my family is fraught with fear—what'll happen if I suddenly die? Well, of course, I go straight to Hell. There I'll burn for eternity. Having sought God her entire life without finding Him, my mother nonetheless gives in to everyone's concerns, and I'm baptized in Marijampolė in 1936. Without my father's knowledge. Now, the Christian God and all his angels will protect and look after me.

...*Our Father, who art in heaven...*

—Where does God live?—asks my granddaughter, twice as old as I was back then.

---

[2] In honor of a famous communist leader.

—In your heart,—I answer her and her little brother without hesitation. I can see clearly that they don't understand.

When we learn how to write, we believe we'll be able to lay out our thoughts in words. When we learn about God, we dare to believe that we know everything about Him. It remains to worship Him and that's all. We're not willing to make further efforts to get to know Him better. To actually seek Him. We behave in ways that are more convenient. We ask Him with sincerity. We thank Him with formality. To Him—we're humble, to our neighbor—we're unforgiving. The gate of our hearts is most often closed.

Granny Žolynas' family after Dita's baptism

Auntie Julija is terribly fond of company and is a great hostess. She especially loves those rare visits from her Kaunas girlfriends whom she refuses to let leave for days, insisting they sleep in her soft beds and feeding them with her most delicious foods. She prepares a true fiesta for her unfortunate friend, Mikuckienė, former first wife of Juozas Mikuckis, poet and Lithuanian military officer, who was later sent to the West by the Soviets. The two women had met and gotten to know each other in the line that formed outside the Kaunas prison, where Mrs. Mikuckienė brought packages for her arrested son. After the guest has stayed a week, Albytė starts getting nervous, and is concerned also about her mother's health. She urgently sends off Mrs. Mikuckienė in the Kaunas train. Tetukė sulks for a long time, Albytė weeps yet again, but it all passes.

A decade goes by, the son-in-law Vytautas Krikščiūnas returns, the daughter remarries the same husband again.

Like a Hollywood star. But this time there was no splendid wedding feast, no fancy guests, *and I was not there, and I did not drink any mead, I did not drink any beer...*

At that time Kapsukas' (i.e., Marijampolė's) almighty ruler was the Communist party's first secretary Žėčius (if anyone today would like to know his surname) who interfered in all kinds of ways with the returning prisoner's attempts at seeking work. No sooner would Vytautas find a job, than he would be fired. But the collectivized people of the Krikščiūnas homeland in the Prienai region at the Ašminta farm, to the best of their abilities, help the son of the former "kulak" and agronomist Pranas Krikščiūnas, nephew of Juozas Krikščiūnas, Doctor of Natural Sciences and former minister of agriculture and a professor—that is, supply him with potatoes, cabbage, and apples. They don't begrudge the "bourgeoisie" of old Lithuania.

Vytautas did not give up, worked outside the reach of the pesky Secretary. An unequal battle simmered between the ex-convict and the omnipotent Soviet functionary. Vytautas used to frequently come to Vilnius on business. He'd stay with us. Those long sleepless nights! I lay in my bed, frozen in horror, squeezed by pain like one of those Žvirgždaičiai fleas under a fingernail. While Vytautas, from his bed, told one after another story of his sufferings in Siberia.

Where was the reasonable and civilized world then? Today, America laments its victims buried among destroyed skyscrapers. Did the world really change only after September 11, 2001? Why not after the Red revolution in 1917? Or after Hitler's holocaust? In Lithuania alone, more than 200,000 Jews died... Where do you draw the line? How many people have to die before it's called the greatest tragedy? A hundred? A thousand? Ten thousand? Or only one, who happens to be the most important to some other one?

After the war, Lithuanians withdrawing into the forests, unable to wait any longer for the promised support from that same America, in 1947, wrote a desperate letter to Pope Pius XII. The letter was widely translated and published beyond the Iron Curtain, but not one state lifted even a little finger.

Albytė was forty when she gave birth to a son, Kęstutis, the descendent of a respected family. In Lithuania there are still quite a few Krikščiūnases. Among them is Kęstutis' son, Paulius, too.

Vytas (that's how we knew Albytė's husband among ourselves) took responsibility to have a monument, a half-

171

cenotaph, erected for his family in the Prienai cemetery. On it are inscribed the names of not only those who are buried there, but also those Krikščiūnases whose bodies should be there but are no one knows where.

Wandering around the memorial cemetery in Marijampolė, near the graves of the famous who rest in peace in their native soil, I found the well-tended graves of some Soviet soldiers. Are they in peace here, coming from the vast Soviet reaches? I find a Russian inscription— "Polkovnik A. Armand." Is this not the famous revolutionary Ines Armand's and the Bolshevik leader Lenin's illegitimate son?

But who cares about him—as Aunt Julija used to say.

My eyes caress a small headstone, very different from all the surrounding markers in its classical simplicity. "Julija Černauskienė" is inscribed on it. It stands straight and strong as Julija herself in photographs of her youth. Auntie died in 1963, eaten up by cancer of the throat. She rests alone, as she lived. For her overbearing and blunt manner she was not loved by all. Prepare your fabulous beds in that other world, Auntie. Wait for us all in your welcoming home. I know, if you have a home there, I can open its door without hesitation.

—Come here, eat, Ditele,—I hear your strong and lively voice.—And I'll pour myself a little drop for health's sake...

For the deliberations of mortals are timid,
and unsure are our plans.
For the corruptible body burdens the soul
and the earthen shelter weighs down
the mind that has many concerns.
And scarce do we guess the things on earth,
and what is within our grasp we find
with difficulty; but when things are
in heaven, who can search them out?

Wisdom 9: 14-16

22
The
Suffocating
Cherry Tree

The spring wind is no joke. It storms downhill, ruffling the lush new grass. In the next second, it runs up the slope, undulating, swirling last year's left-over leaves. Next, it transforms into a furious twister and bends a young cherry tree almost to the ground. The young cherry tree is in bloom for possibly the first time and even before enjoying its new whiteness, almost all its blossoms have been torn off and scattered on the slope.

The girl looks through the window. All the windows are closed but the twister shrieks, wanting to get in wherever there's a gap. It's rattling the door, as if it had a hand.

—Stop being so furious—the girl orders silently.—Can't you see the cherry tree is barely alive?

The twister, keeps raging, again and again returning to the cherry tree, growling and spiralling around it in ever tighter circles. The cherry tree bends down almost touching the ground, swaying left and right, tries to straighten up, is knocked down again.

Next morning the tree lies broken, its uppermost branches flat on the earth. Outside all is calm.

The clouds scattered by the twister are now regathered into bunches heavy with rain.

The girl, leaning on the windowsill writes a poem which she entitles "Spring Storm." But it has nothing to do with the slogan left on her schoolroom wall by the retreating Nazis: *Steh gerade oder zerbrich* (Stand tall or be broken). The slogan is like a gunshot—in German harsh and straight to the temple. I don't want to be broken, but I have yet to learn how many times in life I will be required to feel fear, to be gnawed by anxiety, to become mealy-mouthed, to pretend and be mistaken.

•

I had seen the barely alive, those who could hardly drag their feet, and for whom nothing mattered. Not too long ago, during the Nazi frenzy, I'd witnessed Soviet prisoners of war. Silently, they went where they were led by their guards. Sometimes they'd be made to dig in the streets of Kaunas. To this day, no one really knows how many died of starvation, illness, how many were killed by the SS.

During the German occupation, my mother works at the power plant. Throughout the entire war, the power station is a vital strategic installation. To manage it, a local German is chosen, Berthold Kruk. Undistinguished from other engineers, he's been an acquaintance of my mother's since before the war. Conscripted into a German uniform, he becomes an important person and is trusted by the Nazis. He doesn't even have to go to the front. He is fat and large. Maybe he has a heart condition. Or maybe he has some special merit. Like a sterotypical German, he arrives at work punctually, pleasantly greeting all the workers. Through the corner window of his second-story office, Herr Kruk looks over the approaches to the power station administration building. And suddenly he observes a scene that angers him. Madame Milda, his employee, approaches a work gang of those Soviet POWs and hands one of them a small package. Most likely it's a sandwich she's brought for her own lunch. The guards pretend not to see it. Madame Milda hurries back to her office, sits at her desk, and begins her usual accounting work. Opening the door, a uniformed secretary informs her that the boss would like to see her.

—Madame Milda,—foams the boss,—have you lost your mind? Have you become bored with living? Do you not have a child? Have you forgotten whose it is? Cease these tricks.

...Along Freedom Avenue's sidewalks the Wehrmacht's officers stride smartly. Their boots shine. There's no shortage of ladies in hats. The hats are pre-war and can be reshaped to suit the new style. But shoes! During spring, summer, and fall, all the streets rumble with the clumping of wooden heels. A new war-time fashion has been invented for women—clogs. Their soles are wooden, sometimes split across and joined with leather so they'll bend more easily. The tops of the clogs are made out of old left-over pre-wartime leather belts. Mr. Tadas even donates some leather for Mama's clogs—Moroccan leather from Czechoslovakia he'd set aside for his book binding. That's real sacrifice.

And so Mama's clogs are the most beautiful ones on our entire street.

Men, until now at least, are walking around in leather shoes. Their wearing down is forstalled by the use of galoshes. Some are pre-war with red lining, some are contemporary, often manufactured in secret. And I find out from the adults that the gardeners at the end of Vaižgantas Street also turned over a profitable business of "boiling up" galoshes. How and out of what they boiled them up is still a mystery to me. To this day, I regret never having seen that mysterious concoction.

Today it may seem funny, but during the German occupation, Uncle Kostas hid out from being arrested nowhere other than at his father-in-law Jonas Smilgevičius' manor. Auntie Hanė had taken me to that manor. We traveled by car to Samogitia, to Užventis. Only the second time I've ridden in an automobile, it upsets me so much I start hiccoughing and I climb out at the *Senas Dvaras*, "The Old Manor," barely alive. I write "The Old Manor" in quotes because this was the very manor that Šatrijos Ragana[1] wrote about in her story of the same title:

> *Beyond the forests, beyond the rivers,*
> *between ravines and hills stands the old manor*
> *building. Not tall, but long and wide with a large*
> *porch propped up by white columns, full of*
> *lovely corners, comfortable and warm, a true*
> *shelter for all our joys and sorrows. In front is a*
> *large sleepy pond with its mysterious depths,*
> *shimmering gold at night with reflections of moon*
> *and stars, and a fragrant dreamy orchard*
> *carrying itself away with song.*

•

At the beginning of the century, Jonas Smilgevičius buys the old shabby manor and starts to farm it. He transforms the manor into an "exemplary farm," which also soon includes a distillery, a cheese factory, a brickworks, a mill, and a lumberyard. But I'm most impressed by that sleepy pond.

•

One Sunday morning a scandal erupts in the old manor. Uncle Kostas along with his wife's brother and other young

---

[1] Šatrijos Ragana (1877-1930) was the pen name of Marija Pečkauskaitė. A writer and an educator, her most famous works are *Sename dvare (In the Old Manor)* and *Irkos tragedija (Irka's Tragedy)*.

men take it into their heads to thin the population of crows perched around the garden. They take their shotguns and start taking potshots at the crows who scatter and start cawing in loud, indignant voices. What a noise there is! The old lord of the manor seethes with anger.

—Halfwits!—he shouts.—Mass is being said at church and they're engaged in killing, right at the very consecration. What will people make of us!

•

When the Bolsheviks occupied Lithuania for the first time, the 1918 Declaration of Independence signator, Jonas Smilgevičius, decided to seek permission to withdraw to Germany along with the re-patriating Germans of Lithuania. At that time, Hanė's mother, Stefanija, lay paralyzed in bed. They moved her in an ambulance. While under care at a specialized hospital she developed a fever and died in the spring of 1941. She's buried somewhere not too far from the spot where Darius and Girėnas crashed and died after crossing the Atlantic. Jonas Smilgevičius' family was put up in a camp not too far from Lodz. When the Germans occupied Lithuania, Jonas Smilgevičius returned to his farmstead in Užventis and was given permission by the German civil authorities to run his own estate, formerly nationalized by the Soviets, not as a landlord but as a trustee (*Treuhaender*) on behalf of the Germans. He ran the estate until the end of 1942 and completed his earthly journey at the Red Cross hospital. With a large crowd in attendance, he was buried at the Užventis Catholic cemetery in the chapel's cellar.

After the restoration of national independence in 1990, and the efforts of his grandson Vitalis Petrušis, his remains were reburied in the Užventis cemetery, his grave marked by a modest headstone. This history was told to me by Kostas and Hanė in a letter from Florida. The two of them also write this:

> *Jonas Smilgevičius' offspring—his*
> *daughters, their husbands, his grandchildren—*
> *intend to claim for recovery of nationalized*
> *property. And, if some day, the free and*
> *democratic republic of Lithuania decides to*
> *return lost properties or wealth in natura or by*
> *compensation, all of the heirs have decided to*
> *donate proceeds to the instigation of a scholar-*
> *ship fund in the name of the "February 16th*
> *Lithuanian Independence Act's signator,*

Jonas Smilgevičius" through Vytautas Magnus
University in Kaunas. So that would be a
monument to one of the creators of Lithuania's
independence.

•

Jonas Smilgevičius' descendents have scattered like seeds around the globe. Maybe that's good. Even an unthinking plant likes its seeds spread widely and may flourish in foreign soil. And it can thrive so long as it finds a place to put down roots. After the war, uncle Kostas and his wife lived in Germany, Australia, Chicago, and for the longest time in Florida. In the end, they moved to be with their daughter in Colorado. Certainly, they planned to return to Petrašiūnai Cemetery, near their parents. As ashes, in urns.

Incidentally, the flower in *The Little Prince*, was convinced that people are blown about by the wind because they have no roots, and therefore they suffer.

...Later, the Russians are herding their prisoners. Up to the very end, the Germans try to look good. One prison gang works on Prūsų Street behind the fence of a furniture factory. They stick their heads through the fence, and stare out with pleading eyes. One is quite young, name of Hans. Everyday on the way to school my friend and I give him our sandwiches and always exchange a few words. Once, the Soviet guard, spying our illegal activity, threatens me:

—Do you know what can happen to you for that?

—I don't know,—I reply bravely, though inside I'm dying of fear.

Nothing happens at all, until one day our Hans disappears from behind that fence.

Not far off, the Jonas Jablonskis school has been converted into an army hospital. Perched on the iron fence young, dark Italians chat up the gymnasium girls as they walk past. We're still a little too young for these Italians, but we like how their attention makes us feel. We each choose one—he's yours, that one's mine. I take the black-haired, blue-eyed one.

—Umberto,—he introduces himself.—*Aus Milano.*

Much later, while reading Heinrich Heine's *Travel Pictures*, where he writes in such an uplifting way about the Milan cathedral, those unusual blue eyes of Umberto appear before me.

Long after we've all been mowed down
by Time's scythe, and the wind has blown us
from the fields like dust, that monument will still
stand, untouched; new generations will spring
from the earth, look on in wonder and lie back
down in the earth; and Time, unable to hurt the
form, will encircle it with misty legends, and its
prodigious history will be transformed into myth.

•

After the war I no longer walk down to take piano lessons from Mrs. Lingvienė. I don't know if she still lives on Freedom Avenue, in the back in a small yard, which you access through Baulas' photo studio and staircase. Gone also Auntie Volpianski's toy store next to the "Metropolis." Gone the be-hatted gentlemen and ladies. Gone the display shop windows of Arkusas and of Markusas. The little colored globes of ice cream, formerly served in a dish along with a glass of water, are now sold in waffled cones. Heavy women stand behind the wheeled carts and spoon the ice cream on to the cones. They seem to pack your cone with ice cream, but when you eat the top off, you find it empty. Mama won't give me any coins for ice cream. She simply has no money. My friend Gija generously buys me ice cream. Her parents are well-off. If they don't give her money, she just takes it. I'm un-comfortable accepting those gifts paid for with someone else's money, but I so want the ice cream.

Even if you have money there's not all that much to be bought. It's all controlled by ration cards. You get a number of different colored squares of lined paper, and at the designated shop you buy what you're allowed to with one of the squares. What a scolding I get when, one time, on my way back from a shop I lose those squares. And the month is only half over. Mama, not having a job, takes it upon her own initiative to do work from home, which right after the war had not yet been banned. She knows nothing about marketing or management, doesn't have any kind of busi-ness plan, nor any start-up capital. She just walks every day to the market in the old town, drags sacks of flour home, and kneads the dough, and then bakes rolls at night so they'll be fresh in the morning. Packed into large bags, in the morning the rolls are carried down from Vytautas Hill to the cafes and bars in the center of town. And then she's off again to the market, and then again the kneading, the late night baking, etc. I also participate in this hopeless

178

business which realizes only a minimal profit—just enough to get us by.

Late at night, when the dough has risen, you have to pinch off a lump and weigh it out on the scales, and then form a roll out of the dough. The dough sticks to your fingers, drapes over the scales. Eyelids also stick together— I so want to sleep.

—Where have I seen this all before?—I ask myself after many years while looking at Salvadore Dali's stretched, melting clocks. I had completely forgotten those nighttime tortures and the dough stretching from my fingers...

For the next morning, a few dozen rolls have been ordered. They don't always rise and bake properly. Sometimes, when the flour happens to be bad, the rolls are ill-formed, and they're not suitable for selling. Loss, stress, helpless anger.

From daily drudgery and deprivation, I was saved by poetry. After the childrens' verses of Vytė Nemunėlis, I read poems by Bernardas Brazdžionis, Mykolas Vaitkus, Jonas Aistis. And, of course, Jurgis Baltrušaitis. His sublime poems during the German occupation were published in the collection *A Garland of Tears*. I knew almost all of them by heart.

> *Little daisy all white,*
> *Beautifying my steps,*
> *From the dust you rise,*
> *Lifting up your luminous head...*

How well I remember that field full of the world's prettiest flowers, white daisies. Now, it's all overgrown with tussocks and bushes, but then... Early in the spring the field is no different than any other of the lawns in Vytautas Park. As green as any of them. All the other fields are mown evenly by the groundskeepers, but that meadow is left alone. It is growing vigorously. Here everything is deliciously aromatic, everything hums and thrusts upward. Until the daisies bloom. During June, I check every morning—is it time yet? Are they blooming? Will I be able to pick myself the world's most beautiful bouquet? Back in those days was there even one cloudy day in June? Everything sparkles, and the sun in the corner of the sky blooms as in a child's drawing, where the ant and the dog are the same size, and the butterfly is larger than the crow.

The day for picking daisies is a special day, though it is not marked as such in any calendar. In June 1941, the peonies have already opened their menacingly red, warlike petals. But the white daisies will be the same as ever. And now it's time. I walk along the park fence and through the narrow gate. And then straight along the path. Then to the right and into that field. It's all blue-green as if full of toy German soldiers. But, no, I see that they are real soldiers— with iron belt buckles, high-top boots, uncovered heads. Having set up something like a field kitchen surrounded by tents, they're brushing their teeth with real toothbrushes and they rinse their mouths and spit right onto the most beautiful flowers in the world. Onto MY daisies. One soldier stands with his back to me; I don't see what he's doing, but I understand this much—that he's peeing. Right onto my holy flowers. I hang my head and return home. I don't know yet, that this will probably be the very least of my losses.

Dita and daisies

After a few days the field has been abandoned—not a single soldier left, disturbingly bare. On the edge of the field there are some daisies left. But I don't want those marginal ones. I don't want any at all.

•

After many years I had the good fortune and honor to meet in Lithuania, when they emerged for the first time, as if from nothingness, the famous émigré poet Bernardas Brazdžionis, and then later Henrikas Nagys who'd arrived from Canada. I respected and loved Brazdžionis' poetry, and held on to his books throughout the entire Soviet period, but Henrikas Nagys I literally worshipped, even though before the war he had not yet published a volume of his poems. I knew his work from the *Kūryba* (*Creative Work*) periodical published during the German occupation. After many years I finally read all his poems collected together in his book. I felt that same pain and serene joy, that same dormant hope inside even the most despairing poems. In every poem slowly grew that which was yet to be. And even that won't be the end, as it will be yet again. I

180

couldn't accept even the slightest correction which separated the original periodical version from the later published book:

My gaze, shaded by my dusty hand,
wanders towards the approaching storm clouds.
How the grain sways, endless waves of grain,
how it ripples from hill to hill!
And bees hum in roadside flowers.
And birds flutter their shiny wings over the birches...

But already from afar approach the tired storm's
sighs and heavy steps—heavy as stone...

•

—And I know you from your voice,—says Henrikas
Nagys after many years when I call him at the Lietuva
(Lithuania) Hotel to arrange an interview. He has heard
some of my cultural broadcasts on the radio overseas and
agrees to meet me. I go simmering with joy.

... And in the distance a fair-haired woman
approaches down the path, gold flaming and
fading in her hair in sunlight and shade;
she carries a bouquet of small blue flowers.
Suddenly, she stops. Shades her eyes.
Was she called?
Oh, yes! She sees him crossing the field:
the wind ruffling his clothes and hair,
his eyes reflecting the soaring spring sky.

•

In the small hotel room, Henrikas Nagys' eyes reflected
his difficult experiences, his physical weakness, and his
life's impasses. But the "fair-haired woman" was by his
side. And I don't let on even with one word how dear his
poetry is to me. After all, I'm not going to fall to my knees
like the film star Marlene Dietrich did once, exalting in
front of the Russian writer Konstantin Paustovski. Nonetheless, my heart does kneel. Nagys' poetic powers were so
strong that even his translation of Rilke and Hans Carossa
are overshadowed by his own personality, and the poems
read as if they were written by Henrikas Nagys himself.

"Literature is the creation of a human being's soul, in
writing, assigned to delight." Soon after the end of the war,
that doctrine is quickly changed into the official
requirement that literature, and indeed all art, be social

181

and class propaganda. Lithuania is overwhelmed with Russian and Soviet art.

I had been hungry not only for a tastier bite, but for better literature. From first to last, and again from last to first, I had read through all the five issues of *Kūryba (Creative Work)* published during the German occupation. They had published J. Keliuotis, V. Mykolaitis-Putinas, J. Baltrušaitis, J. Balys—you can't name them all. I learned about the fine poet Hölderlin, saw many reproductions of Lithuanian and foreign artists. Among them—the great Norwegian artist, Edvard Munch's, "Scream." For a long time I couldn't pull my eyes away. It's as if I realized how much life will force me to cry out, and how no one will hear.

In 1946 Balys Sruoga's translation of Heinrich Heine's collection of poems, *North Sea* came out. I had not yet seen the sea then, but with the help of that small book, I got myself ready.

> *The hot red sun sets*
> *Into the silvery ocean,*
> *The earth-flooding sea.*
> *Crimson nets of air,*
> *Billow behind, and opposite,*
> *From veils of glimmering autumn clouds,*
> *Death-like, breaks*
> *The sad moon's face;*
> *Behind it—like sparkling motes,*
> *In the far mist, stars shimmer.*

I was familiar with poetry long before I was with the Bible. But the Bible, right from my first acquaintance with it, has been a serious competitor of poetry.

> *Remember, O Lord,*
> *what has befallen us;*
> *behold, and see our disgrace!*
> *Our inheritance*
> *has been turned over to strangers,*
> *our homes to aliens.*
> *We have become orphans, fatherless;*
> *our mothers are like widows*

> Lamentations 5: 1-3

23
The Fence That Is Long Gone

Kaunas view

Much is long gone. Sometimes that's an improvement. But then there's what no longer is but *could* still be there. Kaunas' centuries old oaks, that once upon a time were shedding buckets of acorns, still stand today. But many of them stand dead. A little bug, a leaf-eater, arrived one day. An untold abundance of his kinsmen followed and fell on Kaunas' oaks, who knows how many centuries old, and gnawed away at them. As everyone knows, the oak can live for more than a thousand years. A shudder goes through me as I look at the king of trees, which, though dried out and fruitless, will still stand a long time. In the meantime, the little leaf-eater and his vast family will take on the next tree.

My favorite oak tree in Vytautas Park is still green. During my childhood, from its foot, you could see the entire panorama of Kaunas. Today, you'd have to climb to its topmost branches to see the Nemunas River. The tree is alive, and I come here to dip into its energy, which it shares with me selflessly. I press my palms, stomach, thighs against its powerful trunk. It's so knotted, I'm afraid I'll scrape myself. However, the oak with its hundreds of warm and gentle hands holds me against its abrasive skin, deeply etched with furrows. Under the bark I hear the oak's dark green blood flow. It flows through me as well. For a short while the oak has plugged me into its bloodstream.

—You can go now—whispers the oak.—I've given you a drop of strength and courage.

—I've loaded up enough for a half year,—I tell my family.

183

When the second Soviet occupation begins, I don't want anything to do with that park. It's used to bury Russian soldiers and is full of red wooden pillars with red stars on them. No one risks going up the stairs in the evening or, during the day, visiting the once pleasant but now trashed public toilet. The entrance door in the Purickis building can no longer be locked, and in place of doorbell buttons gape open holes bristling with stiff wires. In the writer Vaižgantas' house, through whose open front door you used to see a large mirror, now glint a few remaining shards.

The only cow which my grandparents brought with them from the farm, we don't keep for very long. We don't have anything to feed her, and it's too cold for her in the winter in our improvised cow shed. Anfisa, a woman of indeterminate age from devastated Belarus who came to live on our street, buys our cow. Never in her life has she seen such a fine cow, and that's why she sells us milk cheaper than any of the other neighbors. And in all of my life, I've never seen a woman with such bowed legs. From crotch to heel her legs were almost a perfect O. She loves the cow and puts her up in her apartment, in a side room. In the fantastical plans of architect Frykas, there were some apartments with rooms you could enter directly from outside, without steps. Here they live together—Anfisa right on the parquet floor, the cow on some straw so she won't slip.

•

...Love arrives unexpectedly. It finds me in a most unromantic place—in the Kaunas sports arena. On the basketball court. Here a band of our school's girls, playing truant, spend hour upon hour under the baskets. We collect a few rubles, pay the arena guard, he unlocks the door and we can stay as long as we wish. And boys come, too. From other schools. I'm not interested in them. I have a kind of abstract ideal, Algis N., whom I don't know, and whom I never did meet. In those days, a famous runner, swarthy, with short curly hair, black eyes, he was the secret object of my awakening desires. So that no one would know who he was, I made up a name for him—Nadis. I start writing poems inscribed with the secret letter N. I shed tears over Ivan Turgenev's *First Love* and Antanas Vaičiulaitis' *Valentina*[1].

---

[1] Antanas Vaičiulaitis (1906-1992) was one of Lithuania's most prominent modernist writers. His novel *Valentina* was published in 1936.

After many years, while working in radio, I met Antanas Vaičiulaitis. Somehow, I'd never expected to meet this writer. Writers on the other side of the Iron Curtain seemed to us on this side as if dead—whether they were alive or not. At the artist Vytautas Valius' apartment, I was introduced to an elegant, slim gentleman with a hand-kerchief in his jacket's breast pocket.

—Your *Valentina,* in my youth...—I began, and some-thing squeezed up my throat.

I think that Mr. Vaičiulaitis had heard words like that before and he understood me. How wonderful that he was still alive when Lithuania regained its independence. In 1992 I wrote an "*in memoriam*" for the radio, into which I put all my respect for him and my own longing for youthful days. I'd even received two letters from him wishing me the best.

•

And so, came the time for first love.

Resting on the seats in the sports hall, I raise my head. Under the basket I see a boy with a basketball in his hands. He jumps up and shoots the ball into the basket. At that moment Cupid awakens and without even rubbing his eyes lets loose an arrow. Anywhere. At random. What's it to him... The boy shoots the ball, catches it, and will shoot it again. He has no idea about any Cupid. What's all this nonsense? The boy's not very tall, dark complexioned, with wavy dark chestnut hair, dressed in black sweats.

—Who is he?—I ask my friends, suddenly realizing he is THE ONE.

High School basketball team—Rah!

185

—He's our schoolmate Liodzė's brother,—says one.

—A terrible hooligan,—explains another.

—He's from the "Tractor" gang. Don't start up with him,—whispers a third in my ear.

But it's already too late for me.

He walks toward us, cocky, with his own individual swinging gait. As if the ground under him was swaying. He doesn't smile, but in his brown eyes there's a mischievous gleam.

Guardian angel of mine, you've saved me from many a calamity. Why then did you not save me from this love?

Those boys of Kaunas' Žaliakalnis (Green Hill) after the war! They were mostly the sons of laborers—poorly dressed, not that well fed, not too educated. Many of them were too much hooked on that most readily available pleasure of the times—vodka, and they failed to develop their talents and remained as unskilled workers.

Not rude, just crude; not cynical, just rough around the edges; not debauched, just proud of their manhood—madcap, unable to contain their own youthfulness. Almost all of them play sports, some play music. A good portion throw themselves into politics, but the State quickly reins them in: some to jail, some to silence, their mouths closed for the duration of their lives, some with the badge of the Young Communist Union.

Neither their parents nor they themselves ride around in cars or on motorcycles, nor frequent fancy restaurants, just dark shabby cafes. Of all the forms of art, they acknowledge only film. And maybe also the then popular Kaunas operetta.

—Silva, you don't love me,—Vytautas Rimkevičius belts out on stage, the best-loved operetta actor in Kaunas at that time.

—Silva, you don't love me,—sings my newly-met friend when I tell him my name—the one I use at school, not at home. And without blinking I swallow the first banality I hear from him.

—Zenka, they call me,—he says.—Short for Zenonas.

And in an eye-blink that name becomes the most beautiful one in the world. The mystical letter N falls over on its side and becomes a Z. Before too long it's throughout all my school notes, my books, on the school desk I sit at in class. The aura of my first love wraps itself around that letter. And around me. And around my home. But there it meets a cold unfriendliness, even a disapproving resistance. It's never said out loud, but I understand that I'll never be able to invite him to my home. Only the poets support me. Especially Salomėja.

> *The first song of spring I give to you,*
> *Beneath your feet may violets bloom.*
> *Through spring winds fly with me this day,*
> *Through aromas bursting along the way.*

And I, too:

> *I'm just a young maiden*
> *With only a single heart.*
> *I give to you that heart,*
> *In hopes we'll never part.*

...Why after several decades do I sadly touch that barely standing Fričas' garden fence on the corner of Frykas and Vaižgantas Streets? That fence, which is now long gone. And from behind which the smell of manure no longer reeks, nor the husky dog's bark, nor Mrs. Fričienė's hoarse tobacco voice. To put it most simply—it's just NO LONGER THERE. But it stood for a long time, propped up by sticks on both sides. It stood for a long time...

Back then, the fence-which-no-longer-is, held its breath and marveled at those two young persons. One was already sixteen, the other just about to be. It's May. Night. Probably without a moon.

First kiss.

—I'm so big and heavy,—I say, just to have something to say.

—I wish you were as light as an angel. But this is fine, too,—he says, just to say something, too.

And kisses my hand. On the wrist.

Is there anyone who doesn't know that you can run and not have your feet touch the ground? I return home. For three days I don't wash my hand. I have a secret. But it blooms in my face. My grades at school plummet catastrophically. Who cares, though? My report card has sprung up with "twos."[2] My talents, real and alleged, developed or not, all wither. I drown in love poetry and in aphorisms about love. I fill my notebooks with them. I trust in the sacredness of what is written, black on white. And many interesting things have been written.

> *Can the heart ever run out of love songs?*

---

[2] "twos"—Lithuanian schools used a numerical grading scale of 1-5, where "2" is unsatisfactory.

A 16-year-old girl and F. Schiller thought not.

—It can,—say I today, bluntly. And perhaps a little less cynically:—Perhaps love wouldn't wound young people so badly, if they had someone to lean on.

I often wonder and cannot understand, how it can be possible to love someone other than you?

The writer Aleksandr Kuprin's character, Sulamita, from the story of the same name, and I thought that it was not possible.

—Of course not—I grin to myself treasonously.—I had many admirers then. Some who were much more gallant than that Green Hill hooligan.

In our youth how little we know about those whom we love the most. But we think we know all. How easily we re-classify their vices into virtues. How frivolously we miss listening to that which we need to hear. How readily we let silly banalities pass through our ears. Or we hope that our love will change the one we love. But not necessarily at all the one who loves.

In our high school, the large hall is called Recreation Hall. It's very grand: on the left and right, huge windows reaching to the ceiling, at one end a spacious stage, and light-colored parquet flooring throughout. On Saturdays, we dance here. And so that those dances would serve a useful purpose, beforehand there would be some sort of an artistic program, and before that a lecture. No one really listens much to those lectures, but the State's representative gets to check a box called "young communist development," and our school's director, "Gangrene" earns one more little plus for a job well done. "Gangrene" didn't like me for asking that question that I wrote about earlier. After the lecture, she summons me to her:

—Go home now. You're being punished. You're forbidden to stay for the dancing. During the lecture you acted without discipline,—she hisses. As always, through her teeth and nose.

I know that arguing is pointless. All of us girls mis-behaved. We chattered, swiveled in our seats, scoffed—such a boring lecture. But why me? Soon...soon the boys' musical band will sit on the stage and play a dreamy tango. Most importantly, HE will come along, and I won't be there. And I won't get to see him. And who will he dance with? He'll dance with other girls. I walk home, barely able to carry—as seen through my eyes then—the terrible burden of pain and injustice. From my shoes, the white tooth-powder flakes off hopelessly. In those days, almost all the

188

girls wore cloth sneakers with rubber soles. There were no others. But after the war, even those poor shoes, the latest word in fashion, were hard to come by. They would quickly become soiled and so before a dance night, we'd carefully whiten them with a paste made of tooth powder and water. Dried out, it blazed brightly and ended up whitening our dance partners' pant-legs. Thankfully, it was easily cleaned off.

My friend Gija, feeling great sympathy for me, sacrifices herself and leaves the Recreation Hall to accompany the luckless one home. "Gangrene" has taught me a good lesson. Long after that, I quail during lectures. Maybe I'm misbehaving somehow, maybe somebody sees me out of the corner of an angry eye, and after the lecture, will come over and say:

—You are punished.

And that somebody will take something from me of great value.

My friend Gija, though she behaves extravagantly, is kind hearted. She promises to get me HIS photograph, and she keeps her word. She sneaks one off HIS sister after finding a pretext to visit their home. And she finds yet another photo at the photographer, P. Karpavičius. This is on the Savanoriu Prospect, where the entirety of Green Hill's youth went to have their pictures taken. I was friends with her for a long time, until some non-youthful gossip separated us for life. I even stole something from her once— when I saw my own postcard with the rose at her place, the postcard I had received before the war from my father. So I didn't really steal, I stole back. But to this day I don't know if stealing back is also a sin.

And why after five decades am I heartbreakingly stroking that blackened fence which is long gone? That's to say, I caress it not with my hands but with my eyes, which still see it clearly. In the same way, after fifty years, my hand strokes the copper plate around the feet of the giant sculpture of St. Stanislav in the master's workshop in Užupis. I know that all three sculptures will soon be put back on the Vilnius Cathedral's roof. Then I'll only be able to touch them with my eyes. But they will really be there. For a long time. But the fence is gone. Not likely anyone remembers it now. So...

Why, memories, do you awaken this night,
Why, hanged men, do you rise from your graves?

189

Jonas Aistis' verse is like a cool palm on a feverish forehead. Then and now. And love today—not the first, but the truest and the last.

Place me like a seal over your heart,
like a seal on your arm;
for love is as strong as death,
its jealousy unyielding as the grave.
It burns like blazing fire,
like a mighty flame.

Many waters cannot quench love;
rivers cannot sweep it away.

Song of Songs 8: 6-7

Students in the Soviet era

S he won't make a good basketball player—says our trainer, Stepas Butautas, at that time a famous sportsman.
—Why not?
—She cares more about boys.
Well, he's talking about me, and it's true. Except not boys, just one particular boy. I leave training because HE invites me to go with him. The trainer is offended and his verdict is later confirmed.

Oh, how I wanted to dress up. Alas, I had only one dress. A blue one, made of itchy half-wool. All my other dresses I'd already outgrown. And here comes the Masked Ball, the New Year's celebration at our school. But I know that at least for one night Cinderella is promised transformation into a stunning princess. Just like her, the one I'd seen in the theater production. The one who'd been gifted with beautiful clothes by her fairy godmother so she could attend the big party dressed in the colors of the sun, moon, and stars. Sparkling with the most precious stones, and silver and gold. With sheer tulle clouds, ruffled and flared sleeves, pinched waist and wide three-layer skirt. I beg my mother to rent me that dress. Trembling, I wait all week long, because the dress is promised for pick up only on the morning of the Masked Ball. That morning, my heart racing, I see my mother off to the theater where the dress waits to be picked up.

—Just don't forget the diadem, and, most importantly, the shoes—I remind her, insistently, as she leaves. Never in my life have I had the chance to wear such silvery, magical shoes.

191

Before long, Mama returns carrying a large package. I'm sizzling with impatience—let's measure and adjust it quickly, let's transform me into a princess right away. I unravel the precious garments—and oh, the horror! My tears spring out immediately as if from a fountain, like those of a clown in the circus ring. A dust-colored fraying dress with some bits of silver paper sewn on to it here and there. Instead of magical moonlight—dirty stains. The ragged lace has long forgotten that it used to be white. Instead of sparkling gems—the cheapest costume jewelry. And the baubles are barely attached, hanging by thin white threads. The diadem—a snarl of wires wrapped in cheap silver paper taken off candy. True, the shoes are tolerable, silver-colored with high heels, but I can barely get my feet into them. I can hardly walk in them, forget about dancing.

Mama and Auntie Prakseda, frightened by my endless heartache hurry to make improvements to that dress. They sew on some tassels left over from making curtains, add some tulle patches, cover the stains with artificial flowers. They fix the diadem onto a straw hat and make it pretty with ribbons.

—How can this be,—I say, still unable to grasp the secrets of the stage.

—The theater is always like that, full of tricks and deceptions,—explains Prakseda.—Maybe you wanted the diamonds to be real, too?

—Don't worry, in the dim lighting it'll be different,—Mama reassures me.—You'll sparkle like a real princess.

And really, I do sparkle! Our Recreation Hall glows in the artificial red twilight. Silver threads glitter on the windows. From the ceilings hang garlands of white and pink apple blossoms. There's the aroma of a real fir-tree, the glimmer of little colored lights. Where are the stains on my dress now! The faux jewelry flashes now like Ali Baba's treasure. Through the cut-out holes in my mask I can see a shimmering fairy land. Beautifying my hands are my mother's pre-war lace gloves, and they're completely without a single tear. It's all just fine, except that the actress who wears these stage clothes is quite a bit thinner than me. In that dress, I can barely take a breath, and those fantastical shoes squeeze my feet as hard as a nutcracker squeezes nuts. I'm ready to faint! But HE must see me LIKE THIS. Truth to say, I don't really know how to walk in high heels. Stepping on my own dress I fly headlong down five steps.

HE sees me in the enchanted half-light of the hall, where the smell of the fir tree and the feeling of dreams coming true linger. The colored little lights glimmer, my fake precious stones sparkle, HIS eyes, so close to mine, dance with mischievous lights. But woe is me! The hooks on my tight-fitting dress, one after another, start popping, unable to hold my trunk-swelling happiness. My feet burn in those tight silver shoes—it feels as if I'm taking my last steps.

I've had enough. That's it. I change into my mother's old black skirt and old pink blouse, and flat not-so-fancy shoes. But I'm just myself again—neither a princess nor Cinderella. Hand in hand he and I run down K. Petrauskas' and then Utenos Street to the Polytechnic School. My skirt and hair fly in the breeze, and even though it's the middle of winter, it's not cold. We make it by midnight, in time to celebrate the New Year with his friends. Here they let you dance longer than in my school under Gangrene's rule. Only as the lights start to wane in the polytechnic's hall do I suddenly remember Cinderella's treasure-trove of clothing left backstage in the school, which this very morning I must return to the theater. Again we run to the school. Now the windows are all dark. It takes forever to find the janitor to unlock the doors. Both of us pick up the scattered precious rags. For a long time we look under benches for the missing silver shoe. I stuff everything into a bag—and only then breathe a sigh of relief:

—Thank God, it wasn't lost...

Our sextet—friends forever

—What happened then?—ask those who like a spicy love story.

Lots happened. But joy, not so much. There was endless pursuing and fleeing, and vice versa. There was revenge, misunderstanding, sulking, pretending, "infidelity," rivers of tears, mountains of hope, files of bad marks, youthful pranks and entirely unyouthful suffering which even today I can't laugh off.

—I'm leaving,—I say to HIM in the polytechnic's hallway.

—When will you be back? —HE asks.

—Never,—say I, filled with self-pity.

In truth, I never did return to Kaunas. We moved to Vilnius. Why was I so unmercifully uprooted from my own environment when less than a half-year remained before my final exams? Was I supposed to be able to adjust myself so quickly to the elite S. Nėris school where the daughters of high Soviet officials studied—and, for balance, the daughters of the most common of the working class? But I was looked after by our class teacher and mathematician Madam Kaunaitė.

My dearest friend from Kaunas, Rena, wrote me long and detailed letters. But above all, I waited for a letter from HIM. I had written, so he did have my address. Why no letter? So long a time... At least it was my good fortune that in the autumn my friends Rena, Alda, and Irena would be coming to Vilnius to study. Somehow I'll get through it.

I was fascinated with Vilnius right away, but it took a while to fall in love with the city. My roots dried out as they blindly wandered in the unfriendly soil, but finally I made my home here. It was not my fortune to be able to open the doors of Vilnius University, or of the Art Academy. That was to be done by my children three decades later. During my time, the study of English at Vilnius University had been discontinued. I could only dream about Art—in our family artists were seen as freeloaders, drunkards, and profligates. By the way, much later our lodger, an artist, would stun Mrs. Milda with her comment on the much cried about fragile Violetta of "La Traviata":

—And what is she after all, this "La Traviata" of yours? La whore, if you'll excuse me.

So only one decent Vilnius academic establishment was left for me—the Vilnius Pedagogical Institute. It was under the leadership of the literary critic and scholar Marcelinas Ročka, a man of feeble character, who gave over the entire reins of management to an angry little man by the name of

194

Ariskin, who had found his way here from Soviet Russia. I have to be true to myself in saying that a portion of its instructors and even professors were neither intelligent nor very highly educated.

•

In Vilnius we settled on Didžioji Street, in the former chambers of the hetmen and noblemen of the Grand Duchy of Lithuania, the Chodkewicz family. Now the estate has been restored, changed into an art museum. In 1600 a wedding was supposed to have taken place there between Chodkewicz's protégée the princess of Sluck, Sofija Olelkaitė and the nobleman Jonušas Radvila. The nobles for some reason fell out with each other. Small armies gathered between the Chodkewicz and Radvila palaces not too far away, and soon a real battle was brewing. It's hard to imagine that in this peaceful yard once stood hundreds of armed foot soldiers and even cavalrymen.

I'm waiting for a letter. I dream, I read Knut Hamsun's *Viktoria* and *Hunger*.

At that time, in the early fifties, in the same building there was also a pharmacy and a polyclinic, along with apartments for University of Vilnius professors and employees. In the large shady yard, in the evenings an old mustachioed Pole would come and play his violin until some of the kind-hearted professors' wives would bring him a ruble or two. In the enclosed yard the echoing of those violin concerts was very pleasing. Outside the window large poplars murmured, while on the window ledges pigeons cooed. Here dwelt the spirit of Lev Karsavin, professor of philosophy, repressed and exiled to Siberia by the communists where he died in 1952. Still evident, too, were traces of the thinker Vasili Sezeman. *The Soviet Lithuanian Encyclopedia* contains the following lines about him:

> During 1940-50 and 1958-63 he lectured at
> Vilnius University in gnosiology, the history of
> philosophy, logic, aesthetics, psychology,
> pedagogy, and various other subjects.

Only nothing is written about where the professor was between 1950 and 1958. Some time after the the country regained its independence, I saw a map of the former Russian Empire, or the USSR, which had marked on it the places where Lithuanian exiles had been sent. Immediately I thought: what a vast number of places there were! For such a tiny patch that Lithuania is on the map! Could all those places ever be visited, described? In a hundred years who will be here to feel the pain of those old wounds?

I sit on the wide window sill of the Chodkewicz apartment and wait for a letter. And it doesn't come, and it doesn't come.

Throughout Vilnius old Polish ladies, born in the nineteenth century, still walked around, dressed in black hats faded grey over time, draped in long coats, and wearing scrupulously darned black lace gloves. After the old ladies died out, the secondhand stores started displaying tables inlaid with ivory, old carved wobbly cupboards, mahogany chests of drawers with dim mirrors and many small drawers. The old ladies' heirs quickly went about selling off their unwanted inheritances. At rock bottom prices they put up for sale their red velvet-lined little boxes, their pictures of melancholy landscapes in gold-plated frames. The inheritors hurried to paint their apartment walls in the then fashionable geometric figures and broken straight lines, furnished them with knee-high, thin-legged tables and desperately tried to acquire a modern radio apparatus made in Latvia.

The vintage objects, willingly bought by folks with an artistic disposition, emit bitterly nostalgic waves. Undoubtedly at night they look around with yellowed eyes at the new and strange world. But the old world is still near by. In the room where I sleep stands an unusual tall, rounded stove. Not made of tile, but of iron, and painted. Many years ago in this part of the house stood the Chodkewicz family's chapel. I wonder what the princess Sofija, kneeling here, prayed to God for? Was she waiting for a letter from Jonušas Radvila, was she happy that an army gathered to defend her?

I wait for a letter.

•

Back in Kaunas, in our school, assigned to design a stand with our class motto, I wrote down a youthful slogan without the slightest sense of propaganda: *"Visada pirmyn!"* "Always forward!" In my childhood I had read the phrase in a book about Mickey Mouse. When she saw it, head-master Gangrene hissed contemptuously and ordered it be removed, and I became one with an anti-Soviet mentality. Later, when I was studying at the Pedagogical Institute, I dared to critique the design of a poster. Just the design. The poster proclaimed that the Komsomol's spirit was unbreakable. I was ratted out to the Administration as one who was intent on breaking that spirit. And I became known as a cosmopolitan, in those days a popular curse word.

—Join the Communist Youth Union,—peremptorily urges the secretary of the Union.—You'll end up with a better job.

Back then, after graduation, work assignments were compulsory and were made based on "merit."

—I'll get one without your Union,—I jab back at him.

He no longer urges. And so I become hopelessly and irretrievably anti-Soviet, i.e. an inferior person. No doubt, during the state exam I was singled out for failure. Stepping into the examination auditorium I see an unfamiliar Russian woman sitting at the head desk. She's in charge of the exam on Marxism-Leninism; she's wearing black high heels and white socks. I see those socks and an inexplicable gut feeling tells me it's going to be bad. After many years, during the very heat of regaining our independence, a person wearing the tri-colors in place of a necktie, also seems to me suspect. After another ten years he now rallies against his own nation—with a brick in his hand.

And at that time, they gave me a "3," a humiliating "Pass" on the exam. You see, I didn't know how Stalin had named the Eastern European Parties (communist, of course) before his death. How could I expect to get a good job, me of little learning, unarmed with the world's most advanced teaching?

I was assigned to the small town of Josvainiai, but luckily circumstances changed and I didn't need to go there after all. I think I might have been a fair teacher. But I became a journalist and a translator. The mask forced on me in the Institute had already grown attached to my face and it didn't bother me. But tearing it off and throwing it away was not easy at all. Maybe those small-time communist party chiefs who now cross themselves in the Cathedral and claim to have secretly baptized their children back then also wore masks. But us they publicly condemned for that and fired us from our jobs, if not worse. Those who were responsible, as always, can't be found. But every mask leaves its mark; even if only a faint line, it's an indelible mark. Like on my foot, squeezed too tightly by the silver shoe. Alas, the shoe did not fit. I had to remain Cinderella, the little ash girl.

And as if that weren't enough, there were still four decades of masquerading left to live through.

Well, and what about the letter? Then, fifty years ago, did I really not get it?

197

All my life I've been afraid of cellars. Even now I won't go into the most pleasantly appointed cellar, not for anything. It surprises me how people, going out for a drink, are willing to climb down into deep, stone-walled underground bars even if those walls are decorated with contemporary fixtures. Deep, too, with thick stone walls was that cellar at the Chodkewicz apartments. Steep, narrow stairs descended into it, disappearing into the darkness.

—Stay at the top of the stairs and wait for me. You can help me bring the potatoes up,—says Mama. Then she calls from half-way down the stairs:—I've forgotten the keys. Run up to the apartment. The keys are in my black handbag in the hallway.

I run upstairs, and probably for the first time unclasp Mama's handbag. It smells of powder and lotion. There's a little notebook, a comb, lipstick. The keys. Some bills. From the notebook sticks out a four-folded piece of paper. The writing on the paper draws me like a magnet. I unfold it. A letter! My name at the beginning, HIS—at the end. There's no date. I already knew what blows to the heart were. I'd received one earlier from the priest in Kaunas. The second was now. Much more painful. Delivered by the closest person to me—Mama. Lies. Falsehood. Trickery. There's no envelope. Everything's over.

...I have no one near and dear anymore. I lie on the sofa without feeling or tears. My Mama betrayed me. The mask on my face sticks even tighter to my skin. It will take me a long time to learn to distinguish what's honest, what's not. What to wait for, what not. Whom to love, whom not.

I lie awake, I am like a lonely bird on the housetop.

My days are like an evening shadow;
I wither away like grass.

Psalm 102: 7, 11

198

25
Eloi, Eloi, lema sabachtani

That's in the Aramaic language, and in Lithuanian it would be *"Mano Dieve, mano Dieve, kodel mane apleidai?"* ("My God, my God, why have you forsaken me?"). Those suffering words of Jesus from the cross are testified to by two of the four evangelists. Would it be sacrilegious of me to utter them in a moment of weakness and despair?

Easter after the war is hungry and awkward. The Church of St. Michael the Archangel called simply the Garrison is full to the limit. People are kneeling, heads bowed. My knees start to bend, I want to kneel like all the others, but next to me Mama continues to stand. Not only does she not strike her breast with her fist during the consecration, she doesn't even bow her head. And seeing her from the corner of my eye, I don't bow mine either. The two of us stick up above all those bowed heads like unwanted stakes in an empty meadow. Stakes with nothing to be tied to them. I'm embarrassed to stand out like that, but I stand out.

> Let us, all Christians, fall to our knees,
> Greatly hungering for God's grace...

The two of us don't fall to ours. But aren't we also hungry? Are we being unfairly punished? Perhaps we're the kind of sinners who cannot be forgiven?

After Mass, as people are leaving through the doors, the organist gives full rein to his emotions—the pipes thunder so loudly you wonder if the walls will contain the sound. Loudly the notes crawl one upon the other, growing one out of the other, eclipsing one another. The stronger storm and overtake the weaker, but they don't give in and grow again, turn into an unconquerable *fortissimo*. And now again followed by another *forte...*

Šunskai parrish priest Vincentas Ambraziejus, who saved Dita from the Nazis by giving her a new birth certificate in a different name

It's good to go out into the sunshine of Freedom Avenue. But the sounds still stirring in my imagination overshadow confidence in God.

Mama stops going to church. I also feel somewhat abandoned by God. I don't go for a while. Later, I go again. It'll be even worse if I'm abandoned completely, I reason to myself.

On the other side of the wooden confessional screen, the Kaunas' priest's glasses flash scarily. That priest—he's a writer, a friend of young people, and an expert of the soul. So he'll understand this 15-year-old sinner, who has come to acknowledge that she hasn't been to confession for almost a year, that in fact she has strong doubts about God's existence. The 15-year-old comes to tell these primitive concerns to a mediator, not knowing they could be spoken directly to the Addressee.

After listening to the sinner, the old priest, glasses flashing again, asks her:

—Have you been promiscuous?

—No,—the 15-year-old whispers, barley audibly, and it's true.

If she'd had any courage, she'd have said:

—Excuse me, but what does that word mean?

In those days, girls took a little longer to understand what was what.

The fifteen-year-old feels humiliated and hurt. As never before in her life. Automatically, she mumbles her assigned penance—ten Hail Marys—and leaves the church. In her daily journal an entry shows up that she couldn't care less about the Archangel Michael decked out in the bright garb of a Roman warrior. That she fears him not in the least. That his image above the central altar is an ordinary artifice of paint and brush. Let him now flash his eyes at that empty space where once stood that girl with her unfounded promiscuity and her romantic love.

Of course, she'll return here, but not for a very long time.

The Sovietized schools were just looking for those kind of malcontents. Potential atheists. Ones unexperienced in God's love. Ones who feared not even the devil. All the more because there was someone nearby to compare oneself to. Like a magnet, the most outstanding atheist in our class, Irena K., fully two heads taller than the rest, drew us to her. An intellectual, as you'd say now. We've been friends up to today. Could I have then imagined that this great anti-religionist would today be on her knees by the Gates of Dawn altar rail? That she would with tears in her eyes pray for relief from her spirit's afflictions?

Back then, the beginning of my unsuccessful search for God was broken off for many a year. But maybe I still went in His direction all those years somehow. Maybe I'll never arrive but always move toward. Is that not enough? I don't believe those who claim they have found Him.

Kaunas' Garrison church of Greek Byzantine style stands out with its five rounded cupolas on Freedom Avenue. The Soviet authority changed it into a museum of stained glass and sculpture. Until the new independence, the Monument of Freedom by J. Zikaras[1] from the garden of the War Museum, was kept there safely. That holy house was built by the Orthodox in the last decade of the 19th century with the belief that this was Russia and all the Catholics here would convert to Orthodoxy. And that all the Kaunites would begin to speak Russian, even the un-baptized Jews, Christ's slayers.

—But Christ was himself a Jew,—I tried to reason with a local bigot.

---

[1] Juozas Zikaras (1881 – 1944), sculptor and professor.

Instead of acknowledging this truth, the woman pro-claimed her own: Jews bake matzos with the blood of Christians—they hang some abducted child in their closet and drip blood from it, collecting it until they have a bowlful. Then they mix it into the dough, bake it, and savor eating it. Having listened to this horrific storytelling, from which my hair was supposed to stand on end, I inquired:

—So why aren't matzos red?

—You poor, uneducated girl,—said the bigot, ending the discussion.

That woman hadn't read a single word of the Scriptures. Just as I hadn't, by the way.

Back then, I didn't know that you could only understand as much as your education and experience allowed. You can't go beyond the boundaries of your comprehension.

•

—Where shall we meet?—says Emanuel's voice from over a thousand kilometers away over the telephone line. Here, now, at the beginning of the third millennium.

—By the Garrison Church, of course. Opposite the main door,—I reply.

—OK,—Emanuel immediately agrees, as if he'd been there just the other day.

Indeed, we recognized each other right away by the church, as if we had seen each other just yesterday. It was the very middle of summer. Thunder claps echoed, warm rain washed the stones of Freedom Avenue. Our parents' and grandparents' footprints were there, not very deep under the surface. In Kaunas, the city of childhood, youth, old age, and death.

—I'll not return here again,—said Emanuel in a steady and hard voice.

He had just been to see Kaunas' Ninth Fort and the remains of the ghetto in Vilijampolė, and had found the house from which he and his mother had miraculously escaped in 1943.

The whole tribe, over the centuries, had taken the path from Padua, to Venice, to Berlin, to Krakow, to Lithuania, to Vilkaviškis... As Emanuel tells it, this was his mother's family's path. His great-grandparents on his father's side had for some time lived within the triangle made by Panevėžys, Kupiškis, and Anykščiai in the town of Subačius. (They say their surname came from that town). Later they moved to Panevėžys, and took up the hat-making business. Their kids were educated in Kaunas, later becoming citizens of independent Lithuania. The men served in the Lithuanian army.

Ultimately, almost all of them perished in the Kaunas ghetto.

—I'll come again,—he said on another day, when it was time to say our goodbyes. His voice was gentle and trembled.

...A relief of the Holy City, beaten out of metal, brought to me as a gift, shines silvery on the wall. Little by little it changes—the silver tarnishes, and the town's cupolas and the houses gleam golden. As if bathed in sunlight. That gold is of various tints. In places I seem to see faded blood stains.

I begin to question whether my eyes still see well. Whether my ears hear. Whether my soul is now free. Whether my heart is not deceived.

•

In the 1950's, at my uncle Vincas' place, I saw a translation of the Bible done by the archbishop Juozas Skvireckas. I fell on it, reading and later writing down sections from the Book of Wisdom; I copied the Song of Songs in its entirety.

His left hand is under my head,
and his right hand does embrace me.

I remember the archbishop's commentary on these lines: "Christ lovingly supports his Church." The contemporary translator, prelate and professor A. Rubšys, makes no individual commentary on each of the Songs but, overall, sees in them God's love for his people. And he also says, "the poem is not an allegory where every word of the lovers' conversation has a symbolic meaning. The entirety of the Song of Songs is a metaphor for the true meaning of mutual love."

In the pages of the Holy Book, the handsome king Solomon with his Assyrian corded beard passionately confesses a not so platonic love.

His left—under my head,
With his right he embraces me.
                              (S. Geda's version)

It's difficult to say it any other way. That time the wise King Solomon brought a lot of doubt into my head, further messing up my already disheveled thoughts.

*I said in my heart, "Concerning the condition of
the sons of men, God tests them, that they may
see that they themselves are like animals." For
what happens to the sons of men also happens
to animals; one thing befalls them: as one dies,
so dies the other. Surely, they all have one
breath; man has no advantage over animals, for
all is vanity. All go to one place: all are from the
dust, and all return to dust. Who knows the
spirit of the sons of men, which goes upward,
and the spirit of the animal, which goes down to
the earth?- So I perceived that nothing is better
than that a man should rejoice in his own
works, for that is his heritage. For who can bring
him to see what will happen after him?*

Ecclesiastes 3:18-22

●

After the war, I look for answers and explanations in the
literary works published by the State press—Pushkin's and
Lermontov's poetry and prose, Chekov's and Dostoevsky's
works. Those books, with soft covers published on cheap
blotter-like paper, urged me to think. But there weren't
many of them. The genuine culture's stream was rather
narrow, like an artery surrounded by bloated Soviet
Russian cultural veins. The school encouraged us in all
sorts of ways to admire N. Ostrovsky's fanaticism in his
novel *How the Steel Was Tempered.*

Acting schizophrenically, the music teacher, whose
name I don't remember, divided our entire music course
into questions and answers. What is a scale? What is a
flat? What is a ... etc. The questions were numbered, and
instead of reading the questions, the teacher would refer to
them only by number and would require a lightning-fast
response. The answers were to be given not only word for
word, but letter for letter. Oh how he crackled with anger if
you modified a word in your answer! And it wasn't easy for
him to work in those days—there was no ideology in the
treble clef, or the five lines of the staff. It was even more
difficult for teachers of literature, who also tried to contain
their literary interpretations within acceptable boundaries.
They were terribly afraid of making a mistake.

The only one who wasn't afraid was the Russian-
language teacher, Banevičius. If I'm not mistaken he was
no Banevičius at all but a high-born white guard, brought

204

from Soviet Russia by our famous writer V. Krėvė in order to save his life. Banevičius idolized Pushkin and was impossibly happy when he would hear Alina K. declaim:

I remember the fascinating moment...

But in Russian, of course.

The teacher was fascinated by all of it simultaneously—Pushkin's passion, the sweet voice of Alina, her moist lips like petals... the eternal vision of love. He gave Alina the highest marks, compensating for her hopelessness with grammar.

Perhaps behind the young girl's downcast, trembling eyelashes he saw his own vanished youth? His own unfulfilled love?

The teacher made no secret of his distaste for how Mayakovsky was glorified in every way. He didn't criticize him for his content, though, just for his form.

—What a hideous word, *gromadyo*. And perhaps *loshadyo*? For centuries the Russian language hasn't known those kinds of words—he complained angrily.

Obsessed with the spirit of contradiction, force-fed with Soviet ideology, the girls in our class were all for Mayakovsky's poems. They would declaim his "My Soviet Passport" with malignant joy. They didn't know that Stalin's glorified poet had shot himself. They didn't know where their teacher Banevičius was soon to disappear to. They couldn't know that after a long illness of the spirit, the delicate Alina would die.

Not long ago I found a yellowed booklet—the 1950/51 school year's final examination questions. For Lithuanian language and literature there are 39 examination papers. Each one contains three parts. The third one—"analyze the sentence" is everywhere the same. So, here's the first paper:

1. Soviet literature—a qualitatively new, higher level of development of Russian and world literature. V. I. Lenin's article "Party Organization and Party Literature."

2. The Social-political and literary activities of N. G. Chernishevski. The new people of N. G. Chernishevski's novel "What to do?" Rachmetov's image.

3. Analyze the sentence.

In those 39 papers, 18 Lithuanian writers are included. Some of them are from earlier times, even Kudirka, but all of them come attached with "lightning rods." For example:

Nationalistic and bourgeois class elements in Kudirka's writings.
Baranauskas' drift away from the people.

The remaining slots are exclusively for Russian writers— Pushkin, Gorky, Fadeyev, Mayakovsky, Gogol, Ostrovsky. In one Chekhov's "Cherry Orchard" is briefly mentioned, with the emphasis on its ideological content. In another— Tolstoy, revealing the Russian people's patriotism in *War and Peace*; and in yet another, Turgenev's novel, *Fathers and Sons*, also with its ideological content emphasized. Of Dostoevsky, not a breath.

From before the war remained the philosopher Friedrich Nietzsche's book, *Thus Spoke Zarathustra*. Nietzsche, slandered by Soviet academics with a supposed connection to Hitler's ideology, would have been someone for me to take a taste of. But I rejected him because of that Nazi association. And also because through Zarathustra's lips he called woman a cow. Not feeling like a cow, and not wanting to be one, I remained completely empty—without God, without any kind of necessary spiritual food for the soul.

Back then I had no idea of the old Hindu hymn from two-and-a-half-thousand years ago. About the efforts to seek enlightenment here and to reach it on the other side. And to stay forever.

Just as a person throws away old clothes
and puts on new ones,
the Soul gives up the old and useless body,
and takes on a new one.

Bhagavad Gita: Ch 2, verse 22

In the children's kindergarten where Aunt Terese worked after the war they also weeded out all sorts of religious manifestations. During holidays and celebrations, hiding beneath some sheets, the educators would spill handfuls of candies over the children's heads. The head teacher would then ask the overjoyed kids:

—Children, from where are these candies?

And having not received from the yet politically unconscious citizens the proper answer, answered her own question for them:

—From Papa Stalin, the friend of all children.

206

They fired Teresė from the nursery, because she was not overjoyed with the "sweet life" in Soviet Lithuania, like those kids.

The apathetic history teacher, placing one of three USSR history tomes on the table, would read out loud every third sentence. Our job was to carefully underline those sentences and use them to learn the lesson. That is, learn it for the moment, spill it out like unwanted crumbs from a paper sack (here's your lesson) and deeply forget it. We had to wait for a long time before J. Marcinkevičius[2] wrote his fateful dramas, before J. Glinskis' play "Priests' Penitentiary" would ring out with "Let Us Fall to Our Knees." It would ring out completely differently than it did then just after the war in the Kaunas church.

•

...A full crowd of people in the Vilnius Cathedral can see the glowing silvery head of Monsignor Kazimieras Vasiliauskas. Of short stature, he walks quickly (not to be disrespectful: he flits around the temple half-running) such that from a distance you shouldn't be able to see him. But it's just the opposite—the white head of the Monsignor seems to float well above everyone else and is quite visible.

The small is not always necessarily smaller than the large.

The Cathedral seems slightly colder when the Monsignor's no longer there. Sometimes it feels quite indifferent to me.

I don't deserve it, but...

> *Why dost thou hold back thy hand, why dost thou keep thy right hand in thy bosom?*
>
> Psalm 74: 11

> *Call unto me, and I will answer thee, and show thee great and mighty things, which thou knowest not.*
>
> Jeremiah 33: 3

---

2 J. Marcinkevičius (1930-2011) a famous Lithuanian writer whose works were vital in arousing dreams of independence under the Soviet occupation.

St. Francis preaching to the birds — Giotto (1299)

No need to be startled or indignant. I'm just paying tribute to a trend of the beginning of the third millennium. From shit, today, it's possible even to create art. Recently a witty journalist, by analogy with cabinet makers and potters, tentatively named those artists who create things from shit, as "shitters." Speaking with her, an art critic assured her that the so-named artists wouldn't mind the name, that their main intent is to shock the viewer. And they reach that goal. The viewers are indeed shocked. But perhaps not all.

In the middle of the dark ages, the genius Giotto would more than likely have been talented enough to depict noble personages in his paintings, seated on toilets of the time. How he would have shocked everyone. But it seems, his talent didn't allow that. Since talent requires one to place a word, an object, or a stroke of paint where it's most appropriate for it to be. It's simple, as is everything that is genius.

•

At the beginning of the '70s, my friend, the poet Pranas (God bless his soul) invited me on a hunt for wood grouse. Deeply in love with the forests of Aukštaitija and all that they contained, Pranas offered to show me in person what a wood grouse is and what a miracle of God his mating call is. To hear that call you have to already be hidden in the deep forest by dawn and have found the place where that loner lives—that large, sullen, and very shy bird. And he has something to be shy about—over the last century wood grouse have become one of the rarer birds. Finding the

208

place where the voracious wood grouse feeds is not too difficult. Cramming himself with pine needles, the wood grouse excretes frequently and abundantly—under his favorite trees you can find green piles of little dry sausages, reminiscent of those Georgian bay leaf granules that used to be for sale.

We're already in the pre-dawn darkness of the forest, a time that's supposed to be scary. Supposed to be, if not for the exultant cries of some strange bird that are like the first chords, calling forth a triumphant fall of voices to come a little later, at sunrise.

Nearby curves the wild little river Uosupys; in confluence with the Ūla, it embraces the village of Pauosupis. You can't say the village has been forgotten by God and humankind—sometimes, from the city (ten kilometers by forest path from the nearest railway station), the most adventurous of fishermen venture here. They cast fly-baited lines into the hidden dark recesses for the trout and fish for the grayling leaping in the clear waters. In those days, the waters of the Žeimena and her tributaries were pure. Fishermen from the intelligentsia used to call the trout a "forelle," and our sharp-tongued satirist, Albinas Žukauskas, wrote a biting poem, thus called "Forelles."

> *I see her on the footbridge,*
> *She's doing the washing.*
> *Most politely,*
> *As befits an intellectual,*
> *I speak to her:*
> *"Good day, dear lady."*
> *I ask her:*
> *"Where around here*
> > *do the forelles reside?"*
>
> *The woman raises her head—*
> *She's a little old, but still good looking,*
> *Her knees are round as turnips,—*
> *She thinks about it a bit,*
> *And says:*
> *"They used to live here but no longer.*
> *They came for a week, drank up*
> *And left."*
>
> *"Ha!"—I think to myself—*
> *"Peasants!*
> *She doesn't get what the*
> *Forelles are!"*
>
> *Hard for the intelligentsia to penetrate*
> *These duckweed-covered nooks.*

209

And so we steal along as the dawn appears. I look as I've been told, not at the branches of the pine tree but at the ground, probably I'll see one of those hastily digested and quickly ejected little leavings piles.

—Wood grouse shit!—suddenly in a whisper from Pranas' full voice. Loudly quiet.

Neither before nor after, have I heard a more inspired, a greater sacred sentence—containing in it fascination, love, the hunter's primitive passion, the poet's inspiration. I believe that in that second there was nothing more holy and beautiful in the world than that little greenish pile of droppings.

And there is the wood grouse. Large and black in the cool light of the sunrise. His thick neck stretched upward, his wings spread out and downward. You can get closer to him only in that instant when he stops his ticking song and starts that strange sizzling sound, which lasts about three seconds. For those three seconds, the wood grouse is truly deaf. The hunter can stride forward a few steps without scaring him off. Then he has to wait again, until the bird repeats his song's verse.

In the beginning of April, the snow in the forest has only recently melted. The awakening earth smells elemental. Thank you, Pranas, for not shooting the wood grouse in the middle of his love song. Even though you had a license, and permission to fire a real shotgun. Was that a tribute you paid to God's blessing on all sentient beings?

•

—Why does a person need a belly-button?—asks my seven year old granddaughter, having discovered the strange little indentation in the middle of her body.

—Now it's not needed at all.

The umbilical cord, once a simple organic tube, has now moved into the metaphysical domain and is securely connected to those who are loved and will be loved. Inhumanly plastic, that umbilical cord stretches hundreds of kilometers when my daughter moves to London. And the stretching is so uncomfortable. But I have to be reconciled with that, since I know I can't just go to the ticket office and say:

—London. At 1:00 p.m.

Fifteen years ago a train with "Kaliningrad" written on it rattled out of Vilnius station with my son aboard, in the direction of a heavily armed area (former East Prussia occupied by the Soviets). The umbilical chord stretches westward, my eyes following the blunt backside of the last carriage. With my hand I cover my mouth, since, as in

Munk's lithograph, a scream is about to gush out of me. I stifle it. I know that a wailing woman on a railway platform would be pathetic, or even not right in her head. That time my daughter was with me so my pain was halved.

Later, the umbilical chord stretched to the east, but not too far—only fifty kilometers. And again the blunt backside of the last carriage, which I follow with a superstitious gaze until I lose sight of it. But I can go up to the ticket window and say:

—Pabradė. At 1:30 p.m.

On the banks of the Žeimena River, there's an army unit. Here we make the acquaintance of the unit's commander, Vadim Aleksandrovich Bogach. The colonel gets into his snazzy (for those times) ZIL, the only one in the small town of Pabradė, perhaps the only one in the entire Švenčionys region. He orders us to wait. After 20 minutes he returns, drops off our son, covered in coal dust, and orders him to go and wash.

—I found him at the railroad station. The company had to unload coal from the wagon,—says the colonel,—Do you know what he was doing?—he asks looking at me and Paulius with round and astonished eyes. And without waiting for us, answers himself:—He was working.

Paulius and I both sigh with relief.

For such good behavior, the colonel lets our son return home for a two-day leave.

And after those two days, again the rear of the last carriage. Again the stretched-out umbilical chord.

So what was I then? What am I today? A little worm who has managed to crawl out of the years' meat grinder and put on a bit of weight? Or maybe I'm a well-off lady who's raised and educated two children? Someone with a beloved and loving husband? But someone slow to get oriented— hence one who never wanted to drive a car. Someone who's collected a large library, the largest portion of which is no longer needed.

Maybe I am an old woman who's lived out her life in vain, sitting by a broken washtub. No, no, not by a washtub, but by a tree stump in Kaunas, on Vaižgantas Street, between houses 12 and 14. Now, because of the changes in numbering, between 14 and 16. In number 16 at one time lived the Bank of Lithuania's senior accountant, Bronius Miniotas, and his wife. His wife Elzė was beautiful as a Madonna. She gave birth to four little boys, had a nanny and a cook, a two-story house and a spacious lot. Throughout that yard and house, two little boys of my own age rampaged—Aloyzas and Ignas, lovingly called Aliukas

and Ignelis by their mother. Later, two others showed up—
Broniukas and Juozelis. As Madonna-like as the lady was,
she had something boyish about her. To me it explained
why she gave birth only to boys. Then came the years of
great change. Mr. Miniotas died during the years of German
occupation. Elzė remained alone with the boys, chased out
of her home by the Bolsheviks. She struggled terribly. In
the end she did give birth to a girl. And she died aged 46,
leaving behind five orphans. From among them, three
remain today. My news is scanty about these dear friends
with whom I spent many pleasant hours in their bedrooms
with their white beds, in their wood-smelling shed or
among raspberry shrubs steamy with damp earth. Everything was transformed by the occupations. Much later,
Ignelis became famous as the captain of the yacht *Lietuva*
that sailed across the Atlantic. Juozelis, of course, wouldn't
remember me. Nor Broniukas, if he were still alive. And
Ignelis, only with difficulty. Maybe only Aliukas.

But the two of them did remember. The miracle of the
telephone brought those same voices, heard over six decades ago. Ignas, truth to say, needed a few seconds to
think. Aliukas remembered right away and said words that
I am grateful for—better late than never.

In Juozas' home, I saw the symbol of Elzė's great
generosity—Israel's recognition of her as Righteous Among
the Nations for her saving of Jews.

Back then, when the brothers and I spoke about the
future, they would start like this:
Ignas:
—When we grow up and Dita marries me or Aliukas...
Aloyzas:
—When we're big and Dita marries me or Ignas...

•

The future came, happened, and now it passes by.

In our childhood years, with the calamities drawing
nearer, Aliukas stuck a poplar switch into the ground.
Apparently, it was the same one with which he'd been
consecrated across his bare hands for breaking a window.
One of Aliukas' hands was scratched and bloody, not from
the switch, of course. Accountant Bronius Miniotas was not
some sort of a brute, but just tried to raise his little boys to
be upright. And so Aliukas' hand bled because he'd cut it
when he punched out the kitchen window. On purpose.
Out of anger.

—Why didn't you use a rock?—I asked the two-time
sufferer as he fought back tears.

—With a rock, both panes would have been broken,—explained Aliukas.—Then I'd have been punished even more.

Aliukas waters the dried out switch by himself, letting no one else near it. And later it starts to bud. Right by the back door. And then the sapling grows and grows, into a tree. And look, it's already reached the former Graičiūnas' balcony on the fourth floor, and it's a meter thick.

But during my last visit along the paths of those childhood years, instead of a poplar, I find a thick stump. Dead between two houses. It once was and now is not. In the space between remains a grayish emptiness. As if scissors had awkwardly cut out a piece of sheltering Kaunas' sky. White clouds dotting the blue sky, gleaming tree foliage. Green, whitish poplar. A quickly growing tree. But I alone notice that emptiness. Only to me does the glass extension to the simple but stylish home of the former bank workers on Perkūnas Avenue look like a cancerous tumor. How many of them around here are like that—suffering from that or other illnesses! Only one home still remains as it was deep in a secluded garden, the modest Neverbickas cottage—still healthy, but very old.

How to Die Healthy—declares the colorful cover of a contemporary book.

And why die if you're healthy? Or, why be healthy, if the time has come to die?

So I stand by the thick tree stump and it seems to me that long accumulated treasure has been taken away from me. Maybe another boy will plant a switch here and again a tree will grow. But I'll already be, healthy or not, long dead and will not know that. Or maybe my grandchild will walk past here. And it'll be all the same to them—a tree here or a stump.

A green tree in Giotto's painting, like a bunch of myrtle, seems to be bending down to look at a flock of birds, to whom St Francis is delivering a sermon. Or maybe he's feeding them? In this flock there should also be a European roller, well, the ancestor of my youth's roller. Instead of a natural landscape and perspective—a cracked golden background. Perspective was unimportant to the master; what was important was life. Here and now.

What language did St Francis speak in? Did he really know how to talk to the birds? Did the birds understand him? They were all one back then—a tree, a human, a bird.

With Paulius, kids and grandkids

That spring a European roller flew in the forest. As brightly colored as a tropical bird. His head, neck, and abdomen blue-green, the wings dark blue with green shading, his back bright brown, his legs yellow. "The colors of spring," as the poet said. Suddenly a shot, a flash of fire, and the bird of spring falls into a pile of bloody feathers, bits of meat and little bones.

—Why?—I asked back then

—Why? Why?—I ask again today.

•

Why, on the high banks of the Nemunas did I then hear my name called? From that great height the little boat slowly gliding on the sparkling waters seemed completely helpless, like a splinter of wood. On the young ferryman's head—a round, blue cap. As blue as the bluest of the roller's feathers.

—Silva!—echoes from the Nemunas. A train goes thundering by, sucked up by the tunnel's greedy throat. The little boat floats slowly to the other side, where stands the pine forest of Panemunė. Already other people are sitting in it. Not me, nor my girlfriends. When I come here again in a few months, the ferryman with his blue cap is no longer here. I don't even know his name. The greedy tunnel still sucks up the trains. Panemunė's forest is the same, winter or summer—a shifting blend of greens. On the same screen of my memory there's a child's storybook, inscribed for me by my father, a roller's feather, and my beloved friend Alė's telegram from Tallin: "I'm not there, but in my heart I'm

214

always with you." And the first of my daughter's drawings, done on sand, which only I knew how to decode—a bird, wings spread, rising.

•

In primary school we all stood and started the prayer: "In the name of the Father..." One of the boys, a year older than us, used to say, "In the name of the toothbrush..."[1] And during recesses he'd stick his smirking face close to mine and say,

—So how about it?

—What does he want?—I used to ask my mother. I sensed something not right, but I couldn't name it.

—Ask him what he wants,—advised Mama.

So it remained unexplained. Undoubtedly the boy couldn't have explained it either. That little boy is now old, too. If he's still alive.

"Isn't that him over there," I think to myself today as I sit on a bench on Freedom Avenue. "After all, the old Kaunites should be at least recognizable to me."

But the lanky old man passes by and I see only his back. Therefore I presumptuously turn my eyes to another one approaching. Of course I recognize him. He used to be the teacher of our "shed." By the way, all the nine city's secondary schools were known as "sheds" by their pupils. That would make a good book title, *Kaunas' Sheds*. No one would know right off what it was about. And reading it they'd see how different these schools were from each other, how distinctive each was, how unrepeatable. If only because no one will ever teach girls and boys separately again.

So, the Third "Shed" teacher. We called him Ramigani— after a character in an American movie, *The Indian Tomb*, full of handsome rajahs and the pretty women they loved. In the film Ramigani was a baddie. I see our former teacher self-confidently strolling along. Not very tall, his formerly black hairdo now grey along with his sexy mustache. On his full lips there's certainly no longer any hint of that little smile from years ago. Today I'd call it sarcastic. Back then it seemed mysterious. Or maybe it was just the distinctive way his lips were put together. In any case, most of the senior girls were crazy about him. That easy and reckless falling in love! How much of it hovered around in the girls' schools!

---

[1] word play: "Vardan Dievo Tėvo..." becomes "Vard-dan-tukų šepetukų..."

215

Ramigani passes me by with just a brief look; his eyes slide past me, and he is gone.

I am already darting my eyes over to the next passer-by. He's young. Not him. And that one's young. Not him.

Suddenly my heart jumps. How silly of me! HE can't be that young NOW. I must look at the old folks.

And here comes and old hag. Pardon. An old lady. Hobbling. Fat. I fix my eyes like leeches on her face. I desperately want to identify her. Of course! Now I see her in her youth—slim-waisted, a dark braid on her shoulder tied with a polka-dotted ribbon. A dancer. A singer. Clearly, she must still have a name and a surname. But I don't remember the names of the past.

And anyway—that's enough. There's nothing left for me to do in Kaunas. However, the past clings to my sleeve.

—Don't leave just yet,—the past begs,—Not yet. Tell more about what you remember.

—Life is rubbish,—I say, trying to sound like the younger generation.—Life is shit, garbage, a pile of crap and even worse. I'm not a writer, I'm not allowed to write unprintable words.

—No,—responds my eternally-at-rest Auntie Prakseda from the great beyond. And she reaffirms me like a real sūduvė[2]—None of these words strike home.

—Of course they don't, confirms my Mama, also from the great beyond.—In my village in my youth even simple folk didn't talk that way.

And I realize one very simple truth—the goodness of your life depends on you yourself.

> *Ask the former generations and find out*
> *what their fathers learned,*
> *For we were born only yesterday and*
> *know nothing, and our days on earth*
> *are but a shadow.*
> *Will they not instruct you and tell you?*
> *Will they not bring forth words from   their*
> *understanding?*
>
> Job 8: 8-10

---

[2] Inhabitant of Sūduva region.

**27
The Sea**

The Baltic Sea

This year we're going to go to the seaside,—said our class teacher, Algis Neniškis, as we were finishing the tenth year of our education.—Just don't collect a bunch of demerits.

The previous year, when we had just finished the ninth grade, we visited Vilnius and Trakai. I had already seen Vilnius before—during the German occupation. In Auntie Mikalina's family, my cousin Virginija had just been born. From that visit, I remember the Three Crosses Hill, the inscription "Salve!" on an old home's doorstep, the Cathedral, and brick walls blocking the old city streets, reaching up as high as the third floor windows. Behind those walls, I was told, lived the Jews. Still lived.

Later I found out that that was the ghetto. Shamelessly set up in the very center of the city, not as in Kaunas, where it was on the outskirts. Many years later on one of those narrow streets, in a restored building, my daughter took up residence.

An aura of multilayered spirituality shelters Vilnius' old town like a cauldron—pagan, Catholic, Jewish, Protestant, and Orthodox. It was there back then also. Under that cauldron, the desperate notes of the foreign movie star Zarah Leander's rich alto reverberated like an omen:

Der wind hat mir ein Lied erzählt...
(The wind told me a song...)

In the evenings the cinemas lit up with German signs "Soldatenkino." Soldiers had a priority into the movies.

But the most memorable was a door at the top of the staircase in Auntie Mikalina's building, now on Vasario 16-sios Street (February 16th Street)[1].

---

[1] February 16th Street—named for the first Lithuanian Independence Day, February 16, 1918.

Up went the gentle stairs, accompanied by intricately carved balusters, the likes of which I'd never seen in Kaunas. I'd never seen very tall, double doors either, only one side of which was in use. But here also was a set, changed by moving the hinges to one side only into a single door and thus extremely wide. My aunt's husband Vladas explained that a big-shot Gestapo official lived there. But he was so fat, that he couldn't fit through one side of the double doors. So they'd been re-made specially for him.

Of all the Vilnius souvenirs in numerous small shops on Pilies Street (Castle Street), I chose my very favorites—two little grey felt mice with curious little eyes, real whiskers, and long tails.

In Vilnius

So, having finished ninth grade, about thirty of us cheeky, mischievous girls, rolled down the Trakai-to-Aukštadvaris-to-Birštonas highway. We rolled along not in a bus (in those days no one went on excursions in buses). We sat in the open back of a truck, hair blowing in the wind, yelling cheerfully, laughing, shrieking. We rowed boats on the Galvė lake, clambered up the then-as-yet unrestored Trakai castle ruins, but were afraid to climb down. And Algis Neniškis, all sweated up, had to help thirty squealing not-so-little girls down from the steep walls.

Somewhere near Aukštadvaris the truck labors up a hill. On the right side there's a slope overgrown evenly with grass. A grey wooden farmhut sits at the top of the hill with a fence, a well, an apple orchard. A little farther on—a pine grove. Nothing very special, you'd say, if... If I hadn't seen that exact little farmhouse several times before. In my dreams, or somewhere else? After all, I'm riding down this

218

road for the very first time. When and in what form had I been here before? Only later I learned that these miracles happen to others too.

Class excursion to Trakai Castle

After a year we find ourselves in the same kind of rattling truck heading towards the seaside. But I well know that I won't be bathing in the sea. I've been warned by a gypsy to be careful around water. After the war, when the railroad station area was linked to the Freda neighborhood by a pontoon bridge laid across the Nemunas, women with very small children would show up in our street. They would ask for scraps. They wore big men's coats right over their naked bodies and looked very much like gypsies. Later the rumor spread that they were Romanians journeying back to their much troubled land.

—Romania, the very poorest country in Europe,—people said. Horrified by their naked bodies, people generously gave them clothes. The Romanian women crammed those clothes into sacks and continued to walk around half-naked with half-naked kids. Later the Romanians disappeared and from beyond the Nemunas a real gypsy woman showed up with a young girl my age. The gypsy woman was tall, slim and beautiful, clearly not naked, and she didn't beg for anything. She made money telling fortunes. Probably because of her I never learned how to swim.

—What's your name?—asked her daughter.

—Dita,—I replied.—And yours?

—How beautiful,—said the girl.—I'm Rose.

"How beautiful," I thought, but didn't say so, not wanting to seem like I was aping her.

And the gypsy woman, after auguring me all sorts of good fortunes, warned:

—Be careful with water.

While she worked the neighbors, I showed Rose my dolls, our yard, and the panorama of Kaunas below us. Waving her hand in the direction of the Freda neighborhood, Rose declared:

—We live over there.

And of course, I had passed by one of the larger ravines in which there was a Gypsy encampment. The ravine was filled with women, children, wagons, horses. Everything there flickered and clattered happily, full of exultant shouting, laughter, and singing. It smelled of bonfires. More insistent than the smoke rising above the edges of the glen, came the resonant clash of metal on metal. Here the gypsies with large hammers beat the sides of gigantic kettles. The kettles were all different shapes, each larger than the one before, all reddish-brown.

Surely they must have been copper?—I wonder now.

The kettles responded to the strokes differently. Some echoed like soft resonant bells, others bawled, screamed, sharply or gently, depending on shape and size. After smoothing and soldering them, the gypsies probably sold the kettles. However, to whom—I never found out.

The little gypsy, Rose, started coming by to play. At first, the household looked on her suspiciously, stereotypically. But Rose stole nothing, only played hungrily with my toys. She turned the pages of my books respectfully, and I only now realize she was illiterate. Her dark Asiatic eyes looked on the world with curiosity. Then the visits stopped. After a couple of months I had an opportunity to drive by that ravine. It was silent, damp, and dark. Stained autumn leaves settled on the trampled black earth.

•

But this time it was the start of summer. As I said, we were going to the seaside. The journey on a hard wooden seat didn't seem long at all, even though back then it took almost twice as long as today. Because it was the sea! I had never seen it, not even in my dreams. At a distance, from the bench in the truck, it looked like a hand-high gray wall. And here it is, that yearned-for sea...

I didn't have time to be disappointed. When I see it up close, the wall is gone. With eyes full of road dust I see the dark blue plane with a clearly drawn horizon line. But the sea, like a dignified lady, did not allow anyone to fall in love with her immediately. I had to come to her many more times before I found I belonged near her, before I could recite the most beautiful of Maironis' verses as my own:

Wide sea, blown from the west,
Surge over my chest with your cold wave,
And let me express what the heart
Desires as powerfully as you, oh Baltic!

Back then, when we were known as Soviet Lithuania, we feared spies like the plague. At dusk green-capped Russian border patrolmen with guard dogs ordered sunset worshippers off the pier. Then, sitting themselves in a burbling tractor, they harrowed the entire length of the beach. The width of those rows separated us from the Western world, swarming (as we thought then) with spies. At night, you couldn't even take a step toward the sea. One jokester decided, when no one was watching, to walk backwards toward the water across the harrowed stretch and then return the normal way alongside his first footprints. Finding those double sets of tracks in the morning, the border guards raised a huge alarm. But they never found the two spies who, they thought, had emerged from the Baltic. So again at dusk with the guard dogs, the burbling tractor, and the rows harrowed where the flood tide couldn't reach them.

You can walk along the seaside now as much as you want, even throughout the entire night until the morning.

I walk along the very edge, through the damp sand. I put my footprint where the edge of the wave leaves a very thin and very temporary line. It's a line you can see on every map of the world or Europe. It's a clear, black line. I move along that line. I can't be seen, but I'm here. To my left, the Baltic Sea; to my right, the small state of Lithuania. Not even a hundred kilometers of that line. In two days you could walk it. From Nida to Šventoji. I'm at the northern end of that line, in Palanga. Right now, Paulius is going farther and farther along the line, while I sit on a bench and follow him with my eyes. At first his head is the size of a coffee cup, later like a ring stone, still later like a match head—I can still tell it apart from other tiny heads. Suddenly it transforms into a poppy seed and then disappears altogether. I know it will reappear soon. But what if it doesn't? The day will come when it won't. Fear grips me from head to toe. And I sit there petrified, until after a half hour I see him again—no, not like a poppy seed, nor like a coffee cup, but my own dearest being, his own real size and shape.

221

Finding a gap between high white clouds, the marbled moon peers with his frail face over the sunset-bathed dunes. I remember Aistis:

Like long-sleeved Pierrot,
broken-hearted...

Paulius' 70th birthday

A long time ago *homo erectus*, standing up on two legs, first saw such a pale face looking down on him. How much more time had to pass before *homo sapiens*, seeing that very same moon, in a discordant voice sang out something like a hymn, something like a legend:

Moone did marrie Sunne,
in that first Springe.
Sunne rose early;
Moone was already gone.
Moone walked about alone,
and fell in love with Dawne.
Furious, Thunder
smote him in two with his sworde.
Why did you leave Sunne?
Why did you fall in love with Dawne?
And walk the night alone?

(Rhesa, *Litauische Volkslieder*)

In the west the declining sun covers the sea with a sparkling path. The water darkens, wrinkles, and the sun's trail on the surface starts to flash with fire. That fire is fleeting and so seems even hotter than if it were real. But, in reality, it isn't hot at all, no more than 18 degrees Celsius. Look, around the trail the sparks of fire grow— flash out and die, flash out in another place and die again.

222

Dancing before my eyes the separate flashes turn into a flood of fire. In this flood's background—two chocolate-colored figures move, are not still even for a second. Two kids long ago, and two grandchildren now, the very creatures of our own bodies and souls.

The sky clears out and the moon slowly yellows (still not split by the sword), the water blackens, the sun's sphere already seeks the smoky horizon. Darkness comes slowly in our northern country, but it does come. The green pine trees begin to loom fearfully and warm beach sand begins to resemble cooled ashes. The beacon of Šventoji harbour is flashing like some will-o'-the-wisp.

—Look,—says my son astonished, pointing to his own son's head,—it glows.

I can see myself that it's glowing. The blond hair of the boy fluoresces as if reflecting something otherworldly. We look on speechlessly. Then the light dims, and we return home down glooming forest trails to have salami sandwiches for supper.

"The full moon blooms," wrote Heinrich Heine in the *The North Sea* cycle.

There is a faint light in the windows of our house. I know that inside Aneta is watching three serials on TV at the same time, each worse than the other. They're shown on three separate channels, but you can confidently flip back and forth among them—the scenes are all similar, such that if you miss something on one you can easily pick it up on the other. And everything will be clear. At my reproachful glance, "again those silly soaps?" Aneta replies:

—They help push away my thoughts.

Those shunted thoughts still come back to her during sleepless nights. Aneta is beautiful. Level-headed. Industrious. Religious. Honest. So why, Dear Lord, did you send her such a trial? For whose sins? It's hard to believe that in the Lutheran families of Penelis, Berčius or Labotakis there had been any murderers or other wicked people. Aneta had raised three children—a son Jonas, daughters Marta and Edita. Except that Marta now lies in Palanga's cemetery. She died in 1993, but was buried in 1995. For those two intervening years she lay in the damp seaside forest in a dense thicket, almost halfway along the road from Palanga to Klaipėda. Two nineteen-year-olds, Marta and her friend Gaivile, were strangled on an evening in early spring. They were thrown into a shallow grave and hastily covered over. After two years, the authorities turned up the killers in Russia, by chance. And how did the killers find the place where they'd buried their victims? By chance?

223

•

—Marta, come with me to live in Vilnius,—I joked some years ago.

—OK,—the six-year-old Marta said innocently and stepped toward me without even glancing at her mother standing by. Now I understand—it was a foolish joke. It's as if you'd give a child, instead of a candy, a piece of colorful paper wrapped around nothing.

—I recognized her from her earrings,—Aneta said.

She had to go through an unimaginable ordeal to identify the remains of the child she'd raised. Is there a greater pain on this earth than burying your own child. I'm not asking. I know the answer. The women in the mortuary swathed the remains from head to toe in thick white gauze—not even the smallest patch of the body was left visible, not the face, not a finger, not a hair. Only a white cocoon, a pupa, from which never will emerge a glorious butterfly. Aneta bought this white cocoon a white bride-like dress, white gloves, white shoes. In them Marta went to the other side in a Christian manner.

The Lutheran priests, Darius Petkūnas and Reinholdas Moras, presided over her burial in the Palanga cemetery. Not with my ears but with my consciousness I listened to the priest Reinholdas' words, meant to stimulate noble feelings and inhibit angry, vengeful thoughts. I tried to plug my heart's cavity with those words, the way you'd stuff your puddle-soaked shoes with newspapers.

But angry thoughts are like weeds in a strawberry patch—you root them out, but here they are again...

The new section of Palanga cemetery is full of similar looking headstones. Here, as of yet, there's no palpable spiritual aura like the one surrounding the village of Kiauleikiai cemetery where Aneta's mother, Anė, rests, and the Penelis, the Kasputis, the Kalvis families, relatives and ancestors from long bygone times. This cemetery, on a mound in the middle of a plane, overgrown with centuries-old linden trees planted in the time of the The Grand Duchy of Lithuania, has ever since given rest to the people of the whole area. But during the Soviet era local rulers were determined to destroy that well-maintained and nicely-managed cemetery, and eventually it was closed. So Aneta had to bury her grandmother separately in Palanga, away from all her other relatives. Not with the ancestors, but only next to her own sister, Urtė. My mother-in-law. Later on, death managed to make peace between the two sisters, and my father-in-law was laid to rest here too. Because they'd all been angry with each other while they were living, as we all have been with someone. We feel that hatred is more powerful than love. But we think we overcome it. Or at least will overcome it. We look forward to the coming of the age of love. Someone will have to announce it.

•

Today, when "the moon's horns are joined in the round full moon" (a translation from Ovid's *Pygmalion*), I say:
—Sea, surge over what was evil with your cold wave.
The sea floods over it all—the good and the evil. Even my deep and significant footprints (so they seem to me). Most of the wave returns, but a tiny part of it seeps into the sand. And again you look for a reason to start again. And again you start anew. Each time from the beginning.

•

P.S. I testify that the sea does not smell of vomit nor rotten horseflesh, as a popular writer recently wrote in the pages of a respectable publication. I do not doubt that he may be familiar with a whiff of the former, but the latter? After all, these are not Napoleonic times. Besides, Napoleon's horse never rinsed its feet in the Baltic Sea, and the horses of his cavalry died on dry land.
P.P.S. I should add that I'm a lover of the sea—from the shore. The sea raises in me a frightening respect, or a respectful fear, what the Anglo Saxons name simply with the word "awe." I have never been so far into the sea as not to be able to see the shore.

Are thy wonders known in the darkness,
or thy saving help in the land of forgetfulness?

Psalm 88: 12

A. Šiekštelė's cartoon
of me, 1961

28
A Jericho Rose

One winter afternoon, when the sun begins setting soon after lunch, Paulius brings me a gift—a greyish-brown shrivelled lump, similar to a baby hedgehog, that fits in the palm of his hand. He gives it to me, palm to palm carefully, as if it were alive.

— What is it?—I wonder.

—A Jericho rose,—my husband says solemnly, clearly proud of his gift. Immediately from behind memory's veil comes the pre-war poem of Bernardas Brazdžionis, since my childhood immersed in a waft of mystical incense.

> *Like the Jericho rose I bloomed for twelve years.*
> *Blossomed like a precious relic.*
> *Then the flower and I*
> *Both withered away.*

In the Bible stories about the blind Bartimaeus of Jericho, and the trumpets and shouting, which collapsed the walls of Jericho, we have the assertion of the magical power of faith. Jericho is one of the world's oldest cities, sprung from a desert oasis near a natural spring.

And now, at last, here's a real rose of Jericho.

Laid in a shallow, wide bowl, and barely having touched water, the lump begins to spread, unclenching leaf by leaf as if opening up the fingers of a fist, at the same time painting itself bright green. By morning the green rose has completely covered the entire bowl. In a hoarse voice it whispers something I don't understand, in the long-forgotten language of the desert nomads.

The lump is alive. And it's in me to put it to sleep again, withdrawing that drop of water.

226

It is now sleeping again wrapped in gauze in a crystal candy jar from the time before war.

•

But back then...back then I was so inexperienced, forever looking for what I could lean my lever against that would help me move the world. At the very least I believed I could move it a little. Woe is me! The place, where I tried to lean, was always either rotten or unstable, and I would plump together with my lever into a lurking quagmire. It would bubble up gleefully like porridge cooking, but it never had the strength to suck me down. I was always able to scramble out of it.

—How will you scramble down now?—Prakseda would ask when I'd climb up too high into the apple tree in my grandpa's orchard.

It didn't enter my head back then that finding a firm place or a strong person would require a different method of searching. Not with erring feelings but with a cynical mind, since the mind is always cynical to a greater or lesser degree. During the Soviet era, I went to work for the satirical magazine *Šluota* (*The Broom*). (It's regular press run of forty thousand would seem unbelievable today.) A bright memory is the editor-in-chief Juozas Bulota reading my first tentative piece and saying to me:

—OK, you can do it, write!

I believed him, but not entirely. I wrote but not very much. I thought to myself—who do I think I am? I thought—only a potter can make pots.

Editing *Šluota* wasn't easy. Juozas Bulota patiently suffered the pranks of motley employees—bohemian artists, writers and journalists. He was no coward, just very cautious, like many intellectuals during the Soviet era. He was a whole head above his subordinates intellectually, superior in his manners and education. As a member of the famous leftist Bulota family, he was relatively safe. However, being lead editor of a satirical Soviet periodical meant walking the razor's edge. The vigilant eyes of Soviet authorities constantly watch over his fortnightly issues. Not their literary level or their linguistic or artistic quality, but their ideological line. Has some higher-echelon party favorite, or some important functionary, or, God forbid, some general Communist party line, been made fun of?... Every cover or a more biting cartoon had what we called a "lightning rod." The criticism of typical and widely occurring problems was blunted by phrases such as "somewhere," "in some cases," "as it happens," or with

227

quotations from the State's five-year plan and Party resolutions.

That journal cover from 1959 also came with a "lightning rod": "Recently, the state Prosecution Office uncovered a series of large thefts." In the caricaturist J. Augustinas' cartoon, entitled "The Expulsion from the Garden of Eden," stand a comfortable little home and a car by the door—all this is in the background. But in the foreground—a weeping woman. She's pushing a soda water cart, next to her is her worried-looking husband with his briefcase. They're both naked except for fig leaves. You understand, they've lost everything. Behind them is an angel with the attributes of a policeman.

Summoned to the highest Party offices, the editor-in-chief of the journal, like an elementary school pupil, has to listen to a lecture from the designated Head of Press Oversight:

—So you're promoting pornography? Shame on you!— says the boss, tapping at the curvy figure of the woman.

—But she's covered,—says the senior editor, trying for a laugh, and pointing at the green fig leaf.

—Listen, this is not your decadent bourgeois press,— insists the chairman, not in the mood for joking,—You're arousing low passions!

But in fact the rub is elsewhere. There wasn't a touch of pornography in that drawing. At the time, most of the big bosses' wives were fixed up in profitable places—as managers of shops or cafeterias. This cartoon ridiculed the cream of the ruling class. How could they not feel offended?

Juozas Bulota comes back from the Party offices all pale from the thrashing he's received and calls everyone to a meeting.

—So there—he begins as if not angry,—we blew it again. It seems that we're promoting pornography...

Although he's head and shoulders above the ones who had recently berated him, now he loses it, swearing at us, threatening to sack us all. But soon he calms down again. Leaving his office we feel safe, the mood is up. Juozas Bulota has managed to absorb the distressing blow from the authorities.

Of course, it's easiest to lampoon janitors, collective farmers, office workers, and ordinary waitresses. The bosses of those satirized in cartoons and pamphlets, would send an "acceptance of criticism." They were published in a special section called "The Scribble."

From *Šluota* in 1960:

In the Skaudvilė region, the State Nature Preservation Inspector, comrade Remeikis informed the editorial offices, that a cartoon in this year's Šluota, issue Number 19 truly suggested that in the Stalin Collective Farm swine gnawed down 90 cherry-trees. The collective-farm's chairman A. Vasiliauskas and the live-stock manager A. Gudavičius have been reprimanded with administrative measures.

And so the circle was closed—we wrote it up, readers had a good laugh, the leaders wrote back, perhaps secretly also having a laugh, and that was that. True, there'd be announcements of firings, and, rarely, legal actions. But who knew how it really was and, indeed, how it all ended.

Through the layers of time the late Juozas Bulota's eyes still glitter intelligently. That spark never dimmed even into his old age, so it was unbearable to see his remains laid out in the end—I couldn't see his eyes.

•

In the eighth century, when Lithuania's name was still not on anyone's lips, nor was there likely a Lithuania or any Lithuanians, in China the brilliant Wang Wei created poems, painted paintings, and wrote the essay "The Art of Painting."

A strange hybrid from the Soviet era—the positive caricature

229

I became familiar with him and other Chinese poets through Russian translations. I tried to translate him into Lithuanian, but I soon abandoned my attempts. I saw that an amateur translating poetry wouldn't ever get close to the original. However, one evening, from a distance of more than a thousand years, the words of a Chinese poet spoke out to me in Lithuanian:

Aš staiga supratau,
kad kenčia tik kūnas mirtingas;
Silpsta jisai,
o dvasia pasilieka sparnuota.

I suddenly realized
only mortal flesh suffers;
It declines,
but the spirit remains winged.

Still not knowing anything about those poems, just feeling the arrival under my shoulder blades of a sense of my own spirit's still-folded wings, I picked up a paintbrush.

Oh, the re-opened world of forms and colors! Oh, the eyes' pain in trying to perceive their nature. The powerlessness to convey what I see. Only after many years, did I learn from the art theoretician E. H. Gombrich that "artists are more likely to see what they paint, not paint what they see." And that is quite normal and natural.

I did not know that Wang Wei urged the artist to be confined to the most basic means of expression, as that would prove to be one of the most important manifestations of talent.

I would not have so strained my eyes with trying to read the unreadable so tightly wrapped around me.

•

And so, Lithuania's Rebirth (new independence movement) arrived, and my heart lurched wildly when I saw three spools of thread by the sewing machine—yellow, green, and red[1]... What had my daughter been sewing that morning? And where did that green band in my son's room come from?

Me—I'm a child of war, I'm easily frightened.

---

[1] The colors of the Lithuanian national flag ("the tri-colors") forbidden to be shown during the Soviet occupation.

Trembling with fear and joy, I didn't believe my eyes looking at the first *Sajūdis* [2] assembly with its smiling tricolors.

A good time before that, when foreign films were inaccessible to ordinary mortals and could be seen only if you were "on the list," in an entertaining Italian comedy we saw a general whose medals barely fit on his chest. When the general turned his back to us viewers, we saw that his back was also full of medals. The viewers (the select audience) were afraid to laugh out loud, so throughout the hall spread a strange noise—the sound of continuous squealing of people trying to stifle their laughter. The leader then was Leonid Brezhnev (the Soviet Union's communist party's General Secretary, the army's highest-ranking marshal, a Soviet hero many times over). The parallel seemed so obvious and comical that the supressed laughter finally burst out into a unified and powerful roar.

I was unconsciously interested in a specific problem in visual art—inverse perspective, and was reading B. Rauschenbach's studies. My reading was probably too shallow, as a deeper understanding of the inverse perspective could have resulted in the idea that the supposed Great Might must stop somewhere near myself or inside myself, shrinking into a tiny dot.

And Might did shrink into a Dot. Besides, with a latent possibility to develop into a sore. Barely noticeable, but disclosing its deadly poison in small, non-lethal doses.

And the enthusiasm of the country's rebirth began to evaporate as if it were a poorly corked volatile liquid.

Every nation has its good and bad points. I wonder if only Lithuanians typically have a pathological hatred of those who are mentally farther advanced, smarter and more intelligent than themselves?

•

—Granny, solve my riddle,—urges my four-year-old grandson, Gerimantas.—What's white, round, and shines at night. In the sky. WHAT is it?
Impatient for my answer, he eases my task:
—Beginning with the letter "M."
—Well, now I can solve it.

---

[2] *Sajūdis*, established on June 3, 1988 and led by Vytautas Landsbergis, was the political organization which ultimately was instrumental in bringing about a restoration of independence for Lithuania on March 11, 1990.

But back at the start of the 1970s, the censor, who had to inspect and give his blessing to every single radio broadcast, was more interested in the little word "WHERE."

—So WHERE are those geese you're talking about flying to?

God only knows. Maybe to southern Europe, maybe to northern Africa. But over Germany for sure.

Stop!

That's a political mistake. And now there's a demerit for the entire radio production team. Regardless of who actually authored the text.

—Do you not know that such a State does not exist?— asks the censor, flashing his narrowed eyes treacherously.

How could we not know. There is the GDR—The German Democratic Republic, and the GFR—The German Federal Republic. But do the geese know? "Silly as a goose," people say. But, by the way, a goose is not at all silly. And it couldn't care less about temporary boundaries. It doesn't give a damn about the Iron Curtain. It's been flying along skyways that are thousands of years old.

During the Soviet era, censors were not ever called censors, just *Glavlit* [3] representatives. What is *Glavlit?*—you won't find it in the encyclopedia. Just a modest little agency, that's all. But without that agency's stamp, which bore a powerful number instead of a name, you could not take a step. Not a book, not a newspaper, not a magazine, not a play nor a concert, not a radio nor a television broadcast could get out into the world without it...

Not all creative artists were considered desirable by the powerful boss of government-owned radio. Of that sovereign autocrat the vast majority of radio employees were simply physically afraid. The lower rungs of management, i.e., the department editors, in order not to take the Lord's name in vain, called him "THE BOSS." Of course, they spoke (and wrote) that title in capitals.

After looking closely at the line-up of programs, one of the senior editors would often attach paper-clipped in-structtions. Such as

> *THE BOSS has repeatedly and strongly*
> *warned against the over generous use of titles*
> *like "talented" and so on.*

---

[3] *Glavlit:* Under the USSR Council of Ministers, the Main Administration for the Protection of State Secrets in the Press and other institutions.

The talented were only allowed if they'd been so designated and approved of by the State.

THE BOSS, without ever having even smelled the poetry of Algirdas Verba, condemned him because of his alleged drinking. We argued in vain that radio waves carry no odors, and the listeners in no way could have sensed the stench of vodka from A. Verbas' poems.

Half a year later A. Verba received the State prize.

One of my frequently quoted authors, Sigitas Geda, had his name written all in large capitals by the chief editor. Not out of respect, of course, but only for my benefit, to show me and instruct me that the letter E in his name required a diacritical mark. So the name Geda became GĖDA— "shame" in Lithuanian.

By the way, a gentleman who himself worked in radio during the Soviet era, but perhaps because he'd never heard the broadcasts we made to foreign countries, quite undeservedly described our department in the press (under no threat) as a "KGB service". (At that rate, every institution of the time could be called a "KGB service"...)

I confess a lot of my mistakes are not mentioned here. I doubt anyone could learn anything from them. We learn only from our own, and even then not always.

But I still don't know what I'm to do with my winged spirit. I've translated a stack of books from English—they're full of good ideas, but none of them are mine. In the hundreds of films I've translated there are hundreds of lives, but none are mine.

Satan doesn't come forward, doesn't offer me my youth for any price.

So I take up my pen.

I just keep in mind that Jericho rose sleeping, wrapped and tied in a gauze cloth. And it's up to me to raise her up again, if I just give her a drop of water.

•

The Japanese poet, Issa Kobayashi, before his death, wrote a haiku—the last one of twenty thousand he'd created. People found this three-line poem after his death under the pillow in his miserable little shack.

> *I say thank you.*
> *On the blanket covering me*
> *snow falls from heaven.*

233

Palanga steps with Eglė and Žilvinas

29
Father-
Grandfather.
Home

Here, here is my home. Under those chestnut trees growing almost in the middle of the street.
I am not yet aware that the real home isn't here, that it will be a kilometer to the north, under those tall linden trees... No, there's still time.

One luxuriant ash, two overgrown cedars, alongside the gate a stupendous bird cherry, and every year blocking more sky an acacia. Let's say these trees are without any use. But others are for beauty: every year the lilac bushes take up more space, in early summer covered with purple clusters from top to bottom. Waiting until the blossoms turn brown, fragrant little white crosses of jasmine blossoms crowd over—all the way to the ground. The graceful Japanese cherry tree produces no more than two berries each year. And then there are the useful ones: three ancient apple trees leaning their branches tiredly against the earth. Each year they drop a hundred or so little wormy apples at their feet. And another three young apple trees, dissatisfied with the thin, sandy, ash-like coastal soil. Only cherries and currants thrive here. This is my father-in-law Jokūbas Pukys' garden in Palanga, now, in 2001.

It was a similar garden back then in the early 1960s, when I saw it for the first time—similar, but not like now. There was a hundred-year-old birch. The garden was filled with flowers—tulips in the spring, gladioli in summer, and dahlias toward the autumn. The house, already a hundred years old, was dark blue and seemed quite gloomy.

Later, when Jokūbas Pukys becomes my father-in-law and I start calling him Father, timidly, I take it upon myself to offer an opinion that the house might look nicer if it were a lighter shade. My father-in-law says nothing, but when I come to Palanga the following summer I find the house has been repainted a blue-green.

234

—Is it OK now?—asks my father-in-law.

—It's fine, but it could be even lighter—I reply.

My father-in-law says nothing again.

After a few years, when the walls have become a little shabby, he paints the house white. The blue-green paint breaks through from beneath, turning the white into a kind of cozy moonlight shade.

—How beautiful—I hasten to tell my father-in-law, not waiting for him to ask.

Alongside the house, for the longest time, there was no paved street, nor a sidewalk. In 1967 my father-in-law wrote:

> *That Maironio Street of ours is like the last*
> *piglet sucking on hind teat in spring and autumn*
> *it's all mud bog and marshes and in summer it's*
> *dusty enough for the convicted.*

From the second story windows you used to be able to view the sea; now it's blocked by new homes and pines along the shore. On both sides of the veranda are three chestnuts, still alive, but now almost in the middle of the street. Because Maironio Street, after intersecting with Kastyčio Street, has been extended, not in a straight line the way it used to go, but rather curving to the left such that no more room is left for the veranda, and the house itself ends up right on the sidewalk.[1]

My father-in-law had principles and refused to bribe the planners, and so he lost the uneven battle with Palanga's Soviet officialdom. The disgruntled town's chief architect (among other things, my husband's grammar school classmate) angled the street on purpose so that the veranda would have to be demolished to give way for the sidewalk and warned:

—If that old man spouts off anymore, we'll demolish his entire house.

While only a few years before that the town's administrators wouldn't even allow for a change to the veranda's roof—claiming that the house is protected as an architectural legacy.

---

[1] Not true. The chestnuts are gone. The current town's administration have shown themselves to be no better than the Soviets before them. It's as if the chestnuts disappeared under the asphalt. Only asphalt is left. Of the shady trees—not a sign (author's note: Winter, 2002-2003).

That's why on the western side of the yard, my father-in-law changed one of the windows into a door and built some comfortable steps down to the garden. On those steps we ritualistically photograph ourselves each summer: all members of the family, the growing and the aging.

I sit on the steps, and in front of me the black summer sky stretches to infinity. From Finland a northwest wind tirelessly tosses and tosses at the hundred year-old ash tree—flipping over not individual leaves but tufts, dark clumps. The birch tree struggles with the wind differently—it rocks its long branches like outstretched hands, on which the triangular leaves are pinned, each one rippling.

In the rich green leaves of this birch, many years ago, I saw the friendly spirit of the house. There she is looking at me as I sit on the steps, leaves shimmering on her face, eyes of heaven, sunlit hair. Her face darkens as a stormy gust from the seaside shakes the branches, and she yet again looks on me approvingly. And I know I'm sitting here in my place, now and later.

At first glance, my father-in-law seems a bit stern and harsh. He tends to be blunt about what he doesn't like, but he also has characteristics that I've valued highly my entire life—tolerance, for one. Even when in the middle of the night the bed made up just for me collapses with a bang, he doesn't say anything to his son or to the guest his son has brought along, i.e., me.

Later, noticing some misbehavior by his grandchildren, he cuts it short, leaving no room for doubt.

—This is from her.

He means his former wife, my mother-in-law. She had died a long time ago and so couldn't oppose him. My father-in-law looked after her in an exemplary Christian manner until her death, even though they'd been legally divorced. He bathed her in a tin coffin-like tub, filled with heated sea water. My father-in-law was short of love his entire life—he didn't get much from his parents, or from his wife, even less from his first daughter-in-law.

Why didn't he ever hear the word "Daddy" from me, only "Father"? Perhaps—I reason to myself today—because he seemed so strong and unbreakable?

But now I know that what causes us the most suffering are not the words that were said, but those that weren't. It doesn't matter why.

Father likes to drive me to a Lutheran church with him on Sundays: to Klaipėda and other neighboring small towns. If the son won't follow the father, well at least the daughter-in-law will. Before we leave he looks me over carefully: am I scandalously dressed? Am I in pants rather than a dress; am I cheekily made up, am I immodestly uncovered? Only three decades have gone by since then and already blue jeans rule everywhere, even in the smallest church in the middle of nowhere.

Father sits in front of the ancient harmonium. On the round white register heads in black Gothic letters are written various ear-pleasing foreign words: "*Vox humana, Viola dolce, Flöte.*"

> *All people must die,*
> *All must rot like hay,*
> *Whoever's alive must fall apart.*
> *Everyone has to accept their fate.*
> *Our body has to decay,*
> *If it wants to be together*
> *In heaven's eternal glory*
> *Waiting for the good.*
> *That's why this life*
> *I leave when dying.*
> *I forget all earthly worries,*
> *Waiting for the joys of heaven.*

Father-in-law Jokūbas Pukys

237

Father-in-law sits at the harmonium treading the bellows' pedals, playing and singing hymns. Paulius and I don't sing along. We're both still young, our children are little, we don't worry about death nor care for hymns. Even after my father-in-law explains singing hymns is very healthy—not only because of praising God, but because of the workout it gives the lungs. Looking back I think we were pathetic, of that variety now called "homo sovieticus," raising our own little identical "sovietchiks." What did Father-in-law think of us, looking at us through much more comprehending eyes (to us, back then, less so)?

—It's all fiddlesticks,—he'd say as if to himself, observing our lifestyles unacceptable to the virtuous evangelicals.

I was ashamed, but it seemed it was meant to be that way.

However, I take down the old Evangelical Bible with the worn leather covers, clasped shut with brass buckles and belts, sit my kids down at the table and tell them to read out loud the small gothic script of the verses:

Before I formed thee in the belly I knew
thee; and before thou camest forth out of
the womb I sanctified thee, and I
ordained thee a prophet unto the nations.

Moreover the word of the LORD came
unto me, saying, Jeremiah, what seest
thou? And I said, I see a rod of an
almond tree.

And I brought you into a plentiful
country, to eat the fruit thereof and the
goodness thereof.

Jeremiah 1: 5; 11; 2, 7

"This Bible includes all the Holy Books of the Old and New Testaments, translated into the Lithuanian language and reprinted for the ninth time in Berlin. Printed by the British and International Bible Society."

We listen to the strange and attractive sounds of the words, not paying too much attention to their meaning.

Their sense came much later, but not too late, thank God.

Only Jokūbas, Father, died too soon.

He did not hear his son's trembling voice, full of tears, after singing with everyone in the clean Vilnius Lutheran church:

Though like the wanderer, the sun gone down,
darkness be over me, my rest a stone;
yet in my dreams I'd be
nearer, my God, to thee;
nearer, my God, to thee, nearer to thee!

Father buried his former wife Urtė next to her first husband, whose bones by then had already moldered.

—That's what she wanted,—he said.

After many years it's where he lay down too.

On the grey oval plaque on the black iron cross, he had inscribed a few lines of an old hymn, or maybe his own. Painful lines, infused with hurt, sadness, maybe even remorse for having so easily shunned true love.

You rest full of peace
Completely free of difficulty.
After the pain of the cross,
No one can dim your joy.

Now having reached his ninetieth year, he tells me the story of the great love of his youth—the seamstress Marikė.

...Here comes Marikė across the field, beautiful, slim ("she wore a corset everyday"—explains my father-in-law), clothes on her were as if sculpted (his tailor's eye knew how to value them). From the right-hand path comes Jokūbas, from the left, another of Marikė's admirers. Jokūbas approaches, his head gnawed by doubts, his heart squeezed by love. And the other one approaches as well.

—What's she to you, landless, without a dowry,—his parent's words ring in his ears.

Jokūbas is pragmatic, he has almost decided, taken by his parent's advice. But his heart remains unquiet, as if to say things are not right. His heart could still hold out, but... Jokūbas decides to leave it to fate—if he's the first one to get to Marikė he'll propose, but if the other one arrives first, well, he'll let it be. It will have to have been fated.

Had he measured the distance with his eyes? Did he know that Marikė loved him? Did he purposely not speed up his pace? No one will ever know now.

His father, Martinas Pukis, harnessed a handsome horse to a buggy, and, after knotting on a necktie, Jokūbas left the farmstead for Palanga to see the bride his parents had chosen for him—Urtė, the widow of Palanga's police chief during Czarist times. Urtė, or Orta as she called herself, was ready for guests in her own way—her skirt rolled up, her feet in wooden clogs, she was painting the palings of

239

the fence in front of her big house. Her hair was combed smooth, with a part in the middle like all young women of Lithuania Minor.

—She suited me, she seemed hard working,—my father-in-law remembered after many years.

He'd already seen her in the Lutheran church in Kretinga. Ms. Urtė has entered, her be-hatted head proudly held high. Her dress is neatly tight-fitting, beautifully enhanced with lace, all of high quality. Her white ankle socks flash below the long dress. The leather of her shoes rustles quietly, while her heels hammer. Urtė throws a critical glance around the church at the potential young men. Among them is Jokūbas. Her glance lingers a little on him; he feels as if suddenly scalded by hot water. Maybe the wealthy lady has already conspired with his parents, and maybe she's already chosen him. And the entire parish with their eyes focused on them, waits to see what's next.

They married in 1922 in June, right when the lilacs were flowering.

They were driven to the church in the borrowed coach of Count Tyszkiewicz.

Urtė Pukienė with my future husband Paulius

His beloved Marikė also married, and later emigrated to America. Ninety-year-old Jokūbas had somehow learned when her husband had died, when she... A prayer saved him from a broken heart—then as now. "A prayer is like a sword, cutting with two sides," he wrote in his memoirs.

•

I feel proud of having supposedly done a good deed—persuading my father-in-law to write down everything he remembered. He bought himself a thick notebook and wrote on the cover, "My Life." He filled it up. Picturesquely. And with sufficient talent. Not with everything, alas. His long life's journey could not fit even into two thick notebooks.

He wrote beautiful letters to us in Vilnius with lovely little errors in them and with very few punctuation marks. In his childhood, during the rule of the Russian Czar, he'd attended a Russian school, where Lithuanian was not taught. One evening he declaimed by heart a Russian poem that sounded familiar to me.

—Pushkin's "The Bronze Horseman,"—he explained.

The next day I ran over to the library to check it—truly, he'd recited it without error.

It warmed my heart to read his letters, written in his small handwriting:

I'm healthy keeping busy with preparations
for summer that is already very close suddenly it's
turned very warm since May 5 up to 22 degrees
Celsius the little flowers have raised themselves up
the blue saffron are in bloom and primroses of various
colors are in bloom tulips grow their leaves and are
putting out buds the whole garden is blooming while
the peas and radishes are not lagging behind, and
Eglė's and Žilvinas' cherry trees have many buds
and will soon bloom well and the squirrel eats bits
of nuts right from my hand sits on my arm and says
tsip tsip tsip that is she's asking when the kids will
arrive from Vilnius and give her a treat [...] and I told
her soon soon the kids will be with you in Palanga,
and so until the joyful meeting in Palanga.

Father Grandfather 1970 V 7 (5/7/1970)

He liked very much to sign himself "*Father Grandfather,*" with those words expressing his love and modestly reminding us that he was the root of the family.

He called himself neither a Samogitian nor a Memellander—only a Klaipedite (pronouncing the "l" softly). He was well aware of his own identity and did not want to be German or Soviet. He always felt sorry for his brother Ermanis, even though he lived well in Germany along the Rhine. After the war, Ermanis had left the region of Klaipėda where his parents had a farm, emigrating as a

241

volksdeutsche. According to my father-in-law, "because he wanted to run from life's irritations." In 1967, Father-in-law wrote to us:

> *Ermanis it seems has not quite extinguished all*
> *spark of nationhood, but for his wife, as for most of*
> *those from the Klaipėda region, national consciousness*
> *is what they are trying to get rid of, that is all signs of*
> *being Lithuanian and the ones who are still here just*
> *can't wait to get back to the "Vaterland."*

He also looked critically at the post-war work of the novelist Ieva Simonaitytė:

> *And I have heard from many others of my*
> *judgment of the writer Ieva Oh they say the Lord is*
> *full of patience to be able to tolerate such drivel and*
> *those radio performances full of our Lutheran hymns*
> *and how many terrible things has she written about her*
> *people so that when you hear such expressions you*
> *see the kind of mentality that has a hold of the majority*
> *of our Klaipėda Memellanders.*

Jokūbas was the Chairman of the Board of the Kretinga Lutheran parrish and so went with a delegation looking for help from the writer favoured by the Soviets. But, though the writer had been greatly honored, she could be of no help at all—the "heroic" construction engineers still built the new Kretinga post office right in the Lutheran churchyard, sticking one wall right onto one side of the holy building.

Father Jokūbas died in 1993 in early spring. In two and a half years he would have celebrated his hundredth birthday. His nonagenarian birch tree in the corner of the garden dried out and died that same year. Now that the birch is gone no one protects the garden from the fierce Finnish winds. On the rotting tree stump Aneta tends red geraniums.

•

Father-in-law taught me to name all the seaside winds. The Finnish (northwest) and the Winter (north) winds prevail here, but there is also the Saxon wind—blowing from Germany, a southwest wind. Probably the song thrush flew here with its help.

Every morning, the bird greets my early rising father-in-law and he, in turn, says to me:

—Why look, it's a visitor from Germany.

—Why from Germany?—I ask.

242

—Don't you hear, how he greets me? He says: *Guten Tag, lieber Herr, der Frühling ist da?* (Good day, my dear sir, the Spring is here?)—marvels Father-in-law.

I don't hear it like that, but I believe him.

•

...Today the Goatish wind blows, raising wavelets with little white crests, which gambol like kid goats. But the old, squeaky house protects my daughter Eglė and me from the wind's southeastern bite. The house martins dart like crazy around the sky. On the television antenna a dove coos. The two of us are sitting on the steps.

Lower down, on the tiled path, my granddaughter acts out an impromptu play, with songs and dances. The two of us, the only spectators of this unrepeatable improvisation, sit and quietly cry. Not from sadness, no. But from the fullness of life, from the joy of being here, on these modest wooden steps, underneath a very high seaside sky. And now the red twilight begins to fade. The whirring of grasshoppers is so thick it shields us like a wall from the rest of the world.

—You acted beautifully,—I say to my granddaughter the next morning.

—And you, too,—says she.—You cried as if for real.

Oh Lord! Not only are adults mistaken, but children, too. Now I cry "for real."

My daughter has already flown off to London, to her husband.

...Enfolding her small, warm body I imagine I hold my little daughter, my little son. Or maybe I am holding myself as a small child, who could easily have not had a chance to grow up.

—You lied to me,—says Vaidilė.—I'm not at all your most beloved.

—Well, then who?—I query.

—Eglutė,—she cuts back without any wavering. And then hesitantly she puts together a complicated thought. She wants to know something:

—Tell me which is better for you: when I'm here but Eglutė isn't, or when she's here and I'm not?

I must decide with lightning speed.

—It's best for me when you're both here,—I answer, and that's somehow closer to the truth.—I love you both very much.

•

...We're sitting again on the steps, our faces toward the evening. This is the best spot to watch the daylight fade

243

away. Above the sea, the sunset fires have been extinguished, and right in front of us the Evening Star is clearly visible, and the slowly wheeling Big Dipper. And the household spirit? I'd become afraid: where will it dwell now, now that the birch tree is gone? Who'll watch over me? Now I see, though, that the ash tree has thrived so that the spirit of the house is quite comfortable there.

—Do you know how to find the North Star, which is the only one who never changes her position—from our speck-of-dust Earth's point of view?—asks the household spirit silently.

—I know,—I reply silently.

Before my eyes the worlds are unfolded, countless times larger not only than our garden stairs, but than the entire Earth.

•

Now here's an experiment you can try. Sit down somewhere near the sea or on the plain, or somewhere you can see the expanse of the sky. Place your hands on your knees, palms up. You can close your eyes. Can you feel how heavy the cosmos is? Or, put another way, can you feel that column exerting pressure on every millimeter of your palm? But the universe is not just an unliftable heaviness. It gives us strength, too. You don't even need as much strength as you get from holding your hands that way in those few moments. And you won't be able to hold them like that any longer.

There are things you can't measure in kilograms, or by any other known measurements.

•

It's dark, and the stars are ripe... I'm solving poet Justinas Marcinkevičius' riddle:

—Where will my thoughts be when I'm gone?

I don't know yet. Perhaps I can say this much: on the way to the star that awaits me. Will God be living in that star? Probably. But most of all, I'd like to leave those thoughts here. So that they might live in those who remain. Or maybe in me, when I return. But will I return?

Still, I don't say goodbye, but until we meet again.

At that time I will bring you home,
At that time I will gather you together.

Zephaniah 3: 20

ABOUT THE AUTHOR

SILVIJA **LOMSARGYTĖ-PUKIENĖ** was born in Kaunas, Lithuania in 1933. She was educated in Kaunas and later in the Vilnius Pedagogical Institute where she studied foreign languages, specializing in English.

She worked as a journalist for the satirical journal, *Šluota* (*The Broom*) and then as a radio journalist for Lithuanian radio for 28 years as editor of overseas cultural programming.

A life-long active translator from English to Lithuanian, Ms. Lomsargytė-Pukienė has translated and had published works by numerous writers, including major fictional works of modern American and British writers like Hemingway, Dreiser, Cather, Greene, Waugh, and others.

Since 1997, she has been a member of the prestigious Lithuanian Writers' Union.

She lives in Vilnius. She has two grown children: PAULINA EGLĖ PUKYTĖ, writer and artist, and MARTYNAS ŽILVINAS PUKYS, a trained physicist.

ABOUT THE TRANSLATOR

A L ZOLYNAS was born in Austria of Lithuanian parents in 1945. He holds degrees from the University of Illinois (BA) and the University of Utah (MA and PhD). He has co-edited two poetry anthologies and published four poetry books, the most recent *Near and Far* (Garden Oak Press, 2019; San Diego Book Award 2021). He has translated poems of a number of Lithuanian poets. Retired from teaching literature and writing at Alliant International University, he resides with his wife near San Diego, California, where he also runs a Zen meditation group.

Trakai Castle
1350 -1991
from Grand Duchy to Independent Republic

An extended family bridges the past to the present

L to R: **Kostas Zolynas** *(Al's father and Silvija's uncle),* **Paulius Pukys** *(Silvija's husband),* **Arlie Zolynas** *(Al's wife),* **Al Zolynas** *(Translator),* **Silvija Lomsargytė-Pukienė** *(Author),* **Ruta Ratajczyk** *(Al's sister),* **Ona Smilgevičiūtė Zolynas** *(Al's mother: her father,* **Jonas Smilgevičius,** *was a signatory to the 1918 Lithuanian Declaration of Independence, a copy of which hangs on a wall inside Trakai Castle; as a young girl, Silvija met Jonas Smilgevičius at his home in Užventis);* **Brian Zolynas** *(Ruta's son and Al's nephew).*

TRANSLATOR'S NOTE

A Very Brief Guide to Pronouncing Lithuanian Words

Unlike English, Lithuanian words are almost always sounded out syllable by syllable. There are no silent letters unless borrowed from other languages. Hence, the Lithuanian name Janė is pronounced *Yah-neh*, with the last eh lengthened out because of the superdot. The city Vilnius has a dipthong in its second syllable (two vowels together—iu) and is pronounced *Vil-nyoos* where the *yoo* sound is run together, rather than kept separate as in *ee-oo*—which is the way most native English speakers would pronounce Vilnius, i.e., *Vil-nee-oos*, with three sounds rather than two.

So, when you come across a person's name or a town, city, river, just try sounding it out slowly, syllable by syllable, and then a little faster, and you'll have it. A few examples from the book:

Silvija	*Sill-vee-yah*
Lomsargytė	*Lomm-sarg-ee-teh*
	("*g*" in Lithuanian is always hard, as in *go, get, big*); remember to draw the length of the last *eh* out a bit.
Pukienė	*Pook-yen-eh*
Teresė:	*Teh-reh-seh*
Eglė:	*Agg-leh*
Milda:	*Mill-dah*
Ona:	*Oh-nah*
Kastytis:	*Kas-tee-tis*
Prakseda:	*Prak-seh-dah*
Žvirgždaičiai:	*Zhvirgzh-dai-chay*

Lithuanian surnames are gendered, male and female: The male form of the name differs from the female form in the ending, which is determined by married and unmarried status. Thus:

> Lomsargis (male):
> > Lomsargytė (unmarried female)
> > Lomsargienė (married female)
> Žolynas, Žolynaitė, Žolynienė
> Rimkus, Rimkutė, Rimkienė

Diacritical Marks

Lithuanian uses quite a number of those little marks above or below letters common in many eastern European languages. They modify the sound of consonants and vowels and can indicate parts of speech. Here are the most common ones: Š Č Ž/š č ž; Ė/ė; Ū/ū. Š is the same as the English *sh*, č the same as *ch*, and ž the same as *zh*, which is a "voiced" *sh*, a sound that causes the larynx to vibrate, as opposed to an unvoiced sound, which doesn't. While *zh* is not a common sound at the beginning of English words, you can hear it in borrowings from other languages, especially French: "garage" *(gah-razh)*, "sabotage" *(sab-oh-tazh)*. Ė lengthens the sound of *eh* to *eeh*. Ū lengthens the sound, as in the *oo* of "book" to the *ooo* of "spoon."

The question of which syllable in a Lithuanian word receives the main stress and why is a maze too complex to enter here.

CREDITS

Cover design: PAULINA EGLĖ PUKYTĖ

Cover:
    black and white inset photo:
        the Silvija Lomsargytė-Pukienė family archive

    background photograph: PAULINA EGLĖ PUKYTĖ

    author photo:
        the Silvija Lomsargytė-Pukienė family archive

Interior: photographs:
        the Silvija Lomsargytė-Pukienė family archive

    Author photograph:
        the Silvija Lomsargytė-Pukienė family archive

    Translator photograph: ARLIE ZOLYNAS

    Trakai Castle photograph (p. 289):
        the Zolynas family archive

ACKNOWLEDGMENTS

First and foremost the translator is grateful to Silvija Lomsargytė-Pukienė (the author of this book) and Paulina Eglė Pukytė (her daughter) for their close and essential reading of every single word in the translation of *The Parallels of Dita: Surviving Nazism and Communism in Lithuania*. As one who was raised speaking, reading, and to a much lesser degree, writing Lithuanian in an English-speaking country, I found myself more than once at a loss in the subtleties of Lithuanian conjugations, declensions, to say nothing of vocabulary. In addition to the usual stack of Lithuanian dictionaries and grammars I had at hand, Dita and Eglė were invaluable in providing corrections to my efforts often with patient and good humored explanations of any failings I exhibited. For more than two years, slowly, one chapter at a time, I would receive their feedback and vital edits. Quite literally, without their help, the book you now hold in your hand would not exist today. A special thanks to Živile Gimbutas, scholar and translator, for her help in translating a particularly tricky sentence from the writings of Marija Pečkauskaitė.

To my wife Arlie, I bow in gratitude for reading the translated manuscript as it took shape chapter by chapter and then again, from start to finish, at completion. Her ear for the English sentence is infallible and helped me avoid more than one awkward or inelegant construction along the way.

To Bill Harding, the publisher of this volume, I am deeply grateful for a number of things: for his sharp eye for the unusual and compelling story, for his recognition that *The Parallels of Dita* is a book unique among memoirs for its individual voice and for the historical context it grew out of—namely, the eras before, during, and after World War II in Lithuania, when the two occupying forces of Germany and the Soviet Union vied for supremacy in the Baltics. Bill is not only a courageous publisher, he is also a keen-eyed editor. I profited much from these qualities and will be ever in his debt.

Finally, to my parents, Kostas and Ona (née Smilgevičiūtė) Žolynas, mentioned at some length in the book (it is, after all, among other things, a family memoir) I have boundless gratitude, not only for all the things associated with a loving upbringing, but for keeping me in touch with my root language—for sending me to Saturday Lithuanian school (a common practice for first generation kids of the Lithuanian post-World War II diaspora) but also for continuing to use the language in the many homes of their long exile: read Dornbirn, Austria; Reutlingen, Germany; Sydney, Australia; Chicago; Ormond Beach, Florida; and, lastly, Boulder, Colorado.

— AL ZOLYNAS

Publisher's Note

A scholar fluent in Lithuanian and English will detect minor differences between the original memoir, *Dita Paraleles*, published in Vilnius, Lithuania [Jotema Press: 2004], and this translation.

The main difference concerns photographic images. Some photographs in the original have been omitted or replaced, due to loss, inferior quality, or uncertain copyright restrictions. Additional photographs, chosen by the author but unavailable for the original memoir, appear in this translation. Higher quality versions of some photographs replace the same images that appeared in the original version.

Secondly, the author corrected some of the original text for accuracy, and helped the translator refine idioms to reflect the same meanings in both languages.

Finally, suggesting the quirks of translations, one name (Sonia) was presented in the original book in its Lithuanian style (Sonja), though the author notes it is not a traditional Lithuanian name. It has been restored in this transation, at the author's direction, to Sonia.

Since my first encounter with this memoir, I have considered it a significant historical document. Chronological and cultural references in the original narrative have been faithfully preserved, augmented in this translation by footnotes to assist readers less familiar with Lithuania's history than those who read the original edition.

Hopefully, readers of both versions, whether scholars or not, will come away with a favorable opinion, noting that the English account conforms to the original Lithuanian in terms of content, tone, style, and, importantly, Silvija Lomsargytė-Pukienė's singular voice.

— WILLIAM HARRY HARDING

Made in the USA
Columbia, SC
13 October 2021

46827038R00139